TEN CENT BEER NIGHT

The Complete Guide to the Riot
That Helped Save Baseball
in Cleveland

SCOTT
JARRETT

**COSMO
PRESS**

A TOAST

For my wonderful Mom and my incredible Dad, Carol & John Jarrett, who love a cold beer and a great ball game - whether it's in Cleveland, or in the green grass of the backyard in Tiffin, Ohio

For Cosmo, Vanessa, Christopher, and Ani - the four best ball players I know. I believe, though, that I am still better at drinking beer. Thank you for putting up with and encouraging me to see this scavenger hunt through.

For Carl Fazio and Kip Horsburgh, the Whiz Kids

THE LINEUP

LEADING OFF

"They were just uncontrollable beasts. I've never seen anything like it except in a zoo." - Nestor Chylak, veteran of the Battle of the Bulge, Hall of Fame umpire, and crew chief at Ten Cent Beer Night, June 4, 1974

THE BEER TRUCK LINE STARTS HERE!

I just flew in from Cleveland - and boy are my arms tired!

Ba-dum-bum-CHING!

In order to finish writing a book about Ten Cent Beer Night, I had to *stop* drinking beer.

Ba-dum-bum-CHING!

(That last one is actually true).

Sorry - I just couldn't resist those. There's something about Ten Cent Beer Night that seems to lend itself to stand up comedy. Please think of these feeble jokes as a nod to Cleveland native and comedy writing legend Jack Hanrahan, who is honored in this book that I thank you for reading. Researching and writing about Ten Cent Beer Night has been a party. It started as kind of a lark and has been part scavenger hunt, part scholarly adventure, part oral history, part pandemic diversion. Hanrahan, a Clevelander who wrote for the famous show *Laugh In*, is one of the many fun rabbit holes I went down. My basic aim was simply that: fun. Was it necessary to try to figure out the name of the left-handed knuckleballer on the 1972 Rangers? I'll answer that with another question. Did Terry Yerkic, who jumped out onto the field to snatch the hat off of Rangers' right fielder Jeff Burroughs, need another beer on the night of June 4, 1974?

Of course he did.

Should the organist have continued to play as the riot unfolded?

Of course he should have.

Ah…beer and baseball: like Abbott and Costello, Baerga and Vizquel…like a Municipal Stadium hot dog and Bertmann's Stadium mustard. You get the idea. These two have been friends for over a century, but really became chummy when baseball began to broadcast games on TV. Then, baseball, beer, and TV created a perfect threesome. In 1946, half of the television sets sold in Chicago went to bars. In the '50s, though, beer advertising on TV broadcasts took off like a Mickey Mantle home run - and with the ads came those catchy beer jingles. Stuff like, "Baseball and Ballantine, Baseball and Ballantine/ What a combination,/ All across the nation/ Baseball and Ballantine."

I grew up a Cleveland fan in Tiffin, Ohio. Naturally, I had always heard about Ten Cent Beer Night here and there. It is a baseball legend and a quick punchline - along with the burning Cuyahoga River, The Mistake by the Lake, and so on and so forth. But is that a fair analysis of what happened on the evening of June 4, 1974? In fact, lots of baseball teams - from the big league squads to the smallest independent teams - offered Ten Cent Beer Night…and, a few years earlier, several of them had Nickel Beer Nights. (Damn you, inflation!) After the riot, some around Northeast Ohio noted that in the Summer of '74, the Growth Association of Cleveland also hosted nickel beer nights at Chester Commons without any trouble. Of course, Billy Martin and baseball weren't there for those gatherings. And many teams also had something called "Hot Pants Nights," encouraging women to parade around in "itty bitty shorts." Can you imagine having a Hot Pants Night at a modern sporting event? Maybe the only thing close to it today is the Victoria's Secret Runway show.

But isn't there often much more to history than those oft-repeated, involuntary, and dismissive summaries? My esteemed professors at Kenyon College always suggested as much and wouldn't it be a disservice to them, myself, and baseball history if I didn't try to dig a little deeper? Besides, it would be fun. In this book, I wanted to try to give as accurate a reflection of what happened as possible. Although, like the day after a party that had spun out-of-control, there were and are different versions of what really went down. And maybe that's why it has reached legendary status. Ten Cent Beer Night sort of reminds me of one of my favorite Jean Shepherd stories[1] - a baseball tale - where he reflects near the end of it, "It did not appear in the box score, my friends. You'll not see it in the record books. There's two kinds of history: there's the kind that's written down, and there's the kind that really happened." In the past 50 years, the infamy of the evening

---

1 For an enjoyable listen/watch, check out Jean Shepherd's *America* "Chicago (White Sox)" on YouTube. It is a fantastic baseball story involving Lou Gehrig and his "old man" (which delightfully kind of feels like the same "old man" from *A Christmas Story*): Jean Shepherd Baseball Story.

also continues to be shrouded in misunderstanding. Quick internet searches of it will turn up headlines like this: "Ten Cent Beer Night: The Dumbest, Most Dangerous Day In Baseball History," and "The Cleveland Indians' Ten Cent Beer Night: The Worst Idea Ever." It's certainly understandable how Ten Cent Beer Night could be reduced to a gagline and swiftly labeled as a horrible "what-were-they-thinking?" idea. But, as is often the case, there was definitely a little more to the story. Yes, at its peak, maybe Ten Cent Beer Night was a little like that fight scene in *Anchorman*[2] - things got a little bit crazy - and if you were out there you probably had to keep your head on a swivel. But no one was out there throwing a trident - or were they? Well, not that we know of! Everyone who *was there* does seem to agree upon at least one concept: on June 4, 1974, in Cleveland, Ohio, a perfect storm - centered around beer - gathered, then unleashed uncontrollable beasts, leading to one of the most infamous nights in baseball history.

The First Beer (is on me)

Poor Cleveland. The Mistake By the Lake. The city where the river actually caught on fire - frequently. The place where the mayor's hair caught fire. Once. The supposedly dreaded destination for a bunch of innocent and colorful fish, including Dory's parents, in *Finding Dory*, the Pixar movie that you may not have

---

2 By the way, when I lie in bed thinking about beer...oops, I mean, Ten Cent Beer Night, I pose the question to myself, "Self, what movie is Ten Cent Beer Night most like?" Naturally, I can't land on any ONE particular movie. So, I'll sum it up like this:

Well, let's go with part *Caddyshack* (particularly the "Caddy Day swim scene" as well as the final scene where Carl the Greenskeeper blows up Bushwood) + *The Warriors* (any scene) + *Animal House* (the party scenes) + that scene in *Coneheads* (which I think should have gotten much better than 35% on Rotten Tomatoes) where Beldar rips the top off of Chris Farley's car + (naturally) parts of *The Natural* + *Bull Durham* + *Major League* + *The Sandlot*. Oh yes, and maybe throw in a little *Lord of the Rings* (any battle scene). And, for sure, throw in some *Nacho Libre* fight scenes. I'm sure I could come up with some more and maybe, dear reader, after reading this book you could, too. Hopefully somebody will make *Ten Cent Beer Night: The Movie*. Affleck and Damon, I'm talking to you! Or maybe Linklater? Or Anderson? I am pretty sure Will Farrell oughta be in the mix, too, so that we get this thing done right. I am looking forward to your phone calls: 1-800-TEN-CENT.

seen. (Don't worry if you haven't caught that one...it's nowhere near as good as *Finding Nemo*). *And,* oh yes, Cleveland: the scene of what almost now seems unimaginable - Ten Cent Beer Night - arguably one of the worst promotions in sports history - or a happening driven by a perfect storm of events?

On a sultry late spring night in Cleveland - one of the first such evenings in the summer of 1974 - fans of the Cleveland Indians drank an awful lot of cheap beer then rioted. Some were angry - perhaps about the Vietnam War and a lack of leadership in America. Maybe some were angry about jokes about their beloved city and the increased challenge of finding a job there. Some were certainly angry about the visiting Texas Rangers and their pain-in-the-ass manager, Billy Martin. Martin was *that* guy - great if he was on your side, but a real jerk if he was on the other. And he never liked the Cleveland Indians, especially that greaseball throwin', cheatin' hick named Gaylord Perry. They were also angry because a local DJ had told them to be angry. "Stick it in Martin's ear!" And why not? Combine it all with cheap, virtually limitless, 3.2 ABV beer, aka "near beer," a full moon on a steamy summer night, and you arrive at Ten Cent Beer Night.

But the tale of Ten Cent Beer Night is much more than just an angry and drunken mob. It's also the tale of a small and focused "front office" trying to save baseball in an American city in the post-Vietnam, Nixon-era '70s. It's the tale of a once-great city trying to regain some smatch[3] of glory. It's partly the tale of promotions, now so much part of the fabric of sports that not having them - bobbleheads to the first 10,000, Dollar Dog Night!, seat cushion giveaways, and on and on - would be unheard of. It's the story of trying to keep your baseball team, which has been there for nearly 75 years, from moving to another city. And Ten Cent Beer Night is also certainly the tale of two ball professional clubs and the quirky personalities that made '70s baseball so great.

So, grab yourself a cold one, relax, and enjoy.

Bottoms up!

---

3 I got "smatch of glory" from Shakespeare's *The Tragedy of Julius Caesar*. As I researched, I couldn't help but conclude that Shakespeare would have loved Ten Cent Beer Night. Is it a tragedy, a comedy, a romance? Maybe all of the above! Turn to the end of the book to find out more! Oh wait, maybe read the book first.

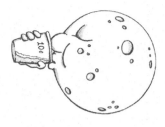

1

THE BIG CANYON BY THE LAKE

"A guy ought to have a horse to play the outfield."

– Babe Ruth

One of the principal characters in the tale of Ten Cent Beer Night wasn't a ball player, an Indians employee in charge of promotions, or a plastered fan (more on them later), but simply a colossal stadium perched on the shores of often frigid Lake Erie. Built in the heart of The Great Depression and representative of a Midwestern city with huge ambitions, Cleveland's Municipal Stadium began to host Indians' games in 1933. By 1974, though - like the City of Cleveland - she wasn't in the greatest of shape.

Cleveland, in 1928, was the nation's sixth largest city, trailing - in descending order - only New York, Chicago, Philadelphia, Detroit, and Los Angeles. And civic leaders had grand plans for the major Ohio city nestled on the shore of Lake Erie - and building an enormous multipurpose stadium, akin to New York's fabled Polo Grounds, was just one of them. Over the next year, Cleveland city officials would achieve one of the many firsts associated with the enormous structure first conceived as "Lakefront Stadium," and ultimately, Municipal

Stadium: a stadium paid for by local taxpayers. Fortune favors the bold - and perhaps those who propose such a wild idea *before* the Great Depression.

On November 6, 1928 voters approved a $2.5 million bond issue 112,448 to 76,975, enabling work to begin. City officials gave local architectural firm Walker and Weeks an unprecedented luxury – a vast tract of landfill right along the Lake Erie shores. Given the history of building stadiums in America, this was another "first" that mattered: "It was thus the first major league ballpark whose shape was not determined or even influenced by its property dimensions, street pattern, or urban context, for there were none of those."

Armed with this freedom, Walker and Weeks designed a 57-sided egg-shaped polygon for another local firm, Osborn Engineering, to build. Osborn had originally earned their reputation building steel bridges, an enterprise which eventually translated nicely into "the design of cantilevered steel grandstands." In the early 1920s, professional baseball had shifted from wooden stadiums and grandstands that could burn down easily, to steel, brick, and concrete buildings. And big ones, at that. Osborn had established themselves as the clear industry leader – five years earlier they finished a $2.5 million baseball cathedral, also known as Yankee Stadium (or, as most New Yorkers called it, then simply "The Stadium"). On April 18, 1923, some 74,200 fans cheered Babe Ruth and the Yankees to their first of thousands of wins there and the first of many over their bitter rival, the Boston Red Sox. Naturally Ruth christened his new house that day with a three-run blast, the stadium's first home run. The new playground of the 20th century's most annoying team was praised as "beautiful, majestic, and practical."[4] From 1909 to 1977, Osborn Engineering built 15 ballparks, including many very notable ones: New York's fabled Polo Grounds, Washington,

---

4 Yankee fans could partially thank famed New York Giants Manager John McGraw for their new stadium. McGraw hated the American League and the Yankees, a team that had begun to outshine the Giants. Both teams shared the Polo Grounds as a home venue, but McGraw convinced Giants majority owner Horace Stoneham to essentially evict Ruth and his teammates. So the Yankees opted to move across the Harlem River to the Bronx. McGraw was delighted and incorrectly predicted that the hated Yankees would wither and die. "They are going up to Goatville. And before long they will be lost sight of," he scoffed. A New York team should be based on Manhattan Island." Ruth and the Yankees would immediately show McGraw how wrong he was. They won

D.C.'s Griffith Field, St. Louis' Sportsman's Park, Atlanta's Braves Field, and Pittsburgh's Three Rivers Stadium.

Naturally, Osborn Engineering got better and better at this type of project. Completed in 1932, Municipal Stadium officially sat at 1085 W. 3rd Street in Cleveland, just off the Lake Erie shoreline. Planners believed that the stadium's "unconstrained layout" would allow it to host over 60 types of events, from religious rallies, to football games, and, of course, baseball. It could even hold a full 440-yard track inside of it (though it would be hard to imagine building a proper track and then razing it in order to make way for other events - but it was an option). Some thought the city hoped to make a bid for the 1932 Olympics. It was revealed later, though, that even before the push to build Municipal, Los Angeles had already been selected as the host city for the '32 Games.

Municipal was "the most functionally ambitious stadium attempted until then." In addition to being the first stadium paid for by taxpayer funding, it boasted the most seats of any stadium (as opposed to bleacher seats), the most architectural aluminum ever used on any building, the most ramps (16), the largest scoreboard, the greatest height (115 feet tall). It was the most expensive stadium to build ($3,000,000) until the early '50s. On its first-ever Opening Day, Municipal Stadium set a baseball attendance record of an extraordinary 80,184 fans. It could host 110,000 for boxing matches and 125,000 for "religious congresses." It was the first field to have permanent field lighting. Yet, because the Indians already had a stadium, League Park, their home since 1909, Municipal also carried the distinction of being the least-used stadium for 17 years. Cozier League Park had served the team fairly well and the rent to play at Municipal Stadium was mighty high amidst tight times. Also, the seating capacity became a turnoff - why host a game there if a small crowd was expected?

At that first-ever affair, virtually all of Cleveland - and then some - celebrated the first baseball game held in the new Municipal Stadium as the Indians welcomed future Hall of Famers Lefty Grove and Jimmy Foxx, stars of the

---

the World Series in 1923. To date they have won 27 World Series titles, 26 of them based at "The House that Ruth (& Stoneham) Built."

Philadelphia Athletics, on July 31, 1932. Indians General Manager Billy Evans[5] proudly declared that the City of Cleveland had established itself as one of the world's great sports centers. Not only did the massive turnout break a record set by the New York Yankees, it also quieted some of the skeptics. "You who said the Cleveland Stadium would never be filled," wrote *Plain Dealer* reporter John Vance in flowery Runyon-esque style, "Can paste the (attendance) figures in your hats, eat them in alphabet soup, stencil them on your bedroom ceiling so you can dream about them at night." The grand opening, according to another headline, proved to be a positive economic sign amidst a gloomy stretch: "Depression Given A Black Eye." City manager Daniel Morgan exclaimed, "The stadium will be an enduring monument to the spirit and aspirations of our people." A press release confidently declared, "It is a stadium that any city should be proud of." And most Clevelanders were precisely that.

Amidst pomp and circumstance, parades of fans bearing banners tumbled out of trains, cars, and buses then proudly marched to the new stadium. There were 450 from Ashland, 500 from Ashtabula, 300 from Fremont, and on and on. A marching band trumpeted its way from Huron Road down Euclid Avenue and into the stadium. On the playing field, various groups presented flowers to the Indians in honor of the big day. Cleveland Fire Chief James Granger, wearing a white linen suit, was perhaps the most striking presenter. Washington Senator clown Al Schact belted out "How Dry I Am," an Irving Berlin song that poked fun at the lack of alcohol in the era. Unlike the game that would take place on June 4, 1974, patrons were unable to enjoy a cool, crisp beer at the initial Opener as Cleveland and the rest of the country neared the end of Prohibition. That didn't mean, of course, that there wasn't alcohol around. Clevelanders did not like Prohibition. Liquor and beer could easily be purchased or acquired in and around Cleveland during Prohibition, which had begun in 1919. Liquor also

---

5 Billy Evans, who hailed from nearby Youngstown, was the first-ever "general manager", serving in that role from 1927 to 1935. Before that teams referred to someone in his role as the "business manager." Evans is credited with signing Bob Feller. Before he was a GM, he was an umpire in the Dead Ball era. He also wrote a syndicated column called "Billy Evans Says." He was inducted into the Hall of Fame in 1973.

came in across Lake Erie from Canada and thousands of people operated stills or simply violated the rules by brewing at home.

By 2:25 p.m., the stands were overrun with fans and dignitaries, including Ohio Governor George White who quipped that he was glad to be there and glad to see that half of the State of Ohio was there too. Standing in front of the Indians dugout, Cleveland Mayor Ray T. Miller spoke into a microphone: "The city administration is happy to announce that all agreements have been concluded to make this the permanent home of the Indians. The Cleveland ball team is a team of courage so like the city it represents. We wish them the opportunity of playing in many world series (sic) games in this stadium."

At that point, the world-famous Goodyear Blimp drifted gently over Municipal. Four airplanes zoomed past the dirigible. Then a "long line of portly gentlemen" walked from Bradley's owner's box in a "somewhat shame-faced fashion" toward the mound. The crowd quieted. The public address announcer bellowed: "One of the greatest batters in history...Larry Lajoie." " 'Larry Lajoie,' the crowd answered." They whistled, they roared and stamped their feet for Lajoie. He was followed by other Indians greats, including Tris Speaker and Cy Young, who was now "large about the middle" and had hung up his cleats some 21 years earlier after recording 511 career wins (a mark that one would think would never be broken). The partisan crowd - as if it were some kind of ritual - echoed the names of Speaker and Young, too.

Shortly before 3 p.m., the band played "The Star Spangled Banner" as the crowd watched the American flag rise. Governor White threw out the first pitch, a "Yukon gold slow one" that reportedly froze on its way to the plate. Miller tried to catch it in the dirt and Judge Keenesaw Mountain Landis, "who never made a mistake in his life," called it a strike. After a massive amount of anticipation and ceremony, the first-ever baseball game at Municipal Stadium was nearly under-way. Home plate umpire Bill Guthrie got ready, but then the public address announcer interrupted the proceedings one more time: "He wanted, he said, to introduce a man who does as much for baseball as any living man. He gestured toward the Philadelphia dugout and there was a roar...out of the dugout came a lank (sic) gray figure, Mr. Cornellius MicGillicuddy, ladies and gentleman,

Connie Mack himself, the old mastermind." Mack, wearing his iconic suit and hat, shuffled out.

The actual game, a pitcher's duel, almost certainly did not run as long as the pregame festivities. It took Lefty Grove just an hour and fifty minutes to shut out the Indians, handing his counterpart, Mel Harder, a 1-0 loss. No matter. Many fans in attendance were simply over-the-moon to be a part of something new and exciting - and utterly fascinated to see so many people in one place at the same time. After the game, the 80,000-plus crowd moved patiently toward the exits, out the stadium, and over pedestrian bridges. "On West 3rd the autos and buses were bogged down. They waited, patient as islands, in a sea of humans."

Everyone declared the afternoon a tremendous success. The stadium doctor reported just one injury - a young woman from Pennsylvania who was hit by a foul ball. Outside of the stadium a young boy waited for players to emerge from the locker rooms. He craned his neck, and marveled at the huge building in front of him. "Some joint," he said.[6]

Unfortunately, there weren't many sellout crowds after that opener. The Indians played 32 more home games at Municipal in 1932 and all of their home games there in 1933. Despite Mayor Miller's Opening Day declaration that Municipal would become the permanent home of the Indians, it did not fulfill that promise. After the Indians finished 75-76 in 1933, attendance began to wane and the Indians opted to return to League Park for virtually all of their home games from 1934 to 1936. Indians owner Alva Bradley called Municipal, which was only a few years old, a "white elephant." Bradley also reasoned that if fans could listen to games on the radio they wouldn't want to attend in person, so he banned radio broadcasts of the Indians. (He changed his mind the next year).

As for its functionality, Engineer Kenneth Osborn had said that Municipal Stadium had "evolved from the study of an ideal baseball grandstand." Others had said it was "the nearest thing to perfection obtainable at the time." But none

---

6 Another wide-eyed boy somewhere among that enormous first-game-crowd at Municipal Stadium crowd was Bob Keefer, future public address announcer for the Cleveland Indians. Almost 42 years after Municipal's first game, Keefer would be behind the mic at Ten Cent Beer Night, imploring fans to clear the field.

other than Babe Ruth, as well as several other players, seemed to disagree with the resulting playing field. In terms of baseball, the central half of the outfield averaged 450 feet, prompting Ruth to joke about the cavernous nature of the outfield and the need for equine assistance.

Seven years later, on June 27, 1939, Municipal Stadium hosted another milestone: the first-ever American League night game, a battle between the Detroit Tigers, who had just traded for a Cleveland fan favorite, Earl Averill. The night before the contest, Bradley gathered with reporters and a handful of players to unveil the 712 individual lights. "The lights blazed and the persons who had been standing and sitting in darkness felt as though a mule had kicked them between the eyes. For a moment no one could see anything, and then each saw that darkness had been replaced by a brilliant summer day."

American League President Will Harridge, spoke glowingly of the experience (and made comments that could have held great irony regarding the fans at Ten Cent Beer Night decades later): "This is the most beautiful spectacle I've ever seen. But do you know what impresses me more than this marvelous lighting equipment? It's the carnival spirit of the fans. I noticed it when I first came in. Everyone seemed intent on having a gala evening. There was a Mardi Gras spirit that you couldn't miss, a spirit that I've never noticed at any day game."

55,305 fans flooded into the park, many of them as early as 6:30 p.m. When the lights were finally turned on at 8:30 p.m., the crowd roared and buzzed. One by one, the six towers 150 feet above the diamond shot out their brilliant whiteness, until all 712 of the 1,500-watt lamps were on. *The Plain Dealer* beamed: "The new lights of the stadium herald a new era in major league baseball. But wonderful as they are, they were outshone last night by a former Iowa farm boy named Robert Feller." Feller yielded just one hit and struck out 13 Tigers enroute to a 5-0 victory. After the ball game, many praised the revolutionary concept of night baseball, which would allow them to work during the day then come to the ball game at night.

Another notable Municipal moment took place just before World War II. In the middle of July of 1941, the *Plain Dealer's* lead stories were generally about the incredibly frightening news from Europe. Nazi tanks edged closer to Moscow, waging intense battles in Smolensk, 230 miles west of the Russian capital. At the same time, acknowledging what seemed inevitable, the United States initiated the second draft, drawing names from some 750,000 American 21-year-olds. As such, the Yankees' Joe DiMaggio provided a welcome distraction to many Americans when he hit safely in a stunning number of consecutive games. For over two months, DiMaggio recorded at least one hit in every game he played in. Not only was DiMaggio proving he was the best hitter in baseball, he was leading the American League's best team to a pennant. Just behind the Yankees, though, the Cleveland Indians held on to slim American League title hopes. Winners of 15 of their last 16, the Yankees rolled into town at 55-27, with the Tribe six games off the pace at 50-34.

On Wednesday, July 16, 1941 at League Park, DiMaggio tallied three more hits in his amazing streak; he now had at least one hit in 56 straight games. The Yankees trounced the Indians 10-3. In anticipation of a much bigger crowd, the series moved to Municipal Stadium for the Thursday evening game. 67,468 fans packed the stadium to watch the drama. The next day, The *Plain Dealer's* Gordon Cobbledick focused first on the loss, then the end of DiMaggio's streak and the role that Indians third baseman Ken Keltner had in ending it:

"The greatest crowd in the history of night baseball – 67,468 fans – saw the Indians virtually eliminated from the pennant race in a bitter battle with the Yankees at the stadium last night. Beaten, 4 to 3, when a ninth-inning rally died with the tying run on third base and none out, the tribe was dropped seven games behind the league leaders – and seven games behind such a team as the Yankees is more than any rival can afford to be at this stage of the race. It was hard to say whether the huge throng that filled all but a few remote corners of the stadium was more interested in the outcome of the game or in the fact that Joe DiMaggio's record-setting hitting streak was ended after 56 games."

DiMaggio walked once and never hit the ball out of the infield, thwarted twice by Indians third baseman Ken Keltner, who made two backhanded snatches of ground balls to throw Joltin' Joe out. After the game, DiMaggio praised the Indians third baseman for stifling him. Pitchers Al Smith and Jim Bagby were also credited with squashing DiMaggio.

Over the years, Municipal Stadium hosted four All Star games (1935, 1954, 1963, and 1981). The Indians played in two World Series at Municipal, winning the series in 1948 (although clinching it in Game 6 in Boston). They also hosted two games there in 1954 only to watch Willie Mays and the New York Giants win the series on Cleveland turf.

Throughout most of its existence, though, Municipal Stadium's size was increasingly a detriment. There was one glorious stretch, when man-of-the-people owner Bill Veeck and the talented '48 Indians drew over 2.6 million fans, a major league record that stood for 14 years. The tireless Veeck understood and embraced promotional opportunities and injected energy into the Indians and the city. That season, games drawing 60,000-plus fans each game seemed almost commonplace.

But the glory days were over by the mid-'50s and throughout the '60s and into the early '70s, attendance at Indians games dwindled significantly. Municipal's mammoth size seemed to highlight the franchise's struggles on the field and at the turnstiles. Photos from those decades showing an on-field play, with a background of vast sections of all but empty seats, highlighted just how bad attendance was. In the early '70s, third baseman Graig Nettles once answered the clubhouse phone. A fan on the other end wanted to know what time the game started. "What time can you get here?" Nettles asked.

Additionally, during stretches of the summer, swarms of insects, pigeons, and Lake Erie seagulls would descend upon the stands and field. "If there is any such thing as an authentic burial ground haunted by lost spirits," wrote Rangers beat writer Mike Shropshire about the building in the early '70s, "For baseball purposes (Municipal) was seemingly cursed and abandoned forevermore."

And yet, despite what seemed like an annual tradition of dismal - losing - seasons, the building's decay, the infamous "trough" urinals in the men's rooms, the dark and dank ramps and concourses, its frigid location on the Lake Erie shoreline, Municipal Stadium, like your favorite dive bar, somehow continued to emanate an unmistakable charm to many. Unnumbered legions still place it in the center of some of their earliest and best sporting memories. Cleveland fan Jimmy Homan remembers taking care of business at the trough urinal in the '80s and suddenly noticing that the man peeing next to him was dressed to the nines. "I said, 'Boy, you look familiar' - it was George Voinovich (Cleveland mayor and later Ohio governor). He had just thrown out the first pitch! He was peeing into the trough urinal just like me. But *that* was the Stadium - we didn't have luxury lodges."

Speaking of peeing, when "The Dawg Pound" was in its full glory at Browns games, fans loved to be near a drain in certain parts of the bleachers so they could drink as much as they wanted and just take care of business right there and not miss a play. (And would it surprise you to know that they drank *a lot* of beer in The Dawg Pound?)

Marty Baker, a long-suffering Indians fan and former president of The Wahoo Club, the Indians fan club, laughs a bit when recalling Municipal through a post-pandemic lens. "You want to talk about social distancing...the Indians invented it during the '60s and '70s!" Baker laughed. "You go into that Stadium that seats 80,000 - and there's only 3,000 - *wow. That's* social distancing!" But apart from that, like many, Baker remembers the enormous energy of Municipal, particularly when things were going well for the Indians. "My father had season tickets in 1954 - right behind the dugout. He said, 'OK, I'm taking your mother to Game 4 of the World Series and I'll take you to Game 5.' Well, unfortunately 1954 turned into 1995." Baker fondly remembers those glorious games in the early '50s when the Municipal was nearly full. "The grass was green and the Indians were decent and they were playing the Yankees. You think it's the greatest place ever." Fan Jim Knuff had the same experience with his Dad. "I remember the first game I went to with my Dad," recalled Knuff, who would later be at Ten Cent Beer Night. "The grass was so green. The sky was blue. Just to be there as a 6 or 7-year-old after listening to the ball games - I died and went to heaven." Dan Coughlin, a reporter for *The Plain Dealer* in the early '70s, remembered the singular impact of walking through the dark concourses and up the ramp to the box seats. "You step out there at night and here's all this green and it was quite a sight in front of you...just to have all this green expanse hit you." "I liked it," said Coughlin, wistfully. "My kids are grown, but when they were little we would go down there at the last minute and park real close by and go right in the press gate and I'd have my three boys with me and we'd sit anywhere and they'd run all over the stadium. There were 5,000 people there at most games - *and they were the same 5,000* - and we knew *all of them.*"

Born in 1951, famed Indians drummer John Adams recalled the bus ride to his very first game at Municipal Stadium in 1954. "We were playing Boston and we won," he said. "I loved that place. I *loved* that place. Every seat in that place faced second base. You didn't have to turn in your seat. That was a great ballpark. Every opening day it was the same feeling: brick and asphalt and concrete and you see the lake. And then you walk through the tunnel and it's like Dorothy in the Wizard of Oz…the green grass and the blue sky and the colorful seats." The mere memories of Municipal made Adams well up with a greater appreciation for the sport. "Why do I love baseball? I don't know…why do you fall in love? I don't know. Just because."

Many ballplayers, however, were not always overjoyed to play at Municipal Stadium.

"Cleveland was not a place where you enjoyed visiting the stadium," said Tom Grieve, who starred for the Texas Rangers on June 4, 1974. "It was cold and the field was crappy." Jack Brohamer, who started at second base for the Indians on Ten Cent Beer Night and many others, recalled Municipal as an "old, cold dungeon." He also remembered the team using the stadium for more than just baseball caused a few problems. "They did a couple of things back then that they would never do to baseball players of today," Brohamer laughs. "One time they had a rock concert the day before a game - and it had rained. They had had Port-A-Pots out there and they'd been knocked over, so it all (the contents therein) soaked into the field. I went out and played (2nd base) and got all soaked and I came down with a foot infection and they wondered why! I couldn't get my cleats on and was out for five days!"

Throughout Municipal, there were ramps and concourses, particularly if you were trying to get to the top of the stadium. Rangers pitcher Don Stanhouse remembered the surreal and dark walk from the clubhouse to the dugout and field. "It seemed like you were walking on a suspension bridge for miles," he laughs. Generally, though, Municipal's playing field was in good shape according to Brohamer, thanks to a legendary groundskeeper named Emil Bossard (aka "The Sodfather") and The Bossard Boys, his sons. *Sports Illustrated* referred to The Bossards as "The First Family of Groundskeeping." Veeck and Manager Lou Boudreau maintained that the Bossards contributed to an extra 10 to 12 wins a year, thanks to little tricks of the trade that gave an advantage to the Indians (or a disadvantage to opponents). In 1948, several of the Indians infielders allegedly had the "range of a grubworm," so Bossard attacked the vicinity of home plate with a pick axe, dug down about six inches, then filled it in with loose dirt to make it the consistency of oatmeal then covered it with loose dirt to conceal it, resulting in ground balls that died. After the Indians and their grubworm infielders won the World Series, they awarded Bossard a share of the winnings, which he used to buy a new Buick. "It's a game of inches, son, and inches are what the Bossards specialize in," *Sports Illustrated* declared. Bossard would allegedly build up the mound height from 15" to 18" for Hall of Fame pitcher Bob Feller. Other tricks included shaving four or five inches off of the visiting team's bullpen mound to try to disorient them so that when their pitchers came into the game, they felt "like they are standing on Mount Everest."

At one point - late in its life - Browns owner Art Modell sought to repaint some of the stadium and add luxury boxes. "Gabe Paul once said that it was like 'putting makeup on an old whore,' " laughed former Indians treasurer Bun Blossom, who was also part of Nick Mileti's ownership group. "You can discern from that what kind of a shape the stadium was in. Apart from the loges, you could say the rest of the place was pretty dreary."

By the early to mid-'70s, Municipal Stadium, combined with chilly Cleveland spring and fall weather, proved to be a significant obstacle in terms of promotions and simply getting folks to come out to the ballpark. "The stadium - with all that steel - it felt like a refrigerator. Sitting next to Lake Erie, which was like a giant bucket of ice water," said Carl Fazio, tasked with filling the seats in 1974 (much more on him later). "It seemed like it held the cold." Be that as it may, as players reported to Indians spring training, workers in Cleveland began prepping Municipal Stadium for the baseball season of 1974, patiently cleaning the yellow slatted seats, one-by-one. At some point in the season fans in the upper deck would hang a banner that proudly declared, "THIS TRIBE CAN BE GREAT LIKE IN '48."

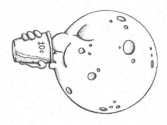

2

THE BAD OLD DAYS

"Pennant fever in Cleveland is usually a 24-hour virus."

- Frank Robinson

Perhaps baseball in Cleveland was doomed from the start. To wit: in 1865 the Cleveland Forest Citys emerged as a respectable amateur and professional baseball organization that boasted 150 club members by 1868. They were highly thought of locally (or at least thought highly of themselves) but then played the Philadelphia Athletics on June 24, 1868. They lost 85 to 11. But the team morphed into a squad called the Spiders in the late 1880s. By 1900, they were owned by Frank De Haas Robison, who also owned another - better - team: the St. Louis Perfectos. Because the team in St. Louis was superior (or maybe this is *why* they were superior), Robison would frequently roster his better players, including a talented pitcher named Cy Young, on the Perfectos. Unsurprisingly, the Cleveland Spiders finished the 1900 season with an incredible 20-134 record.[7]

---

7 Robison was unhappy about a Cleveland "blue law," which prohibited baseball on Sundays. He did, however, have an enormous impact on Cleveland baseball as the driving force behind League Park, the home of the Indians for the first few decades of the 20th century. League Park also hosted professional football games and was the home of the Negro League Cleveland Buckeyes in the late '40s. The Browns also practiced there into the '60s.

As for the origins of the Cleveland Indians, backtrack briefly to 1894 and Grand Rapids, Michigan and the birth of the Grand Rapids Rustlers. The squad moved to Cleveland in 1900 then renamed themselves the Cleveland Lake Shores. It was good timing as Ban Johnson just rolled into town seeking a team to join a new venture he called the "American League." In 1901, then, the Cleveland Bluebirds became one of the eight charter members of the AL. In these early days most squads were simply referred to in terms of their league affiliation: the Boston Americans, the New York Americans. Thus, the Cleveland Americans were born. Eventually, though, they became known as the Cleveland Naps (in honor of star player Napoleon Lajoie). But in 1915 they traded the fading Lajoie away, briefly flirted again with "Spiders," then, upon the suggestion of sports-writers, settled on the "Indians."[8]

In 1908, the franchise missed out on winning the American League and going to the World Series by a scant half a game. The squad finished 90-64, second to Ty Cobb and the Tigers, who actually played one *less* game because of a rainout (in those days teams were not forced to make up rainouts). In 1920, though, the Indians finally *did* make it to the World Series, their first-ever. They were almost certainly guided there, in part, by the spirit of shortstop Ray Chapman, the only major league player ever killed in a baseball game. On August 16, 1920, Chapman dug into the batter's box at New York's Polo Grounds against Yankee right hander Carl Mays, who was widely known to throw a spitball and had a reputation as a headhunter. Shadows and sunlight, a misguided pitch, a dirty ball, Mays's sneaky submarine delivery - they were all factors that seemed to play a role in an utterly horrifying moment in sports history. Chapman, apparently unable to pick up the pitch, never moved and Mays's pitch thud-ded sickeningly into the shortstop's temple, dropping Chapman immediately to the ground. Chapman was conscious and, ever-the-gentleman, was actually forgiving of Mays as they rushed him off to St. Lawrence Hospital where he died early the next day. Upon hearing the news of her husband's death, Chapman's pregnant wife fainted.

---

8 The team name was frequently said to honor Louis Sockalexis, a Penobscot Indian who played for the Spiders for three years. Whether that is why the team became the "Indians" or not is a matter of debate.

In the 1920 World Series a few months later, thanks to Tris Speaker's hitting, pitcher Stanley Covaleski's three wins, and an unassisted triple play by Bill Wambsganss (the only one in World Series history), the Cleveland Indians finally won their first World Series title. The team would not win another World Series for 28 years. In 1948, energized by Veeck, amazing attendance, and a core of stars - Feller, Larry Doby, Satchel Paige, and Lou Boudreau - the Indians won it again. Six years later, the team won a record 111 games and appeared poised for another title, when they ran into Willie Mays and the New York Giants, who swept them in four games.[9]

It was around this time - the mid '50s - that what late late '60's manager Alvin Dark once referred to as "the bad old days," began. In truth, it was a phrase that could have applied to a nearly 40-plus year stretch for the franchise, starting in the mid-'50s and leading up until 1995 when the Indians finally returned to the World Series, but lost to the Atlanta Braves. Even as of 2024, the organization still seeks another World Series title, a drought going on 76-plus years.

And though they were largely hapless from the late '50's until the mid '90s, the Indians certainly rostered their share of colorful characters. In October of 1995, Bob Sudyk, a longtime beat reporter for *The Cleveland Press,* sat in the brand-new Jacobs Field stands anxiously and excitedly awaiting the start of the first World Series game played in Cleveland in over 40 years (a game between the Indians and the Atlanta Braves). Sudyk sat high in the stadium, marveling at

---

9 One of the most colorful characters on the 1920 team was Ray "Slim" Caldwell, a veteran pitcher who had been around since 1910 who certainly would have loved Ten Cent Beer Night. Recognizing Caldwell's penchant for a drink or two, the Indians wrote the following in his contract: "After each game he pitches, Ray Caldwell must get drunk. He is not to report to the clubhouse the next day. The second day he is to report to Manager Speaker and run around the ballpark as many times as Manager Speaker stipulates. The third day he is to pitch batting practice, and the fourth day he is to pitch in a championship game." Caldwell In 1919 at League Park, Caldwell was pitching a shutout. He was just one out from a victory when he was struck by lightning on his head. Caldwell later said it felt like someone had whacked him over the head with a board. After the chaos settled, Caldwell got up and (like a true Cleveland Indian) got the final out to record a complete game shutout. The team finished second in the American League to the Chicago White Sox, who infamously became the Black Sox when they threw the World Series.

the moment about to unfold in front of him, while simultaneously reflecting on the decades of futility he had witnessed while covering the franchise. In addition to being a fan, Sudyk covered the Indians from 1962 to 1977, arguably some of the worst years in the franchise.

In particular, he remembered these notably zany Indians, some of the "stars" of the bad old days:

- Gene Green ('62-63), who dropped three consecutive balls with the bases loaded, then, when the inning finally ended, dropped his glove on the way off the field.

- Roommates Gary "Ding Dong" Bell ('58-67) and Jack Kralick ('63-67), who had a fist fight in a Washington hotel room over what Saturday morning cartoon they should watch. Ding Dong apparently won as he knocked out one of Kralick's teeth.

- Chico Salmon ('64-68), who was afraid of ghosts, and thus preferred to have the lights on while he slept.

- Lou Johnson ('68), who visited a Cleveland car dealer on the last day of the season, test drove a Cadillac and loved the car so much that he promptly drove it all the way to Los Angeles without telling the dealer.

- Charlie Spikes ('73-77), who was so excited about getting called upon to pinch hit, that he leapt up and bashed his noggin into the roof of the dugout, knocking himself out.

- Harold Morris "Gomer" Hodge ('71), nicknamed thus because he looked very much like the loveable buffoon "Gomer Pyle" from *The Andy Griffith Show* (and the spinoff *Gomer Pyle, U.S.M.C.*). Hodge labored for 8 seasons in the minor leagues but finally got his cup of coffee in 1971. He promptly made the most of it when he had hits in his first four pinch-hit at bats, including a game-winning single with two outs and two on to win the 1971 home opener against the Red Sox. The team carried Hodge off the field. Gomer, as if wholeheartedly embracing his namesake, gushed to reporters, "Gollee, Fellas, I'm hittin' four thousand! Ain't that somethin'?"

And who could forget "Sudden" Sam McDowell, the incredibly gifted and lanky lefthander, who could allegedly throw a cocktail olive through a wall? "Unfortunately, he always downed the cocktail first," Sudyk wrote.[10] McDowell was also so enormously talented that the Indians gave him a $75,000 signing bonus after he graduated from a Pittsburgh high school. McDowell used part of the bonus to buy a Ford Thunderbird, which he drove to spring training. McDowell, cracked longtime sportswriter Terry Pluto, was blessed with a "million dollar arm and a ten cent head." Yet, for his part, McDowell probably delivered more than any other Cleveland player in the '60s and early '70s. For more than a decade, from 1961 to 1971, he won 124 games and lost 99, all while the franchise struggled mightily with its offense.

McDowell was larger than life. In 1969, he won 18 games for the hapless Indians, who finished 62-99 (only a divine intervention final game rainout in New York prevented them from losing 100 games). Late that season, Umpire Larry Barnett threw McDowell out of a game in Baltimore - the first ejection of McDowell's career. After the game Barnett told reporters that McDowell had called him, "a gutless blankety-blank." McDowell disagreed with the accuracy of Barnett's comment. "I didn't call him just 'a gutless blankety-blank'. I called him 'a blankety-blank gutless blankety-blank' - and that's just what he is." Following McDowell's ejection, and en route to the 3rd base dugout, the frustrated southpaw drew back his left arm like an archer trying to shoot a flaming arrow to light up a mountaintop cauldron. McDowell launched the baseball high into the upper reaches of the upper decks - almost over the stands. A few days later American League President Joe Cronin, having read Barnett's report about the incident, called the ump for clarification about McDowell's reaction. "How far did he throw it?" Cronin asked Barnett. "I told him the best I could figure was that it landed about 10 feet from the top of the grandstand, about 205 rows up." Cronin, tapped into his own sense of humor, scribbled down the numbers, did some math, then promptly fined McDowell $205, or roughly a dollar per row. "But anybody who knew McDowell, knows what Sam did next," Barnett

---

10 McDowell wrote and published *The Saga of Sudden Sam: The Rise, Fall, and Redemption of Sam McDowell*, in which he refers to himself as the "worst drunk in baseball," and describes how he has rebounded to become a professional counselor and helps others with addiction.

said later. He sent Cronin a check for $216 because, McDowell claimed, the ball cleared the top of the stands and out of the park - and there were 216 rows in Memorial Stadium.

But when the Indians traded McDowell to the San Francisco Giants after the '71 season, they got another character in return. His name was Gaylord Perry and, like McDowell, he was an absolute workhorse. Perry joined the Indians before the '72 season. He was 33-years-old and the Indians maintained that they were more excited about infielder Frank Duffy, who came with him in the deal. But Perry proved that he was far from having peaked as he continued to churn out quality innings and became the bedrock of the Indians pitching staff. He had been in the major leagues since 1962, but always claimed that it was during a 23 inning game at New York's Shea Stadium in 1964 that he really found something. Always coy about the keys to his success (although he also published an autobiography brazenly titled *Me and The Spitter*), Perry came into that game, on May 31, 1964, in the 13th inning. The game was tied 6-6. He proceeded to pitch 10 shutout innings until the Giants eked out two runs in the top of 23rd. Perry had given up 7 hits, walked just one, and struck out 9. What was most significant, perhaps, is what he told those gathered for his Hall of Fame induction decades later: "When I got to the mound to start the 13th inning, my catcher Tom Haller says, 'Kid, it's time to put something on the ball.' " (The Cooperstown crowd loved that one.) Perry also noted that, thanks to their many mound visits, he knew pretty much all of the umpires by their first names. He also joked that, "My catchers (sic) was the one that called all those pitches" (particularly, we assume, the spitters).

In 1969, the Indians lost their final game to cap off a 99-loss season, the most losses since 1914. Pitcher Luis Tiant[11] lost 20 games. Even Manager Al Dark

___

[11] After his 20-loss season, in which he gave up 37 home runs, the Indians traded Tiant and Stan Williams to the Minnesota Twins on December 10, 1969, hauling in Dean Chance, Bob Miller, Ted Uehlaender, and, most notably, Graig Nettles (Nettles eventually declared that he would be happier playing some-where other than Cleveland. He got his wish when the Indians traded him to the New York Yankees in November of 1972). The next season Tiant said, "If you pitch for the Indians, and you give up one run, you tie, and if you give up two runs, you lose." Tiant charged out of the gate in 1970 with a 6-0 record by the end of May, but ultimately finished the season just 7-3 and was released

admitted that it was a "lonely year." Things had gotten so bad, Dark noted, that even the sportswriters wouldn't accompany the Indians on the road. "It's been real lonesome here the last few weeks," Dark reflected. "It didn't seem natural."

The team bounced back a little in 1970 (76-68) but returned to dismal form in 1971. At the dawn of the 1971 season Dark had promised that he and the Indians would play every game that year like it was the 7th game of the World Series. After they lost the opener to Mickey Lolich and the Billy Martin-managed Tigers in Detroit, Cleveland's Ken "Hawk" Harrelson said, "This team has a lot of spirit. It's going to do alright." The Indians boarded a bus in Detroit and headed back to Cleveland with a day off before the home opener against the Red Sox, who were also expected to be one of the top squads in the American League. GM Gabe Paul predicted success at the turnstiles: "The Indians are going to do something for Cleveland," Paul told the Cleveland Advertising Club's 42nd annual beginning of the season "welcome luncheon" at the Hotel Statler Hilton. "Attendance increases through a spontaneous desire to see a team. Emotion creates this desire. This squad will do this. I'm looking for a dramatic increase in attendance. There is going to be excitement, and that should be in capital letters, in our great city."

Unfortunately, Paul, Harrelson, and many others were terribly wrong. In 1971, the Indians managed to lose a stunning number of contests - 102 games. They won just 60 games and notched the franchise's worst attendance numbers in quite some time. Just 591,361 fans attended home games - amidst 24 teams in Major League Baseball, only the San Diego Padres turned in worse numbers. Owner Vernon Stouffer had set up a deal to share the Indians with the City of New Orleans for 30 of its home games. Rumors with a great deal of substance circulated about a move to another city - New Orleans, Seattle, or possibly Dallas.

Many attributed the woes of the '60s and '70s to an anemic farm system. The Indians finally gave Dark[12] his walking papers in the middle of the horrific

---

by the Twins on March 31, 1971. After a 1-7 year with the Red Sox in 1971, Tiant finally hit his stride from '72-79 with a 134-82 record (a span that included seven seasons with the Red Sox and one with the Yankees).

12 With the right talent, Alvin Dark proved that he could manage quite capably. After the Indians dismissed him in 1971, Dark did not manage in the majors in

'71 season and his replacement, Johnny Lipon, proved not much better. In 1972 they tried something a little different. Rather than hiring a manager outside of the organization, they named Ken Aspromonte to lead the team. Aspromonte, or "Aspro" to many, had played second base in the major leagues for several teams, including the Cleveland Indians. As his career wound down, he crossed the Pacific to play in Japan and was delighted to be relevant again. "The only person higher than me in this country is the emperor," Aspromonte reflected. "That's the way it is here, being a major league ball player. You're right below the emperor as far as the people are concerned. Most of them can't name the top people in the government, but they know all the ballplayers, and they really idolize us. I never saw anything like this in the States."

After hanging up his cleats in 1966, Aspromonte did a variety of things - including some broadcasting in Washington - until Indians GM Hank Peters called him in 1968 and asked him to manage the team's rookie league in Florida. Aspromonte loved it, excelled at it, and was soon promoted to run the Indians' Class A squad, the Reno Silver Sox, in 1969. The organization liked what they saw in Aspromonte - a tough but motivated manager. In 1970, he took over the Class AAA Wichita Aeros. Again, he proved himself to be quite capable and though he had turned in two sub-.500 seasons, the organization seemed to recognize that the manager could only do so much with the talent he was given and that they generally kept moving the better players up to the big league club. Finally, when Indians needed a manager to replace Lipon, they loved that they could bring in a manager that had proven himself and one who had established a positive relationship with many of the players. Under Aspromonte, the '72 Indians did show some improvement, winning twelve more games than the

---

'72 or '73. He reemerged, though, in the spring of '74 and led the seemingly dysfunctional A's, who were known for clubhouse disputes - even physical fights - to the 1974 World Series title. A few days before Ten Cent Beer Night, the "Mini Page," a sort of kids insert that appeared in newspapers nationwide, focused on the A's: "Would you believe a championship team made up of unhappy coaches, players, and managers who fight, fuss, fume, bicker, and scrap among themselves still manage to win two World Series in a row? The team is the Oakland A's, one of the most unusual teams in the history of baseball."

year before (they finished 72-84).[13] The 1973 season proved about the same (71-91), though attendance continued to languish, hovering just above 600,000 for both seasons. Yet, the team felt Aspromonte had the team headed in the right direction.

Unfortunately, Dark's "bad old days" assessment might have applied to the City of Cleveland, too. Beyond the losing seasons and as the 20th century progressed, larger trends that were wearing on several once-great American cities began to lead to a loss of population from the city centers. Better highways, including the interstate system, meant folks could live farther away. Mass exodus to the suburbs, a trend that began in the '20s, accelerated in the '50s and '60s. Businesses left as well, and downtown Cleveland - littered with vacant parking lots - generated less and less taxes for the city. Higher crime rates within the city didn't help either. In 1950, the City of Cleveland listed 914,808 residents then saw a rapid decline. By 1970, though, the city population was 750,903 and in 1980 just 573,822.

And then there was the Cuyahoga River. The Cuyahoga partly originates, modestly, in Hambden Township - near Chardon - then meanders around Northeastern Ohio through Akron and Cuyahoga Falls before gathering volume and heading north into Cleveland and out into Lake Erie. In 1795 Mad Anthony Wayne incorporated the Cuyahoga River in the Treaty of Greenville, formally titled, "A treaty of peace between the United States of America, and the tribes of Indians called the Wyandots, Delawares, Shawanees, Ottawas, Chippewas, Pattawatimas, Miamis, Eel Rivers, Weas, Kickapoos, Piankeshaws, and Kaskaskias." After George Washington signed the treaty and the United States Senate ratified it, the Cuyahoga River essentially became the western border of the United States of America - albeit briefly. A few months later, in the summer of 1776, a surveyor from Connecticut named Moses Cleaveland sailed along the Lake Erie shoreline and noticed the Cuyahoga. He stopped, ascended the bank, and decided it would be a good spot for a city (and probably a baseball stadium and an infamous baseball promotion). "I believe, as now informed,

13 The 1972 season began (or, rather, *didn't* begin) with baseball's first-ever strike. The Indians and most teams played 156 games. The Tigers played one more game than the Red Sox, enabling the Tigers to win the AL East by a half game.

the Cuyahoga will be the place," Cleaveland declared. "It must command the greatest communication either by land or Water of any River on the purchase or in any ceded lands from the head of the Mohawk to the western extent or I am no prophet." (Somewhere along the way the city founder's name got misspelled and "Cleveland," as it is spelled now, was born.)

Growth was slow. During the first year, there were just four settlers. In 1800, the population shrank and only one official resident, Lorenzo Carter (who was probably no relation to future Cleveland Indians star Joe Carter), lived in Cleveland. Carter and his wife had 9 children, three boys and six girls, and got involved in all sorts of things, including running a jail and building the first tavern in Cleveland. But Carter also invited and controlled a band of desperadoes who lived "under the hill" that apparently discouraged would-be settlers. Samuel Huntington, who eventually become the third governor of Ohio, wrote to Moses Cleaveland, that Carter was "gather[ing] about him all the itinerant Vagabonds that he meets with out (sic) whom he gets all his labour done for their board and Wiskey: over whom he has an absolute control—organizing a phalanx of Desperadoes and setting all laws at defiance." Gideon Granger, another would-be settler wrote that "Cleveland has a Thousand Charm, but I am detered (sic) from pitching on that place by the Sickness, the poorness of the Soil and the Inhabitants under the hill." Granger added that he was also dissuaded from settling there because of the massive amount of sickness. Indeed, an abandoned channel of the Cuyahoga had caused stagnant water to pool, breeding malaria-carrying mosquitoes.

In 1820, the city notched a population of just 150. But, obviously, things picked up. From the start of the Civil War to the beginning of the Great Depression, Cleveland prospered, growing from a modest city of 43,000 to an industry-heavy metropolis of nearly a million people. As Cleveland grew, the Cuyahoga River flourished, at least in one respect, by becoming a crucial shipping lane. Also, the river connected to the Ohio and Erie Canal, which would allow goods brought in from Lake Erie to make their way all the way to the Ohio River and beyond. But as industry and commerce expanded, so did pollution in the river - resulting in fairly predictable damage to the watershed. Perhaps this abstract from a 1968 Kent State University symposium sums up the state of the Cuyahoga River around that time period best:

> The surface is covered with the brown oily film observed upstream as far as the Southerly Plant effluent. In addition, large quantities of black heavy oil floating in slicks, sometimes several inches thick, are observed frequently. Debris and trash are commonly caught up in these slicks forming an unsightly floating mess. Anaerobic action is common as the dissolved oxygen is seldom above a fraction of a part per million… *Animal life does not exist*. Only the algae Oscillatoria grows along the piers above the water line. The color changes from gray-brown to rusty brown as the river proceeds downstream. Transparence is less than .5-feet in this reach. This entire reach is grossly polluted.

The Cuyahoga River actually caught on fire many times throughout the 19th and 20th century, a casualty of Cleveland's industrial growth. But it was a 1969 conflagration that made the river - and Cleveland - infamous worldwide. On June 22, 1969 - a Sunday morning - a fire broke out on top of the oily sheen, scorching a few bridges and resulting in $50,000 in damages. After the City of Cleveland's Fire Department, using equipment on land and a fireboat, extinguished it, the city moved on. The world, however, did not. Shortly after the fire, *Time* featured a 1952 photo of the river on fire, accompanied by news of the most recent blaze. The world suddenly began talking about Cleveland in the context of a larger global interest of taking care of the planet. "The nation, it seemed, had suddenly woken up to the realities of industrial pollution, and the Cuyahoga River was the symbol of calamity." Less than a year later, on April 22, 1970, 20 million people celebrated the first-ever Earth Day. Many environmental blights throughout the world surely contributed to Earth Day's birth, but the abhorrent state of the Cuyahoga - and the publicity from the previous year - certainly provided a current event poster child. Later that year, President Nixon and Congress established the Environmental Protection Agency. And two years later Randy Newman released *Sail Away* featuring "Burn On" (which plays at the start of *Major League*, a 1989 movie in which the Indians miraculously beat the Yankees to win the division title). The song is a mournful and slow nod to the burning Cuyahoga. Many, too, still couldn't process the notion that a body of water could actually catch on fire.

In addition to the burning Cuyahoga, the hair of one of the more prominent local politicians, Ralph Perk, also caught on fire. After running for mayor and losing twice in the '60s, Cleveland's voters finally elected him to the post in 1971. A year later, Perk's barber slathered his head with a hair product just before he was due to appear at an American Metals Society and use a blow torch. Perk, standing in front of a small crowd and the media, dutifully took an acetylene torch, applied it to some metal - eliciting a shower of sparks - then stood back to smile. Meanwhile, Perk was unaware of what the audience saw: his hair was on fire. The cameras caught it all as someone slapped Perk's head to quickly extinguish the fire. Photos of the mishap hit the news wire nationwide and everyone laughed at Cleveland - again.

But beyond the cannon fodder of both the Cuyahoga and the mayor's noggin catching on fire, Cleveland also emerged as the butt of jokes on national TV, a phenomenon largely caused by an actual Hollywood joke writer - and a native son. Consider these zingers:

- The definition of a plush Cleveland cocktail lounge: A bottle of Seagram's with a brown bag around it.

- In Cleveland, St. Patrick's Day parade consists of 50,000 Jewish onlookers watching the help walk by.

- Attention Cleveland! Your lake just died.

- The best steak on the menu at Cleveland's classiest steak house is an all-beef wiener.

- And, of course, the easiest one of all: Attention Cleveland! Your river is on fire.

These jokes were the product of Jack Hanrahan, a Cleveland native and writer for the enormously popular TV show *Laugh In*, which ran from 1968-1973. After the show had banked on a number of Polish jokes, Hanrahan later said that he and the writers had received a note written in crayon from a

Milwaukee anti-defamation league. It read, "If Youse keep up dis here smart ass jokes about us Poles youse are gonna get yerselfs in deep trouble."

Naturally, a joke writer like Hanrahan laughed at such a missive: "Upon reading the note I mused over what 'deep trouble' they had in mind," says Hanrahan. "The worst deep trouble that I could conjure up would be a forced march from beautiful downtown Burbank to Pulaski Square in Cleveland, where we would be chained and left to the merciless attack of 5,000 dysentery-ridden pigeons." But Hanrahan and the writers also understood the message, particularly after an NBC sensor urged them to go easy on ethnic jokes. So, they turned their attention to American cities. "We were already getting a few laughs with Burbank, but we needed something to cinch the ratings in the East and Midwest. We had already written off the South because the show was slightly offensive to most of the cotton gin and white lightning set. Anyhow, we were running through the list of cities like a dose of salts. We even considered reviving earlier useables. Someone sent up a test balloon for Anaheim…'How about a shot of the little guy on the tricycle, with the raincoat driving up the freeway and we see him run into a city limits sign that says: YOU ARE NOW ENTERING ANAHEIM … SET YOUR WATCHES BACK ONE HUNDRED YEARS, someone suggested." A producer said that Anaheim jokes would be too "esoteric." Hanrahan recalled in *Cleveland Magazine*, "Things deteriorated to the point where we were all ready to laugh at anything anyone said just to get the meeting over with. Several pages of foolscap with every city in the Atlas written, scrawled or typed on them were scattered about amidst butt-filled paper coffee cups. By midnight we had gotten down to Schroone Lake, New York, and Lake Titicaca, which is somewhere in the Andes." The writers and bigwigs continued to brainstorm and bicker. Then, approaching "terminal boredom," they decided to put it to a vote. It was, Hanrahan recalls, around this time that producer George Schlatter quipped, "Don't pay attention to Hanrahan's ravings, he's from Cleveland."

It was a seminal moment.

"Suddenly, the room grew hushed. Twelve demented writers stared at each other, knowingly, cunningly, sagely. First it came as a little giggle of relief, which soon spread to a rumbling chuckle and then swelled and crescendoed into a fit of crazed, uncontrollable gutshaking, relief-giving laughter. Of course, *Cleveland,* naturally Cleveland. Cleveland ... it was there in front of us all the time. All we had to do was go through the script and drop the word Cleveland into the openings vacated by the Poles, and the script laughed, chuckled and guffawed back to life like a beached whale revived by a tidal wave." Thus, Hanrahan (and others) made America laugh with stuff like: "In Cleveland, Velveeta cheese can be found in the gourmet section of the supermarket."

Likewise, in April of 1974, an enormously popular Cleveland rock station, WMMS (100.7 FM), chose a buzzard as its station mascot - largely to reflect Cleveland's shaky economic status and the sense of death and decline in the air. American Greetings artist David Helton created an iconic caricature of a buzzard that quickly became more recognizable than the Coke logos and certainly the mascot of the Indians, Chief Wahoo. The choice of the buzzard proved shrewd as the City of Cleveland made national news in December 1978 when it defaulted on loans, making it the first major American city since the Great Depression to do so. The default resulted in a reduction of city services and another black eye for Cleveland's reputation nationally. In the '70s the city lost 23.6 percent of its population.

Perhaps it is no wonder, then, that in the early '70s, the Indians, discouraged mostly by poor attendance and a decaying stadium (and maybe a smidge by *Laugh In* jokes?), considered moving the team. Team owner Vernon Stouffer had an agreement in place to play several of the "home" games in the new and shiny New Orleans Superdome. He simply needed to act upon it.

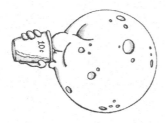

3

FROM A CROWN TO
A FROWN

(The Cleveland Indians: 1947-1973)

**"When you're playing for Cleveland, at least you
don't have to come in there on the road."**

– Dick Bosman

To many Clevelanders, it must have felt like the city and their baseball team had
hit the rock bottom of the burning Cuyahoga River at precisely the same time.
How had the city's baseball fortunes come to this low estate in 1973, 25 years
after being the toast of America's sports world, led by a promoter extraordinaire,
winners of the 1948 World Series, and the proud possessor of an all-time major
league attendance mark of over 2.6 million fans?

After his short - but wildly successful - three-year ownership, Bill Veeck,
needing money for a divorce settlement, sold the franchise soon after that
remarkable 1948 season. The team's success on the field would continue for
almost another ten years under General Manager Hank Greenberg[14], who was

---

14 Greenberg had been an outstanding player for the Tigers and was elected
to the Hall of Fame in 1956.

also part of the new ownership group. Greenberg hired Al Lopez as field manager, who would go on to a Hall of Fame career with the Indians and White Sox. From 1948 to 1955, though, the Indians were no slouches. They averaged 94 wins a season, achieved eight consecutive first division finishes, won another American League pennant ('54), and finished no lower than second place for six straight years. But, like everyone else, they just couldn't beat the (damn) New York Yankees, finishing second to them five times in a span of six years.

With all of that, maybe the fan base had begun to take such success for granted. Despite all those winning seasons, attendance in the massive Municipal Stadium dropped steadily - and it showed. Compare 2,620,627 in 1948 to 722,256 in 1957. Even the most enthusiastic Ten Cent Beer Night drinker, in a post-game press conference, could make some logical conclusions about such numbers. In 1957, then, tired of second place finishes, and surely feeling the dramatic reduction in gate receipts, the ownership fired Hank Greenberg (although he remained a shareholder).

Over the next 15 seasons, then, four different ownership groups would struggle to regain the Indians' winning touch. In retrospect, it appeared that the management of the team was deeply flawed. They never seemed to have a plan, or, if they did, were able to stick to one. Short-term thinking led to a seemingly endless stream of player trades and repeated attempts to keep the fans and media engaged and optimistic. Such efforts may have produced short-term excitement, but ultimately made little difference, mostly resulting in clubhouse instability. No real attention was paid to building an organization that could return the organization to its winning ways.

Greenberg had correctly believed that a productive farm system was the key to long-term success. He did stock the farm with some notable talent: Rocky Colavito, Roger Maris, Ray Fosse, and Tommie Agee, for example. And strong pitching emerged from the system: Sam McDowell, a true ace of staff for eight seasons, Herb Score, Luis Tiant, Sonny Siebert, Steve Hargan, Jim "Mudcat" Grant, and Tommy John, to name a few.

But with management's lack of focus on chemistry and leadership, and an almost endless obsession with trades, the Indians had little to show for all this talent. In 1958, the owners signed Frank "Trader" Lane to a three-year contract, replacing Greenberg as GM. Rather than developing players through the farm system, Lane seemed to pin the team's hopes on, well, trading (thus the nickname). Also, ownership was so focused on attendance that Lane's contract called for a bonus of 5¢ per head for each fan over 800,000. Although Lane was the architect of one good season in 1959 (89-65), his chaotic management style (to wit: 51 player trade transactions involving 118 players, in just three years), led to his downfall. In 1960, Lane moved on.

Gabe Paul followed Lane as GM, but also as part-owner, which made him incredibly difficult to fire. Over the next 12 years, Paul served as GM, President, and owner (along with several others). Owner William Daley, then the next owner, Vernon Stouffer, put their faith in Paul, who always said his teams were "just about to gel." But they never seemed to do that, and in Paul's 12 seasons, the Indians only finished above .500 twice. Paul also hired six managers and presided over some of the worst attendance marks ever; during his tenure, the Indians never surpassed 935,000 fans in a season, and dipped as low as 591,361 fans in 1971.

The span of Lane's and Paul's team management years, from 1958-72, coincided with Cleveland's general decline as a city. Only civic pride and responsibility, as well as dogged determination by two ownership groups, kept the team from being moved to another city. One of those owners was Stouffer, who had made millions through a food-service operation most famous for frozen meals like French bread pizza. Stouffer bought the Indians in 1966 with the express purpose of assuring that it would not be moved to another city. In a terrible stroke of bad timing, though, his net worth cratered after he agreed to become part of a conglomerate, Litton Industries, whose stock plummeted. Stouffer spent most of his ownership simply trying to keep his own personal finances above water. He also, Sudyk and others noted, drank to excess and would pass out during Indians games, in full view of the fans. In the early '70s, Stouffer decided that he wanted to sell the team (and, most famously, nearly did sell to George Steinbrenner), but kept holding out for what he thought was a fair price. When the final out of '72 was recorded, the Indians and its fan base could only reflect upon a sad state of affairs: a 5th place AL East finish, a meager season attendance of 626,354 fans, financial disarray, and rumors (which had a great deal of substance) of the franchise leaving town. The team and community needed a change.

In 1972, Stouffer finally got the price he wanted as an ownership group of *50 people*, led by Clevelander Nick Mileti, paid $10 million for the team. "It ensured that - at least one more time - the Indians would remain in Cleveland." Mileti was a young, optimistic, and incredibly driven Cleveland native, prone to enthusiastic aphorisms like, "How do you eat an elephant? One bite at a time." The son of Sicilian immigrants, a graduate of Bowling Green State University, Mileti was a "borrow and buy businessman" and yet another much-needed savior of Cleveland baseball. Unlike owners who simply inherited a team, or who were fortunate enough to have amassed significant wealth in business and were able to simply buy franchises outright, Mileti was a different kind of "owner." Specifically, he was the master of uniting dozens of investors in order to purchase a team. In 1969 Mileti did just that to buy the AHL Cleveland Barons and their home, The Cleveland Arena. In 1970, he cobbled together $3.7 million in order to buy a new basketball franchise called the Cleveland Cavaliers. And for this he was lauded throughout the greater Cleveland community. In 1972, he again pooled money together to buy a minor league hockey team called the Cleveland Crusaders. After selling the Barons, he proceeded to his next magic trick, breaking ground on The Coliseum, a brand new state-of-the-art facility strategically located in Richfield, midway between Akron and Cleveland. The Coliseum would be the home of the Crusaders and the Cavs, as well as the venue for a number of big-name acts. And as if this weren't enough, Mileti somehow found the time to buy AM radio giant, WWWE (1100), the broadcast home for the Indians and the Cavaliers. Running all three teams, Mileti believed, created a "synergistic concept," whereupon all three franchises would "work in concert to woo the public."[15] What he had accomplished in four short years was remarkable. And he had saved the Indians. As one might expect, though, running all three teams, a world-class arena, and a radio station, simply proved to be too much.

---

15 In many respects, this led to a franchise resurgence in the '70s. The Indians were nursed along until the 1986 purchase by Richard and Dick Jacobs, who had the resources and negotiation skills to rebuild the team and get a new modern stadium built.

But Mileti was stretched too thin and "in the red." And a team owned by 50 people was certainly not an ideal blueprint for success. The 1973 Indians, in the first year of the Mileti ownership, had lost another million dollars and needed some guidance. Enter Alva "Ted" Bonda, a part owner of all three teams. He was perfectly positioned, with the blessing of Mileti and the other investors, to serve as the team's executive vice president. Bonda, who had invested in the Cavs and the Indians, also knew a thing or two about running businesses.

The employees loved Bonda. Named after Alva Bradley - remember that Indians owner from the Great Depression and when they first played at Municipal? - Bonda was a Clevelander and a self-made businessman who had made significant money in a number of ways, including partnering with Howard Metzenbaum in an airport parking company (APCOA). As a leader, he conveyed a "don't panic" perspective - and liked to have fun. Bonda also loved tennis and golf and, at one point, decided he would like to see if he - or anyone - could hit a ball using a 5-iron from home plate over the top of the centerfield scoreboard. He invited Charlie Sifford, the first African-American to play on the PGA tour, to join him in the challenge (neither were successful). Bonda injected new energy and faith into the front office.

"Ted was a real gentleman," remembered Randy Adamack, a young public relations assistant with the team.[16] "He always treated me well." Adamack, who would go on to have a long career in baseball, noted how Bonda had a "different kind of job" because the Indians were owned by 50 different people. Jackie York, the Indians' '74 director of promotions, said Bonda was one of the finest people she ever worked with. "I respected him immensely," York recalled. "He empowered you to do the work and he gave you the flexibility to do the job. He had an amazing sense of humor. He could give it and he could take it." Drummer John Adams remembered Bonda as a man of the people, perhaps more of a baseball executive in Veeck's mold - the kind of guy who liked to watch the Indians with the fans. "I first met him beating the drum out there (in the bleachers).

16 Adamack graduated from Wittenberg University and was one of the first students in the Ohio University Sports Administration program, one of the first such programs in the country.

He would walk around the ballpark. He was just 'Ted.' He'd come by and say hello and he'd sit out there. And he'd always be screaming, 'Bunt! Bunt! Bunt!' " Adams laughed. "So, one time we're sitting there and he goes, 'John, I'm gonna be serious. Anything you want, *anything* you want...I will get it for you.' I said, 'OK, Ted - Here's what I want: Every time you say, 'Bunt,' I can call you a stupid son-of-a-bitch and we're still friends.' And he said, 'OK, asshole.' "

Early in 1974, Bonda and his team faced a task taller than a thousand of Cleveland's Terminal Towers stacked one upon another. Attendance at the Indians games in the late '60s and early '70s was sometimes so sparse that fans were fairly confident that if they yelled at a specific player or umpire, they would be heard. "We got on the case of the Umpire Ron Luciano," recalled Bun Blossom, who was an Indians fan and served as treasurer for the team in '74. "Between innings he turned around and tipped his cap to us. Fom that moment on, he had endeared himself to me. There were so few fans there that he could actually hear us."[17]

Blossom and his brother, Bing, were also major investors in the ownership group. In fact, Mileti's initial proposal to major league baseball was turned down as additional capital was required. The Blossom brothers provided it. As treasurer, Blossom was obviously also privy to the financial challenges the franchise had in 1974. "One day," Blossom said, "Ted came into my office and said 'How are things going?' and all I did was open up the bottom drawer of my desk that had a half million in checks that we couldn't release because we couldn't cover it. He just sort of laughed. I knew then that it wasn't the end of the world." Blossom added that the franchise had taken out loans from Cleveland banks and it was very frequently a precarious situation, but Bonda knew that from a public relations standpoint that the banks wouldn't "call in the loans" on the Cleveland Indians. "As treasurer it was my job to manage the internal financial stuff and not being able to pay bills was horrible. We muddled through," Blossom reflected. "Someone more naive (than Ted Bonda) - who had no idea - would not have known how to deal with the banks when they rattled their swords."

---

17 Footnote: Luciano once threw Earl Weaver, Manager of the Elmira Pioneers, out of four consecutive games.

"He had the toughness to fend off the other limited partners who from time-to-time wanted his job. Bonda had to keep the 50 partners together, despite occasional attempts at mutiny," said Fazio.

The Indians had just 16 people in their front office in 1974. Yet Bonda, who was one of them, put tremendous confidence in each person. Despite the barebones budget and a squad that again might struggle to finish over .500, they would do their best to promote the Indians and to save baseball in Cleveland. And to help them do that, they would lean on 24-year-old Carl Fazio Jr., a young and energetic native son and die-hard Indians fan.

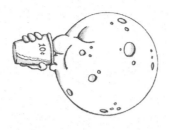

4

THE WHIZ KIDS

"Don't laugh. Two young men in our community, one 19 and the other 22, intend to own the Indians within 10 years and put them on top of the baseball world. If anybody can do it, these two boys can."

– Hal Lebovitz, The Plain Dealer

Carl Fazio, Jr., marketing director for the 1974 Cleveland Indians, was the son of a highly successful Cleveland-area supermarket founder, Carl Fazio, a 20th century American success story. Fazio was born in 1917 in Sant'Agata di Militello, a picturesque coastal town in Sicily, then moved to Cleveland in 1920. Growing up in the roaring '20s and not-so-roaring '30s, Fazio loved few things more than going to Cleveland's League Park where he cheered heartily for Indians stars Hal Trosky and Earl Averill. He attended John Adams High School, but dropped out in the heart of the Great Depression, primarily to help his parents run their small fruit and vegetable store on Lee Road in Cleveland Heights. In the decades that followed, Fazio and his brother John surrounded themselves with good people and expanded Fazio's. They bought Fisher Foods, Cleveland's supermarket leader at that time, but one that had lost its edge. They grew the business into a grocery empire that had 200 supermarkets in three states and was traded on the New York Stock Exchange.

"He had a great life, lived to be 102, and enjoyed the fruits of his labor. My father believed if you love what you are doing, it's not work," Carl Fazio, Jr. said. "He led by example. He was energetic, a hard worker, focused and competitive. The supermarket business happens every day, the profit margins are razor thin so you have to take care of the customer. He always said, 'the customer is always right, even when she's wrong.' - that's the culture he built. That customer service ethic really hit home with me and in my baseball career I always put the fans first and tried to give them a great value."

Carl Jr., born in 1950, grew up loving sports and in all things Cleveland sports - and despite the Indians' struggles during his formative years, Fazio remained a passionate fan. In the summer of 1967, Fazio captained a summer baseball team made up of classmates from Hawken School. The team was coached by Kip Horsburgh, an older Hawken schoolmate. The pair quickly discovered that they had something in common: baseball, yes, but more than that - very specific plans within the industry of baseball. That summer, fueled by their enthusiasm for the Indians (who were struggling again), Fazio and Horsburgh attended an impressive 30 games. They weren't just watching as casual fans, though. They analyzed, dissected, discussed, and looked carefully at all of the details - everything that goes into running a team: how quickly you got into the ballpark, how good was the service at the concession stands, were they integrating the young players into the team - *everything*.

"We looked at it like, 'What would we do if we were running the team?'" Fazio recalled. Oh, and add Horsburgh to the list of young men who fell in love with baseball thanks to Municipal Stadium. "My father took me to my first game to see Bob Feller - probably in '55. I remember walking up the ramp at a night game and then you see that beautiful grass under the lights," said Horsburgh. "I didn't think it was a 'mistake on the lake.' " "I always thought the game had a wonderful beauty to it," Horsburgh said, "It made sense and all fit together. I loved the trappings of it. The first thing you saw was the field and I had that experience when your mouth drops seeing all that perfect green. I started scoring games. For some reason I liked the business aspect of it."

Horsburgh, like Fazio, absolutely *loved* the Indians, despite the franchise's long spiral downward through the late '50s and throughout the '60s. "It was the best of times. You look back and you don't think about how bad the team was. It was just 'our team.'" Horsburgh especially revered Rocco Domenico "Rocky" Colavito. Colavito, a 6'3" slugging outfielder, was a star for the Indians during a stretch when they had few others to brag about (other than McDowell).[18] And in the early '60s Horsburgh remembers the Yankees coming to town and going to a near capacity and electrified Municipal Stadium. Despite his passion, Horsburgh concluded early on in the affair that he wasn't destined for the majors - at least as a player.

"I was such a poor athlete - overweight," he said. "I played on an intramural team with Marty Feller and Steve Greenberg (sons of Hall of Fame players Bob Feller and Hank Greenberg). Feller was the greatest living Indian, while Greenberg was a member of the Indians front office. "Their dads would come to our games," Horsburgh recalled. "But it was very clear to me: I couldn't even dream about playing in the major leagues." But that didn't dampen Horsburgh's love of the national pastime. Like Fazio, he was a loyal Indians fan and extremely proud of his scrapbook full of photos of him posing with Feller, Doby, and other stars. Undaunted by his own lack of major league potential, sometime around 6th grade, Horsburgh stumbled across another idea: if he couldn't *play* major

---

18 Rocky "The Rock" Colavito emerged in 1955 and anchored the Indians lineup until 1959 when, much to the dismay of the fan base, General Manager Frank "Trader" Lane swapped Colavito for a player he had long coveted, Detroit's Harvey Keunn. Cincinnati General Manager Gabe Paul quipped, "The Indians traded a slow guy with power for a slow guy with no power." In 1959 Colavito had hit 42 home runs and driven in 111 runs for the Indians; Kuenn had led the league in hitting with a .353 average, but had just 9 home runs. The Indians, led by Paul, traded for Colavito, enabling the outfielder to make a triumphant return to the city he loved. In '65, he drove in 108 runs and was one of the starting outfielders in the All-Star Game. He continued with the Indians through part of 1967 when Paul traded him to the White Sox. Colavito had felt Paul and manager Joe Adcock were colluding to keep him off the field in order to prevent the player from reaching incentives that were in his contract. He remains one of the most impactful and memorable players for fans of that era, including sports writer Terry Pluto whose book *The Curse of Rocky Colavito* celebrates the man and the frustrations of being a Cleveland sports fan.

league baseball, why not *run* a major league squad? "I had decided in 8th grade that I wanted to work in baseball and eventually run a major league team," recalled Horsburgh.

After graduating from Hawken, Horsburgh attended Bowdoin College and eventually Stanford Graduate School of Business, while Fazio finished at Hawken and then eventually attended Hobart College in Geneva, New York. During the winter of '69, while home for Thanksgiving break, the pair found themselves in the Cleveland Arena, a 10,000-seat venue most famous for being the site of Alan Freed's 1952 Moondog Coronation Ball, often considered the nation's first major rock and roll concert.[19] They were there to see the Cleveland Barons, the American Hockey League franchise owned by energetic sports entrepreneur Nick Mileti. Excited about the organization and the everything sports, the pair approached Mileti during a game and immediately caught the young owner's attention.

"He was all ears - had owned the team for two weeks," remembered Fazio. "And on the spot he offered a job to us for the coming summer - straight commission and no expenses - selling tickets. We were wild-eyed about the opportunity. We were on top of the world because we had a job in professional sports in a city that we grew up in and loved." The following year, 1970, building on their success selling season tickets for the Barons the previous summer, Mileti channeled their enthusiasm by adding Fazio and Horsburgh to the first front-office staff of another one of his teams, an absolute sports franchise baby - but one with tremendous potential: the NBA expansion franchise Cleveland Cavaliers. Simultaneously, someone tipped off *Plain Dealer* writer Hal Lebovitz to Fazio and Horsburgh, and their ambitions, and he began to champion them to his readers. It turned out that Mileti, their new boss, was slightly jealous of the press the pair were receiving. "I thought I was going to work for Nick Mileti the rest

---

19 The Moondog Coronation Ball was another Cleveland crowd-gone-wild situation due to more tickets (including counterfeited ones) being printed (than the venue held). An estimated 20,000 (or some say 25,000) tried to get into Cleveland Arena, which held only about 10,000. Concerned about a riot, police shut down the concert after an opening song by Paul "Hucklebuck" Williams. As such, the concert was really only about 45 minutes long. But it gave birth to Cleveland's "rock and roll" identity.

of my life," said Horsburgh. "All he did was work and all we did was work. After some of the articles (by Lebovitz), he called us in and sat us down and said, 'I need you to know this: I run this team and you're not gonna run it.' "

But Mileti had hired the pair and genuinely liked the young men - and believed in them - even if their goals threatened him a little bit. After Mileti felt he had made himself clear regarding the teams he owned (and the ones the young men did not own), he offered Fazio and Horsburgh some helpful and timely advice: "Here's what you should do," Mileti told them. "Baseball is your first love. Go *buy* a minor league baseball team and get the experience you need running it."

And in the early '70s, simply buying a minor league team to use as a training ground, was not common. Most minor league teams were owned by civic-minded local business people. On the other hand, most minor league teams didn't cost thousands of dollars. Fazio and Horsburgh chewed on Mileti's advice then took it to heart, concluding that their plan to someday run a major league team had just one probable path: just like that of an aspiring ball player - they had to earn their chops in the minor leagues.[20] "That was back when Major League teams were hiring front office people that came up through the minors, as scouts or players, not smart guys from Harvard and Yale," recalled Horsburgh. "We were ahead of our time. We were business people and college educated."[21]

Ask and ye shall receive: word spread that a pair of ambitious young men were looking for an opportunity - any opportunity - to own and operate a minor league team and. They set off on a joyous and enthusiastic road trip, checking out opportunities in Bend, Coos Bay, and Medford, Oregon as well as Watertown, South Dakota. Minor league team operators were an unusual bunch in those times, presenting a wide range of opportunities. "For example, the guy that owned the team in Medford drove the bus on road trips to save money so there

20 Check out Netflix's fantastic documentary, *The Battered Bastards of Baseball,* which celebrates how Bing Russell and his son, actor Kurt Russell, blazed into Portland in 1973 to set up the independent Portland Mavericks. Bing Russell bought the Mavericks for $500. In 1978, Russell was compensated $206,000 (after arbitration) for the Mavericks, as the Beavers returned to Portland and the Pacific Coast League.

21 In 2020, NBC sports reported that 43% of baseball operations personnel were Ivy Leaguers.

was no one back in Medford selling tickets and promoting the team," said Fazio. Enter the Twin Falls (Idaho) Magic Valley Cowboys, a team in The Pioneer League. "Magic Valley" was the nickname for the area because they grew wonderful potatoes (and never had a crop failure). A group of local businessmen there had each chipped in $100 to keep the local team afloat but were tired and more than willing to hand over the reins for a season to two energetic dreamers. So they leased the team to Fazio and Horsburgh for a ceremonial price of one dollar.

Poised on what may have at one time seemed like the edge of the Western frontier, the Pioneer League was a half-season rookie league made up of six teams. They were stocked each summer with first-year players from the June amateur draft. Five of the franchises were affiliated with major league squads: the Great Falls Giants (San Francisco), the Billings Mustangs (Kansas City), the Idaho Falls Angels (Anaheim), the Caldwell Cubs (Chicago), and the Ogden Dodgers (Los Angeles). And then there were the Magic Valley Cowboys - affiliated with no one. For Fazio and Horsburgh in 1971, the Cowboys roster was patched together from the five other teams, on loan to the Cowboys, to create a much-needed sixth team in the league.

"We were part of a 'League of Nations' arrangement - they called us a 'bastard club'," Horsburgh recalled. The teams were definitely not giving Fazio and Horsburgh their best players - far from it. "They were giving us their less desirable - draftees - and their lower level prospects," recalled Fazio. "They kept the best ones." And sometimes diamonds emerged: future Hall of Famer George Brett played his first professional season with the Billings Mustangs that year.

The Magic Valley Cowboys were blessed with an excellent manager, Art Mazmanian, a scrappy junior college coach from L.A. He had been the starting second baseman on USC's 1948 national championship team. "Art was great," said Fazio. "He came for the summer and brought his wife and two kids. They worked in our concession stand."

Fazio and Horsburgh were like kids in a modern-day MLB souvenir shop. "We were so confident that it never occurred to us that we wouldn't succeed," said Fazio. They were blessed with a quaint but tiny wooden stadium, Jaycee Park, tucked into a municipal park in Twin Falls. It had been built by the WPA in 1939 for $30,000, was all wood and incredibly charming, but "could have burnt down at any time," recalls Horsburgh.

Loaded with enthusiasm and bursting with promotional ideas, but lacking an enormous budget, they ran a tight ship. A long-time Cleveland friend and teacher, Marianne Relic, volunteered to spend her entire summer break, contributing to their operation in every conceivable fashion. Together, they formed the Cowboys' entire three-person front office staff.

"We did absolutely everything," Horsburgh continued. "We printed the tickets and ran the concessions. We placed ads, set up accounting systems, spoke to the Jaycees, the Lions Club, the Rotary Club, and the Chamber of Commerce. We handwrote the payroll checks for players while the bus was waiting to leave on a road trip, even watered the infield one night when our one groundskeeper didn't show up. Jaycee Park had no ice machine, so to properly run the concessions - in the summer heat - we made a nightly ice run to the local 7-Eleven, filling two 10-gallon containers with ice. I thought I was running the New York Yankees. It was a great experience."

Horsburgh flew to Los Angeles to see the Dodgers' uniform outfitter, W.A. Goodman, who helped him pick out and design uniforms for the squad. After sorting through all of the traditional options he landed instead on an iconic look: cherry red. When the Magic Valley Cowboys finally trotted out in public, it didn't take long for a local writer to dub them "The Big Red Machine." Since they were their only uniform, the Cowboys wore them at home and on the road. Drawing on their Cleveland and Hawken connections, they even convinced Feller to come all the way to Twin Falls for the opener. They also gave stuff away, a relatively new concept in baseball, Horsburgh recalled, and certainly something new to Twin Falls.

"We had a T-shirt giveaway night sponsored by Twin Falls Mortuary," he laughed. "We had all the kids running around in mortuary T-shirts." They had caps, bat, and ball giveaways - as well as a Polaroid night where fans could pose with the players. "Sounds like such normal stuff today, but it just wasn't done back then," said Horsburgh. Overall, though, the entire experience proved invaluable.

After 35 home games, Fazio and Horsburgh proudly totaled up the season's attendance: just over 27,000 fans, almost 800 fans per game in the 1,800-seat ballpark. It was a significant improvement in attendance over previous years. Better yet, Fazio and Horsburgh picked up the utterly invaluable experience they had so desperately sought *and* they had interacted heavily with executives from five major league teams. The Magic Valley Cowboys finished a respectable 36-34 in 1971, tied for third place, and ahead of two teams that had provided them with players.[22]

"It was a different time, something not even close to duplicable in today's world, but an unbelievable opportunity for us to experience every single aspect of franchise operations, in a place we didn't even know existed a few months before we started," Fazio marvels nearly 50 years later. "We were on an uphill climb and ready for the next step."

Fazio and Horsburgh (and others) declared the venture a success, and the pair decided they were ready to climb the next rung of the baseball ladder; they wanted a bigger market, a higher level team, and more challenges. So, in 1972, thanks to referrals from baseball executives they had met, the pair hustled their way into Class AA baseball, taking over the Eastern League Elmira, New York Pioneers. The Pioneers were an Indians affiliate and blessed with a rich history in a quaint town. Like many ballclubs in a town of its size, The Pioneers had been affiliated with a variety of Major League clubs over the course of their existence: the Dodgers, Cardinals, Browns, Phillies, and Orioles. In 1951, while affiliated with the Brooklyn Dodgers, Elmira Pioneer Don Zimmer married his wife, Soot, at home plate. From 1962 to 1965 future Hall of Famer Earl Weaver managed the club. In the late '60s, the Pioneers were shared by the Royals and the Padres. In 1972 it was the Cleveland Indians' turn to be the Pioneers' major league affiliate. Fazio and Horsburgh each kicked in half and bought the Pioneers for $2,500 from the Kansas City Royals, who no longer wanted to own and operate minor league teams. A decade later a AA ball club would have cost them a great deal more than that. Heartened by their early career success in Twin Falls and the enthusiastic backing of Mileti and Lebovitz, the duo rode into another

---

22 Fazio and Horsburgh (and the visiting Bob Feller) weren't the only Cleveland connection to the Pioneer League. In 1968, 18-year-old Oscar Gamble, a future Indian, hit .266 for another team in the league - the Caldwell Cubs. Gamble had been scouted by famed Negro Leaguer Buck O'Neil, who said that he was the greatest prospect he had signed since Ernie Banks.

challenging, sleepy, and declining town. Fazio and Horsburgh had progressed from Idaho's Pioneer League to Western New York's Pioneers.

"The dash and optimism of these young men is encouraging and so is their desire to learn the business from the ground up," Lebovitz wrote. "Too many baseball promoters and owners today are not well-schooled in the business. They come into baseball with fortunes and reputations established in other fields. Very few have made baseball their life's work. But Horsburgh and Fazio are coming up the ladder of success by using each rung."

The Elmira Pioneers played baseball at Dunn Field, an old stadium nestled in southwestern New York near the generally peaceful Chemung River, which wandered some 46 miles east and southeast through the likes of Corning, Big Flats, Elmira, and Waverly before pouring into the Susquehanna River in northern Pennsylvania. Along its banks were quaint pre-colonial towns that had been founded in the 1700s. Named after a tavern owner's daughter, Elmira, New York was dubbed "The Queen City." The Chemung Canal, finished in 1833, helped connect the town to the Erie Canal and the likes of Rochester, Buffalo, and Albany, leading to growth in the 19th and into the 20th century. In 1950, Elmira boasted 49,716 people, but when Horsburgh and Fazio arrived in 1972, the population had dropped to around 39,000. Mark Twain, who married an Elmira girl, had spent many summers there and wrote in a quaint octagonal-shaped study that was moved from his sister-in-law's farm to the campus of Elmira College. It was in Elmira that Twain wrote much of *The Adventures of Huckleberry Finn* and Twain's final resting place is Elmira's Woodlawn Cemetery.

Fazio and Horsburgh thought that Elmira certainly met their criteria: a loyal populace that valued a rich baseball tradition. Also, it was located just 60 miles from Geneva, New York, where Fazio was finishing his degree at Hobart. But not everyone had a rosy view of the town. While covering a Pioneer game against the Pittsfield (MA) Rangers, a *Boston Globe* writer wrote, "Mark Twain lived in this industrial town of 39,000 people on the junction of the Erie and Lackawanna Railroad and the Chemung River, and it's a good thing he had a sense of humor. It is dreary and bleak; its sidewalks deserted by people who apparently have enough sense to be elsewhere. As the Pittsfield Rangers' bus rolled over a bridge on its way to the park recently, the players recalled that the last time they had been in town the authorities were dragging the river for a body. It was a general consensus that the body had been fortunate."

But of course Elmira wasn't that bad - and what did a snooty Boston writer know anyway? To the contrary, it was a hard-working, slightly declining, but enthusiastic American town - a little, in that respect, like Cleveland.[23] Most importantly, in the eyes of Fazio and Horsburgh, the Queen City loved its baseball.

"A baseball team is one of the pillars of the community. When you own the baseball team you meet everybody - the fans, the business people, the media, the mayor, and community leaders - this great diversity of people in the town," said Fazio.

Thanks to his understanding and cooperative Hobart College professors, Fazio was able to accelerate his final semester and spend most of his time in Elmira. He and Horsburgh set their sights on an audacious but lofty attendance number: 100,000 fans for the season. They already had a head start in one crucial aspect: they had brought with them the cherry red uniforms, with black and white trim, that they had acquired in Twin Falls. They simply tore off "Cowboys" and stitched on "Pioneers." Up next: time to sell some tickets.

Just as they did in Twin Falls, Fazio and Horsburgh put together sponsorship and ticket packages and went door-to-door, introducing themselves to businesses. They spoke to local organizations and clubs. They met with Mayor Ed Loll. And they, of course, planned promotions. Loads and loads of promotions: Valley Baseball Day, City of Elmira Employees Night, Valu Makers Night, Bat Day, Hospital Day (ticket admits hospital employee's entire family), Marine Midland Bank Day at the Ball Park, Businessmen's Luncheon Day, and on and on. They passed out foldout wallet-sized schedules, sponsored by Genesee Beer, brewed in nearby Rochester. The schedule highlighted the home dates and declared the

---

23 One ambitious resident of Elmira was a young man named Tommy Hilfiger. In 1971, Hilfiger opened a hip clothing store called The People's Place, in downtown Elmira. Hilfiger and a pal would drive to New York City to get clothing - bell-bottoms, leather jackets, and peasant blouses - to stock the store. Eventually, though, he began designing his own clothing. Today, the Tommy Hilfiger Fashion Business School is part of Elmira College.

team's ambitions: "100,000 OR BUST!" (also, "The Pioneers Want You in '72"). A hundred thousand fans translated to just under an average of 1,500 fans over 67 home dates.

"These guys never give up, never lose enthusiasm," Elmira sportswriter Al Mallette wrote, "Which is the greatest thing that's happened to Elmira baseball since Ward Goodrich, whose 10-gallon hat and cowboy boots, lured 94,000 fans to Dunn Field in 1962." Goodrich, who took over the Pioneers before the '62 season, managed to more than double the season attendance from 40,000 to just over 80,000. (Perhaps it didn't hurt that he had a young and fiery Earl Weaver managing that ball club.)

Despite all of their determination and energy, though, the 1972 Elmira Pioneers opening weekend may have been an unfortunate harbinger of things to come. After a massive amount of legwork and buildup (including a return engagement from Feller), Fazio and Horsburgh hoped for a 6,000-fan sellout for the opener. Instead, bitterly cold and persistent spring rain, and a brisk high of just 40 degrees, prompted the postponement of the game after two innings. The crowd of 3,024 scurried home to their fireplaces. The next day only 1,497 fans showed up as it continued to drizzle. Finally, on the 3rd day - the series finale - the pair had to cancel the game and series.

The rain in Elmira, it seemed, was only just beginning.

On June 18, 1972, 70 games into the season, thousands of miles south, a hurricane of epic proportions - eventually christened "Agnes" - gathered strength across the Yucatan Peninsula and Gulf of Mexico, ultimately slamming into the Florida coast, and unleashing 26 tornadoes throughout Florida. Two days later, legendary baseball clown Max Patkin frolicked across Dunn Field in front of a respectable crowd of 927 fans. The Pioneers beat the Pittsfield (Massachusetts) Rangers 8-5, while, well south of Elmira, Agnes had diminished to tropical storm level. Yet the meteorological die was cast: in the days that followed, tropical storm force winds and massive rainfall overwhelmed 15 Eastern states and Washington, D.C. - from Florida to New York. Horsburgh and Fazio canceled T-Shirt Night planned for June 21st. In a matter of a few hours, in Elmira and throughout New York's Southern Tier, Agnes-generated storms dumped a record amount of rain. The Chemung River, just 200 feet from the ballpark, quickly overflowed its

100-year-old dikes, prompting floodwaters to rush through Elmira's streets and especially the quaint and quiet Dunn Field. A torrent of water ripped through the grandstands, knocked over part of the outfield wall, and carried the Pioneers' concession stands out into the parking lot. The normally gentle waters of the Chemung River waters rose up and overwhelmed the playing field, submerging it in eight feet of muddy water. The stadium and field, in Horsburgh's words, were "a real mess...an unbelievable mess."

"We had just stocked up the concession stands with hot dogs and buns and peanuts for an upcoming 14-game home stand. It was late June - it should have normally been a strong attendance weekend and then the flood hit." The Whiz Kids, understandably, were personally devastated, but undeterred and accepting. "Baseball is unforgiving - you simply have to play the games," Horsburgh said. "And you certainly can't control the weather. But it was nothing compared to the thousands whose homes and businesses were damaged or destroyed." They quickly declared that they would not seek any help from the City of Elmira, which had many other priorities in helping the citizens of Elmira and the entire region in a long road to recovery. They also had no idea where their team was. "It took us two days to find our players," Horsburgh recalled.[24]

Both realized that a natural disaster of this magnitude was out of their control. As the days passed, they decided that Dunn Field would be unplayable for quite some time. They scrambled for a place to play. Finally, they found a converted football stadium in Waterbury, Connecticut - over four hours east of Elmira, but geographically a good fit for Eastern League travel - that would host them for as long as it would take to make Dunn Field playable again. Ultimately, the Pioneers lost 23 home dates, and had to play 14 consecutive doubleheaders. By mid-August they had cleaned the stadium - thanks in part to the help from many player wives. When they returned to play at Dunn Field, in cooperation with the city fathers, they offered free admission for "Flood Recovery Night" and enjoyed the kind of night they had always imagined: a jammed stadium. "It was just one of those really great feel-good moments, a packed house of happy

---

24 From the Caribbean to Canada, Hurricane Agnes killed 128 and led to $2.1 billion in damages. It was the costliest hurricane to hit the United States to date. One of the Pioneers had lost everything and just decided to call it quits on his baseball career.

people enjoying baseball on a beautiful summer evening and temporarily putting their travails aside," recalled Fazio.

It had been an exhausting season in many ways. In addition to experiencing a flood of Biblical proportions, the team of Indians' farm hands had been in last place from the first day of the '71 season to the last. The Pioneers finished with a 46-91 record, 36½ games out of first place. Needless to say, Fazio and Horsburgh did not meet their goal of 100,000 fans. When the Elmira Pioneers recorded the final out of the '72 season, the pair sold the franchise for $25,000, barely recouping their losses. The team would be moved to Waterbury, Connecticut. Elmira was the smallest city in AA baseball - the Pioneers were destined to be a better fit for the shorter season offered by the New York/ Penn League (Class A baseball).

Horsburgh and Fazio had certainly grown professionally from their two seasons as minor league owners. Their minor league mission had been successful and both returned to Cleveland. Horsburgh took a job with Cleveland Trust Bank, while Fazio returned to the supermarket business. Within a year both had calls from two major league teams: Horsburgh from the Texas Rangers and Fazio from the Cleveland Indians.

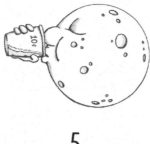

5

THE TEAM THAT COULDN'T HIT[25]

"Once again the fact was underscored that the Texas Rangers were not really a baseball franchise but rather a Kurt Vonnegut novel."

– Mike Shropshire, *Seasons From Hell*

When Kip Horsburgh, one of the Cleveland Whiz Kids, agreed to work for the Texas Rangers in 1974, he joined a "very tired, depressed front office with a few folks that had moved over with the Senators." Today the Texas Rangers front office has hundreds of front office employees. In 1974, they had 17. Very few sportswriters, employees, fans, and even players would disagree with Horsburgh's assessment of the general vibe, although 1974 would actually turn out to be much less depressing than their first two seasons in Texas. In 1974, the Texas Rangers were in their third year of existence, well, sort of, at least in Arlington, Texas. The Rangers were born when the Washington Senators, who had been in the nation's capital from 1961-1971, decided that they had enough. More specifically, frustrated Senators owner Bob Short, who had bashed the city saying that the crime-ridden area near the stadium was just one reason they had poor attendance, issued an ultimatum: if someone didn't buy the squad for $12 million,

---

25 *The Team That Couldn't Hit*, published by the Society of American Baseball Research, focuses on the futile first several years of the Texas Rangers.

he would move the team to another city. No one took Short up on his demand. (Amazingly, in hindsight, George Steinbrenner bought the New York Yankees in 1973 for just $8.8 million dollars.)

Both Short and his manager, Ted Williams, often thought of as the greatest hitter of all time, wanted out of DC. In his autobiography, Major League Baseball Commissioner Bowie Kuhn recalled a conversation with the defiant and angry Short. "No one can keep me in Washington, not Nixon, not Cronin (AL President), not Kuhn," Short said. "I will cannibalize the club if necessary. I own it and I will take it to St. Paul if I want. I have lawyers, too. I will move wherever I want...Ted (Williams) says Washington is a horseshit town and I've gotta get out. I'll go elsewhere before I'm forced into bankruptcy like Seattle. I know I had my eyes wide open when I went to Washington, but I told the American League that I wouldn't keep it there forever." At one point, the President of the United States even wrote a note to the American League owners who had gotten together to consider the proposed move of the Senators to Arlington, Texas. "I implore you," Richard Nixon wrote, "Repeat: I implore you: Do not move the nation's national pastime from the nation's capital." But the majority of the owners voted to allow the move (the White Sox and Orioles dissented). Washington, D.C.'s media and its fans - including Nixon - were enraged about Short's intentions.

As the Senators limped toward the finish line of an eventual 63-96 season (in which they drew just 666,156 fans), Short made his decision: he would move the Senators to Arlington, Texas for the 1972 season and they would forever thereafter be known as the Texas Rangers. Senators fans and the DC media were upset and couldn't understand how they had lost the franchise to "a dinky nowhere town between Dallas and Fort Worth with all the big league stature of an anthill."[26]

The American League owners ignored Nixon's plea and voted 10-2 to allow Short and the Senators to move. On September 21, 1971, some 14,000 fans paid to attend the Senator's final game in Washington, D.C. - a tilt against the New York Yankees. The somewhat angry crowd at RFK Stadium, though, ballooned

---

26 Short had experience in these types of dealings. A few years earlier, as owner of the NBA's Minneapolis Lakers, he moved the franchise to Los Angeles.

to some 25,000 after the ticket takers and security guards abandoned their posts. Fans unfurled two narrow vertical banners that simply declared, "Short Stinks!" Mike Kekich pitched for the Yankees while Dick Bosman toed the rubber for the Senators (and both would later pitch for Texas and Cleveland). Bosman gave up five runs and Kekich yielded three, but the Senators, thanks to a Frank Howard home run, rallied late and were leading 7 to 5 headed into the ninth inning. Poised for one last win, the Senators had two outs in the ninth when the charged up fans could apparently no longer take it. Or, perhaps, some later reflected, they were just drunk and confused and thought the game had actually ended. A young man sprinted onto the field and tore first base off its moorings and ran off with it. There were apparently no security guards around to stop him, which may have encouraged what happened next. Thousands of fans followed the base stealer, overwhelming the infield, stealing bases, digging up dirt, tearing numbers and lights from the scoreboard, snatching anything removable. WWDC radio broadcaster Ron Menchine hoped, in vain, for order to be restored: "So we certainly hope that this ballgame can be concluded...The players now are clearing the field...as pandemonium has broken loose...and the field is filled with many souvenir hunters...The Senators lead, 7 to 5, with two outs...Police are trying to restore order, but the crowd continues to mill all around the field... Some fans are scooping up dirt...more and more now are converging on the field." The umpires declared the game a forfeit, adjusting the score (one run for each inning) to 9-0 in favor of the Yankees - a result that foreshadowed the final score in Cleveland in early June of 1974.

"Well, it's a strange way to lose a ball game," a defeated Menchine told whoever was still listening. "It's a strange way to wind up major league baseball in the nation's capital...but I guess it's been a topsy-turvy season, no one believed that there would not be major league baseball in the nation's capital. But it's sad to report there no longer is."[27] [28] [29]

And with that the Washington Senators morphed into the Texas Rangers. The team packed up and headed some 1,348 miles southwest to Northern Texas

---

27 If it's not confusing enough, baseball nuts might be interested that the original Washington Senators were one of the charter member teams in the American League and existed from 1901 until 1960, when they moved to Minnesota to morph into the Twins. In 1961, the American League, recognizing that Washington, D.C. could not be without baseball, awarded a new expansion franchise to the city - the Senators were back! Washington, D.C. would not host major league baseball again until the Montreal Expos moved there in 2005 to create the Washington Nationals.

28 In 1973 former Senators radio announcer Shelby Whitfield excoriated Short in *Kiss It Goodbye,* scorning him for his "robber-baron, public-be-damned, let's-make-money-without spending-any-attitude."

29 Combining beer, baseball, and fan frustrations, just before Short moved the Senators to Arlington, a fan allegedly poured a beer over Short's head to fully convey how he felt about the team leaving. Yet, the superfan known as "Baseball Bill", Bill Holdforth, claims he never did that. "If you knew me, you knew it wasn't me who did it. I'd never waste a beer like that." But Holdforth and other Senators fans definitely showed their disgust. A 21-year-old clerk at the Library of Congress, Holdforth was also an usher at RFK Stadium, but had lost that gig in 1971 when he and some friends found a Short dummy in the stands and paraded around with it. So, when Short and the Rangers came into town in May of 1972, Baseball Bill and some friends were there to greet him. "We couldn't let him get into town without doing something," Holdforth said. Armed with another effigy - a large white-shirted, tie-bearing dummy with *The Sporting News* stuffed into it, Baseball Bill snuck down to Short, who was in the first row. He stood behind Short, hanging the dummy and a sign bearing "Short Stinks!" and posed for photographers. In the photo, a portly Holdforth, who has been described as Bluto from *Animal House* because of his tremendous beer-drinking abilities, smiles while Short leans forward looking miserable. In 1978, Holdforth learned that Short was running for a Minnesota seat in the U.S. Senate and teamed up with some friends to establish the "Keep Bob Short out of Washington" committee. They held a fundraising party at Holdforth's apartment, charging $10 a person to get in, then placed an ad in the Minneapolis Tribune: "Bob Short held our trust for three years, and we were SHORT CHANGED." Short won the primary but lost the election.

and, as one writer called it, "the world's biggest open air roaster," also known as Arlington Stadium.

In 1965, city officials in Arlington, Texas built Arlington Stadium, originally dubbed "Turnpike Stadium," with the clear goal of eventually attracting a professional baseball franchise. Longtime Mayor Tom Vandergriff believed that the city's location - not exactly equidistant between rapidly growing Dallas and Fort Worth, but close enough - would ultimately draw a suitor. For several years it served as the home of the Fort Worth Cats. Vandergriff nearly convinced Charley Finley to move the Kansas City A's to Arlington, but they headed to Oakland. Even Vernon Stouffer, rumor had it, considered moving the Indians to Arlington. Vandergriff was right, he and Arlington would entice a team to come there, although the process took several years. Finally, Short and the Senators bit.

Built for just $1.9 million in a natural bowl some 40 feet below the Texas landscape, Arlington Stadium had a coliseum shape, offering seats to patrons near the infield and wrapped around foul pole-to-foul pole. Across the outfield, fans could sit in bleachers - the largest bleacher section in the major leagues. Originally built to host 10,500 fans, it had been primarily those bleachers that were expanded in order to beef up the stadium's capacity to 35,000 to make Major League Baseball happy. What the Stadium did not offer, however, was shade. Theoretically the subterranean construction was intended to help combat the vicious summer heat. Players in the home dugout enjoyed air conditioning, however, as Mike Hargrove recalled, the Rangers would shut it off during the game. And over in the visitor's dugout? No AC at all. To get from the dugout to the clubhouse the players had to pass underneath the stands. "And the rats were big," Hargrove recalled. A stiff wind generally blew in from right field just about every night.

Texans love a good saying more than, well, more than a clam likes high tide - especially quips about how hot it gets in Texas. One can only imagine, then, the rich sayings about trying to enjoy a baseball game while sitting on metal bleachers in Arlington Stadium must have elicited. It was more often that not "hot as Hades, hot as the hinges (or hubs) of hell, hot as a depot stove, hot as a two-dollar pistol, hot as a billy goat in a pepper patch, hot as a summer revival, hot as a pot of neck bones, hot as a stolen tamale, hot enough to fry eggs on the sidewalk, hotter than whoopee in woolens, hotter than a honeymoon hotel, hotter than a burning stump, hotter than blue blazes, hotter than a fur coat in Marfa.

And that was in April.

Like Cleveland's Municipal Stadium, Arlington Stadium had its flaws, but also a strange allure. "It was a dump, but it was *our* dump," remembers fan David Williams. Between the frequent playing of the "William Tell Overture," "Cotton Eyed Joe" (in the 7th), ballpark nachos (the first in the major leagues), and a Texas-shaped scoreboard, *some* fans loved coming to the park. In the late innings, too, scantily clad dancers and "bodyguards" would circulate through the crowd to let folks know that their ticket stub would get them free admission to their nearby establishments.

In terms of architectural aesthetics, *Fort Worth Star Telegram* writer Mike Shropshire described the building as, "Drab, squat, and lifeless". Shropshire also noted that civic boosters liked to suggest that the feel of the stadium was "'intimate." He added, "...And it was - intimate like a drunk tank in the Bronx on New Year's Eve." Pitcher Pete Broberg, who came with the team from Washington, said that Arlington Stadium looked like it had been built with an Erector Set.

And, as a team, perhaps the '72 Rangers were perhaps the equivalent of an Erector Set. They are immortalized in a Society of American Baseball Research collection *The Team That Couldn't Hit* as well as Mike Shropshire's outstanding *Seasons In Hell*. Their inaugural season began with a strike that led to the loss of eight games from their original schedule (which was a good thing for the franchise). When it was all said and done, the Rangers finished 54-100. The season was marked by a particularly brutal September in which the Rangers were 3-23, lowlighted by a 15-game losing streak. After '72 concluded, Williams seemed to conclude how dire the situation was and quit. Somehow, things got worse in 1973. Whitey Herzog took over for Williams and tackled the job with a sense of humor, but the Rangers, playing more games than the previous year, also had an opportunity to lose more contests. They finished a dismal 57-105.

The '73 Rangers pitching staff included a left-handed knuckleballer and a pitcher who had shot himself in his pitching hand while cleaning a gun. Over the course of the season, Herzog was completely unafraid to tell the truth about his squad: they were bad. Twice he replaced his entire starting pitching staff of five. But the benefit of being so horrible in 1972 was that it gave the Rangers the top draft pick in 1973. That, in their opinion, was a little bit like hitting the lottery. In the spring of 1973, a stellar Houston high school lefty named David Clyde wowed not just the City of Houston but impressed most major league scouts. Rangers Owner Bob Short salivated like a Texan waiting for a plate full of brisket. Clyde, he decided, was precisely what the franchise needed: a Texan boy blessed with a Sandy Koufax-like curveball. During his senior season of high school, Clyde registered an 18-0 record, 0.18 ERA, and struck out a whopping 328 batters in 148 innings. The Rangers drafted Clyde on June 5, 1973.[30] A little more than three weeks later, Clyde toed the rubber at Arlington Stadium against Rod Carew and the Minnesota Twins. And beat 'em. The Rangers were just 24-43 and Short decided he had found at least one way to fill the stands. Ultimately, though, Clyde struggled - as did the entire ball club. The team had an August akin to the September of '72: a dismal 6-24.

As for Short, though, as he had done with the NBA's Lakers, he was ready to turn a profit and get out. And like Stouffer, he wanted a fair price. Finally, in May of 1974, he sold most of his shares to Brad Corbett, who had made a fortune in his thirties through a business that provided PVC pipe to the oil industry. Corbett was certainly willing to spend money, but also got heavily involved in personnel decisions. From a promotional standpoint, the Rangers turned to one of the old Cleveland Whiz Kids, Kip Horsburgh. Horsburgh had been hired by Rangers Vice President Dan O'Brien, who had been brought into baseball by Branch Rickey in 1955 and had served in a variety of minor league roles. O'Brien reached out to Horsburgh in Cleveland and told him over the phone that he had a very limited budget. Horsburgh laughs, "He said, 'If you decide to interview, you have to promise to take the job because I can only afford to interview one person. So, if I fly you down here, you better accept the job.'" Horsburgh accepted.

"I remember that season like it was yesterday. They got incredibly lucky," Horsburgh recalled of the '74 Rangers, whose media guide featured a smiling

---

30 The 1973 draft featured several Hall of Famers - Robin Yount and David Winfield, drafted 3rd and 4th, and Eddie Murray, drafted 63rd. The draft also featured future solid major leaguers Lee Mazzilli (14th), Len Barker (49th), Mike Flanagan (159th).

Martin beneath a movie marquee that shouted, "Manager Billy Martin Starring in 'The Great Turnaround of '74'. " The organization hoped for it, predicted it, and got it. And the fans turned out. As of June 4, 1974, the Rangers were leading the American League in attendance with just over 400,000 fans showing up to 26 home games (quite a turnaround, too, after they had notched just over 686,000 fans in all of '73). "The fans down here are just great," Martin told reporters. "All they ever needed was a reason to come to the ball park (sic) and we're giving it to them. This team isn't a bunch of losers."

Maybe the craziest luck in 1974 came in the form of Mike Hargrove, an extremely talented athlete from a small Texas Plains town called Perryton, located just south of the Texas/Oklahoma border. Hargrove had played football and basketball in Perryton but his town's high school did not offer baseball. Hargrove had played some YMCA and American Legion baseball and had some baseball lineage: his dad had gotten offers to try out for the Dodgers and Giants, but opted to work the family farm. When Hargrove accepted a basketball scholarship at Northwestern State College and enrolled there, his father encouraged him to also try out for the baseball team, ultimately delighting the coaches. Yet Hargrove didn't exactly rise to the top of scouting reports, so when he graduated with a degree in education, he took a job at a meat packing plant in Liberal, Kansas, just north of Perryton. While there, Hargrove played for a semi-pro team, the Bee Jays, and planned to become a high school coach. But he had popped up on the radar of the Rangers, who drafted him 572nd overall (the 25th round). After spending time in A ball in Geneva, New York, then in Gastonia, North Carolina - and hitting very well (.351) - the Rangers sent him to a fall instructional league in Florida in 1973. The Rangers, meanwhile, were coming off of the 57-105 season and Martin was determined. "Bob Short and Billy were coming in to watch a series of games - you can imagine how excited us kids were that they were coming to watch us," Hargrove recalls, adding that he had a solid spring training. When the team broke camp, they stopped in Houston for one final tune up.

"There were four or five of us young guys and we went and played in the Astrodome and we were wondering where we were going and had decided we would go ask Billy. I got busy doing something and the guys went without me.

I was pissed. So, I go to the ballpark and I'm walking out on the field and Billy was walking beside me and I said 'Billy I know you talked with the other guys about where they were headed' and he said, 'Well, I thought I'd take you with me to Arlington. But if you don't want to go, let me know.' I was just flabbergasted."

Hargrove called his high school sweetheart and wife, Sharon, who was subbing as a teacher in Perryton. It was April 1st and she told him that she was done with April Fool's Jokes. Once Hargrove (and his wife) finally acknowledged that he was in the major leagues, he told reporters that he actually liked batting there as opposed to the minors "because the pitchers have so much better control."

Like the Indians - and seemingly all teams in the '70s - the Rangers also had their share of characters. Pitcher Don Stanhouse liked to bring a stuffed gorilla to the stadium and shout out with primal screams. He also had a move called "the sleeper" where he would fall asleep on the mound until the batter got frustrated.

And they had veteran Alex Johnson, who had been an All Star in 1970 and was perhaps the only player in World Series history who was eating a sandwich in the clubhouse when called upon to pinch hit (while with the Cardinals in '67). Johnson had much in common with the Indians' George Hendrick: he was very talented but seen as aloof. He had led the American League with a .329 batting average in 1970 with the Angels. But he was also a bust with the Indians in 1972, batting just .239. They traded him to the Rangers in March of 1973 for Vince Colbert and Rich Hinton, two pitchers who never saw action for Cleveland. The Rangers had high hopes for Johnson to rediscover his 1970 form. They were also hoping that a player development seed they had planted several years earlier (when they were still the Senators), would blossom - and it did.

In the midst of a West Coast swing in early May of 1969, the Senators had invited an 18-year-old named Jeff Burroughs to take batting practice before one of their games against the Anaheim Angels. Burroughs, who was just finishing his senior year at Woodrow Wilson High School, had impressed major league scouts in school boy action, but he definitely sealed his fate by hitting five home runs in front of the Senators' brass. It was more than enough for Williams and Short, who selected Burroughs #1 in the June amateur draft, ahead of J.R. Richard (#2 overall), and future Hall of Famer Bert Blyleven (Round 3). They paid Burroughs an $88,000 signing bonus, officially qualifying him as one of the favorite terms of the age: a bonus baby.

Williams loved what Burroughs could do at the plate. "He doesn't have an outstanding arm or outstanding speed," said the Splendid Splinter after the Senators picked him, "But he has an outstanding bat." Burroughs went through the 1970 spring training, started the year in the minors and by summer was ready to make his debut. Williams waxed eloquent again: "He's the best looking right-handed hitter for his age that I've ever seen. He can be as good as he wants to be."

Like most rookies, Burroughs struggled when the Senators suddenly asked him to play third base for the AAA Denver Bears (he had been more accustomed to playing in the outfield). At the plate, he stumbled early on but eventually began to hit prodigious home runs. "Please don't make me sound boastful but I know I can do it," he told reporters. On July 20, 1970, although he was leading the Pacific Coast League (AAA) with 85 strikeouts, the Senators gave Burroughs a chance, calling him up to face the Milwaukee Brewers. Batting 6th in the lineup, he went 0-3 with a strikeout. He played right field and late in the game with the Senators clinging to a two-run lead, Williams considered replacing him defensively. But he didn't.

"If there had been 25,000 present and Jeff was from Ziltsville, Arkansas, I'd have taken him out, but there were 4,000 there and he's from Southern California," Williams said. After the game, President Nixon visited the Senators in the clubhouse, hoping to meet the young slugger. Williams, though, didn't let Nixon in until after a 15-minute "cooling off period," which Nixon supported. While the President of the United States waited, Coach Nellie Fox politely offered him a plug of tobacco, which Nixon declined. After ten days the Senators sent Burroughs back down. "It was a lesson for Short," *The Sporting News* reported a few months later, noting Williams' objections that the 19-year-old just wasn't quite ready.

By 1974, though, Burroughs *was* ready.

Sportswriters loved to wax eloquent about him, too. "When Burroughs, 6'2" and 193 with the arms of a blacksmith, swings, it's a sight to savor. Rip... crack...line drives fly off his bat." Even Indians players were impressed by the young Ranger. "You ought to see him hit a golf ball," Buddy Bell said. Burroughs, though, was not a fan of Arlington Stadium, which could be very windy and especially discouraging to right handed hitters. He once said that if he got ahold of some dynamite he would "blow the park into the next state." The 1974 Texas Rangers also had Lenny Randle, a speedster who could play several positions. A former punt returner at Arizona State, Randle was also Martin's kind of guy - a product of a tough Watts neighborhood in Los Angeles who bubbled with bravado. "We feel we'll win the whole division by a wide margin," Randle told *The Sporting News* a couple of weeks after Ten Cent Beer Night. "We're looking at the teams in this league from a different point of view this season. We used to be the pushover. Now we think they are."

But the biggest reason for the Rangers turnaround was perhaps due to their new manager, Billy Martin. In early September of '73, though, despite their winning record that was a far cry from the hapless Texas Rangers, the Detroit Tigers fired Manager Billy Martin. And the Cleveland Indians had played a small but exciting role in the firing. Angry and sure that Indians pitcher Gaylord Perry was throwing "greaseballs," Martin had told two of his pitchers to doctor the ball in a meaningless game. After the game he bragged to reporters about it. The American League promptly suspended Martin, who had also butted heads with his GM. Ultimately, the Tigers had had enough of him and gave him a pink slip. Hundreds of miles south, Short was immediately interested in Martin. According to Herzog, Short had said he would "fire his own grandmother if he could hire Martin." He got what he wanted. "I'm fired," Herzog said. "I'm the grandmother."

Martin rolled into town like a character of a Clint Eastwood western. He completely embraced the cowboy image and was delighted to be relatively close to his old drinking pal and teammate, Mickey Mantle, who lived in Dallas. He said he was honest and determined. "I've been fired twice. I'm a two-time loser. I know losing. But I also know winning. And I know how to get from one to the other," Martin declared. "The days when the Rangers are patsies are over."

Outfielder Tom Grieve agreed. "When Billy took over the team in 1973, he told the team that he didn't come to Texas to finish .500 and anyone who didn't believe that could come into his office and he'd make sure they were gone the next day." But Grieve laughed and added, "Some of us veterans said, 'Man, he hasn't seen us play!' " According to Grieve, the players rallied behind Martin. "You can't underestimate the impact that Billy Martin had on our team. He was *our guy* and he was a tremendous manager."

Martin managed just 23 games to close out the Rangers' '73 season - he was 9 and 14 - but Rangers fans generally loved him. As the Rangers gathered for spring training in '74, there was a new sense of optimism about their squad. In addition to Martin's arrival toward the end of '73, in late October the Rangers traded Bill Madlock and Vic Harris to the Chicago Cubs for pitcher Ferguson Arthur Jenkins Jr., a bona fide ace. From 1967 to 1972, Jenkins had won 20-plus games in every season. In 1971, he was 24-13 and won the Cy Young Award. When he didn't hit those high standards in 1973 with just a 14-16 record and a dip in total innings pitched, critics concluded that the 30-year old Jenkins was on the decline and the Cubs traded him. Martin took the parts and pieces he had been given - Hargrove, Grieve, Randle, Burroughs, Jenkins, and others - and assembled a team that had a fighting chance. And if there was one thing that Billy Martin loved, it was a good fight.

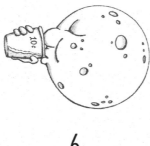

6

THE NEW SHERIFF IN ARLINGTON, TX

"I may not have been the greatest Yankee to ever put the uniform on, but I am the proudest."

– Billy Martin

Billy Martin, the manager of the 1974 Rangers, was a lightweight but cantankerous, scrappy, bar-lovin' former 2nd baseman. He had played for the New York Yankees during one of their most dominant stretches and he wanted nothing more than to someday manage them. He got his chance to do that - many times. He also lost his chance to do that many times. But before he would return to the Big Apple, he would have to prove himself in distant locales like Detroit, Minneapolis, and Arlington. And throughout that journey, a familiar pattern would accompany him: initial success followed by eventual self-destruction (aka, being fired).

Martin had grown up fighting, earned his place in the sport through scrappy play, and demanded that people notice him and the teams he managed. He often referred to himself as "The Little Dago," although he had Portuguese/Hawaiian heritage on his father's side and Italian on his mother's. He was born Alfred Manuel Pesano, Jr. in Berkeley, California on May 16, 1928. But Alfred Martin Sr. abandoned the family when Alfred Jr. was just eight months old, so his mom changed their last name to Martin. Martin's grandmother used to call the young boy "bello" (beautiful), which morphed into "Belli," and eventually into "Billy." One of baseball's most colorful characters, a future World Series champion, and a future World Series-winning manager, Billy Martin had been christened.

Fighting - verbal and physical - or one followed by the other - seemed to be simply part of Martin's DNA. Growing up in an impoverished area of West Berkeley, Martin grew accustomed to battling for everything. He played baseball on the local sandlots, in high school, and eventually played for the Oakland Junior Oaks, an amateur baseball team backed by Oakland's Pacific Coast League squad. When he wasn't playing baseball, though, he also took part in amateur boxing matches in the Bay Area. When he and his mother would walk down the street in Berkeley, men would whistle at her and Martin, 11, would want to fight them. But his mother, who was all of 4'11", would reassure him, "Billy, don't you ever forget that I got the best-looking fanny in town."

In the minor leagues, Martin once drove in an amazing 173 runs in a single season. He also learned a lot from Oaks Manager Casey Stengel, who was like a father to him. Stengel had played under John McGraw, one of the great managers of the game, in the early 1920s. In the dugout, Martin would dog Stengel and ask him why he had made certain managerial decisions. Once, angry with his mentor about something, Martin pouted until the old manager came over to him and slipped into baby talk: "Ith Li'l Bill-wee mad at naughty Ol' Case?" It seemed to diffuse the situation and Martin didn't take any swings at a man he worshiped. As a minor league player, famed manager Stengel had Martin bat 8th for the Oakland Oaks. Martin didn't like that spot but Stengel convinced him that he should simply think of himself as the team's "second cleanup hitter."

After more than five years of minor league seasoning, Martin began to flourish. In 1949, the Oaks traded him to the New York Yankees, who were managed by Stengel in 1950. Martin debuted on April 18, 1950 with two hits in the 8th inning as the Yankees thumped their rival, the Boston Red Sox, 15-10. For the next five years he mostly held down the starting job at 2nd base, playing stellar defense and delivering timely hits for four-fifths of the Yankees historic five-year run of World Series titles ('49, '50, '51, '52, and 53).

Martin just didn't appear in the World Series - he thrived. In his five World Series with the New York Yankees - a total of 28 games - he tallied stunning numbers: 33 hits, two doubles, three triples, five home runs, and 19 RBIs - all while posting a .333 batting average. In 1953, Martin batted .500 in the October classic and was named MVP. After his performance, Stengel marveled at his protege: "Look at him. He doesn't look like a great player—but he is a helluva player. Try to find something he can't do. You can't." From 1950 to 1957, the Yankees played in seven World Series - the only year they didn't, 1954, Martin was in the military.

Martin's fighting spirit also blossomed. Taking exception to players who slid aggressively into him at 2nd, he would throw down without hesitation. From an early age, fighting was an integral part of Martin's life. As a little kid he fought with other boys. As a player he fought with other players. As a manager he fought with his players, opposing players, fellow bar patrons and most famously, at one point, with a marshmallow salesman. All his life, though, Martin maintained one thing: that he never *started* a fight.

But the Yankee brass did not like Martin's late night/early morning activities, which included heavy drinking and partying with teammates Mickey Mantle, Whitey Ford, and others, taking full of advantage of New York's night life. So, after Martin and several Yankees took part in a brawl at New York City's Copacabana Night Club, the team promptly traded him to the Kansas City A's in 1957. It crushed him. His Yankee teammates were equally upset. Mickey Mantle cried in the clubhouse and mentor Stengel said, "Well, you're gone. You're the smartest little player I ever had." Martin was also so angry at Stengel after the trade that he didn't speak to his mentor for six years. He did play another six seasons for the A's, Tigers, Indians, Braves, and Twins. On October 1, 1961 Martin played 2nd base and batted 2nd for the Twins. He was 0 for 4 in his last game as a player. He hung up the cleats, still longing for those pinstripes.

Upon retirement, Martin was initially just a special scout. But then he began coaching at third base and eventually the Twins invited him to manage their AAA team in Denver in 1968. He wasn't sure he wanted to and only accepted the job after praying feverishly about it. The next season the Twins tapped him to be the manager of the big league club. The Twins went 97-65 that year, winning the American League West. They lost the American League Championship in three straight games to the Orioles, but few could deny that Martin had the

Midas (managerial) touch. And yet, despite his success, the Twins fired Martin, who had insisted on starting a 5-5 pitcher in the playoffs, irking Twins owner Calvin Griffith. Martin had also gotten in a vicious fist fight with one of his own pitchers, Dave Boswell, outside of a Detroit bar. All of it - the success, the disagreement with the owner, and the fight with one of his own players - was a harbinger for Martin's career.

As Frank DeFord wrote,

> The world is always out to get Billy Martin - he is right - because the world cannot afford to tolerate Billy Martin. It would all come apart at the seams if we acted like him. This is another reason why we have commissioners. But nobody is going to do Billy Martin in, because he believes in himself as surely as he believes in the other things he fights for.

Martin believed that he was the force about which the team resolves and that a manager could effectively impact the outcome of between 20 and 50 games a season. As a manager, Martin was proud that he didn't "just fill out the lineup card." "I call everything myself. Infield in, halfway, back; all the pitch outs; whether to throw through or not. I call a lot of the pitches, too. There's someone out there looking at me before every pitch."

After the Twins fired him, Martin took a year off then got back in as manager of the Detroit Tigers in 1971, who finished in 2nd place in the AL East (91-71). The next season the Tigers won the AL East (86-70), but lost to the Oakland A's in the playoffs. Again, though, Martin showed he could turn around a ball club - and generally inspire team unity and loyalty.

"Martin is perfect for baseball because it is the belonging that counts so much, the camaraderie, the men in groups," wrote DeFord. "Football coaches are generals, but baseball managers are master sergeants. It is difficult to talk to any player who has ever worked for Martin who does not start off by referring to his loyalty: Billy Martin is behind you. That sort of thing matters very much on (baseball) clubs."

Hargrove understood clearly what Martin wanted from his players. "He told us, 'The biggest way to get in my doghouse is if there is something going on in the field and you are not out there in it'," recalled Hargrove. "When I saw the big brawl start, I was out there." Martin also allegedly had one rule for spring training: anyone who skipped a workout would be fined - unless he could prove that he had been fishing.

Martin's players, though, loved him - well, except when he got into fist fights with them (see Reggie Jackson). Lenny Randle described Martin as "like a godfather of baseball." He loved the pugilistic and hard scrabble approach to the game, as well as his sense of humor and strategic knowledge.

"Billy Martin was like General Patton," Randle waxed eloquent in 2019. "He was like Yogi, Mickey Mantle, and Ted Williams all into one. Guys bought into him, we'd take a bullet for him. He was a leader. We knew the score was 1-0 before we stepped on the field. Billy Martin should be in the Hall of Fame. He was a winner." (As of 2024, Martin is not in the Baseball Hall of Fame.)

When he arrived in Arlington, Martin told the mayor exactly what car he drove - a black Continental with a white vanity plate and the #1 on it - and that cops should simply leave him alone. He told Vandergriff to tell his cops that if he drove on the sidewalk, so be it.

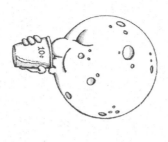

7

THE MOUTH THAT ALWAYS ROARS

"How can you dial a phone and wear a straitjacket at the same time?"

– Pete Franklin

If Billy Martin did whatever he wanted to do in Arlington, Texas, sports jockey Pete Franklin behaved in a similar manner - at least on the airwaves - in Cleveland, Ohio. Confrontational and irascible, Franklin ushered in a new era of sports talk radio - not just into the Cleveland media market - but on the national stage. He manned the mic for Cleveland's WWWE (1100 AM), the station that famously bragged that it could be heard in "38 states and half of Canada." Franklin often utterly eviscerated callers on his radio talk show, *Sportsline*. And most listeners (and maybe some of the callers) *absolutely loved it*. According to *The Plain Dealer*, Franklin thrived on being "loud, boastful, rude, fawning, mercenary, exhibitionistic and overbearing." To this, *Sports Illustrated* added that the *PD* writer was only "half right." "Sweet Pete is also brilliant, vulgar, informed, profane, fascinating, cruel, leering and funny - once you realize that 90% of his insult-the-caller routine is contrived to keep the show moving."

While in the Marines, Franklin started small as an Armed Forces Radio broadcaster. Franklin debuted on the public airwaves in the early 1950s at NBC Studios in New York's Rockefeller Plaza. Buoyed by a post-World War II

Veterans Administration scholarship, he sold BVD underwear by day and studied broadcasting at Columbia University by night. But upon graduation he had to settle for a radio job in what must have seemed like the farthest reaches of a radio broadcast market in the United States: Oakdale, Louisiana.

"There is nothing between Lake Charles (Louisiana) and Alexandria," Franklin reflected in his aptly named and entertaining autobiography, *You Could Argue But You'd Be Wrong*[31]. "I worked in Nowhere, Louisiana, which was swamp country. I worked 70 hours a week, and my main job was to get to the stations early in the morning and kill snakes. I'm not talking about the guys who acted like snakes. I met them later on. But real, honest-to-goodness, crawl-on-their-bellies with-their-tongues-sticking-out-snakes."

Franklin earned $45 a week broadcasting the farm news and discovered that killing snakes was probably the most useful skill he had honed. Eventually he advanced to a station in McComb, Louisiana, which "had even more snakes than Oakdale." "One day when the snakes decided to sleep in, the station manager asked, 'Pete, did you ever broadcast baseball before?'" He had not. Franklin and a producer trekked to Jackson, Mississippi to cover a Millsaps College baseball game. When he discovered that there weren't even any bleachers to sit in, Franklin grabbed a mic, hoisted himself into a tree and broadcasted the game while sitting on a branch. It was the perfect assignment for the young man who had loved baseball since his youth.

As a child, Franklin's uncle had once sprung for box seats close to the field at a Yankees game and called out to Lou Gehrig, who, to their surprise, came over to them. "My uncle didn't know Lou Gehrig, but he acted like he did. He introduced me to Lou and Lou said something like, 'How ya doin' kid?' and tousled my hair. That was it. Lou then said goodbye and walked away. After Lou left I was still trembling. I wanted to say something to Lou Gehrig, but no words came out of my mouth. I bet you find it hard to believe that Pete Franklin was speechless."

But it was more than Lou Gehrig that drew him to "the national pastime". (Ultimately Franklin grew to hate the Yankees with such tremendous passion that he'd help arm 40,000 Cleveland fans with 'I Hate the Yankees' Hankies). Franklin loved the theater of baseball, the pace of the game (and the fact that

---

31 Franklin teamed up with Terry Pluto for *You Could Argue But You'd Be Wrong*.

there was no clock, unlike the clock that ran most sports and most people's lives). He also loved the "egalitarian aspects of the game," its persistence throughout the 20th century, the unbridled joy of spring training and the sense that every team, at least in late March, had a chance. Even the Texas Rangers. Even the Cleveland Indians. And he loved the sense that baseball symbolized America. And baseball, like Franklin, had an unmistakable and vibrant personality.

Over the years, the young disc jockey sailed his way over the AM broadcasting waves, docking at progressively bigger and bigger ports: Ahoskie, North Carolina, then Sylvania, Georgia, followed by Savannah, Georgia, on to Freeport, Texas, then Houston, next to Trenton, New Jersey, followed by Bakersfield, California, then Las Vegas, Los Angeles, San Francisco and finally, in 1967, Cleveland, Ohio. He first hosted shows on Cleveland's WERE - *Sportsline* on weeknights from 7:30 to 10:30 but also a lighter and popular show called *After Hours* from midnight to 3 a.m. As such, he had a kind of Jekyll and Hyde role - bashing sports fan callers in the evening then sort of comforting those who phoned in during the middle of the night.

Franklin was a perfect fit for Cleveland, offering a challenging voice in a disrespected city and downtrodden fan base. *Sportsline* captivated sports-hungry men between 25 and 54 - he typically averaged 250,000 listeners, who seemed to love Franklin's refreshing bluntness. To delight Browns fans, he loved to refer to Pittsburgh as "Pittspuke." Franklin loved sports and loved discussing them, though he had little patience for the minor ones or for callers who didn't seem to know what they were talking about. For example, *Sports Illustrated* chronicled such an encounter in an article titled "The Mouth That Always Roars":

> "Hello Pete? This is L-L-Lenny from Akron. I'm a first-time caller."
>
> You can tell poor Lenny is nervous. He has the voice of a Parris Island recruit addressing his drill instructor. "P-P-Pete, I'd like to talk about truck pulling," he says. "You know, where they put r-r-ropes on trucks and pull 'em around?"
>
> Franklin recognizes a loser when he hears one. He can sense if a caller is about to whimper. "Well," Franklin says, "Let me

articulate here. Don't just say 'trucks.' What the hell kind of trucks you mean? Double bottoms? Twelve-wheelers?"

"P-P-Pickup trucks, Pete. You know, you put ropes on 'em and pull."

Franklin pauses for effect and then swoops in for the kill. When it comes to interrogating witnesses, he makes Howard Cosell sound like a choirboy.

"Tell me something," he says. "Has anyone ever pulled your brain and found anything there?"

"No," the caller says tremulously.

"That's what I figured!" Franklin roars.

Boom! His finger hits the red disconnect button, and Lenny the truck puller is sent deadheading, as it were, into the night, never to be heard from again unless he's a glutton for punishment and calls back for more.

Franklin mostly stuck to discussing Cleveland football, basketball, and, his favorite, baseball, notching an overly impressive market share compared to his counterparts in other major sports cities. Each show, he declared, began with three simple premises: "1.) I know more than anyone else about sports. 2.) You know nothing. 3.) I say 'I told you so' whether I did or not."

He gained confidence, and listeners, by simply telling it like it was and absolutely flaying any callers who disagreed with him or who simply - in his estimation - said dumb things. He would sometimes end calls with the sound of a flushing toilet. The public loved it. "Some are out-and-out morons who deserve to be treated as such," he told *Sports Illustrated*. "A lot of it is show business. I yell at some guy, dress him down, call him a Communist, that's what people will remember – the social faux pas. What did I do? I spoke to some anonymous person and called him a dum-dum. All I did was violate someone's sense of propriety."

In a 1969 *Plain Dealer* article, Franklin acknowledged that he criticized callers, but asserted that he also respected them. A few years later, though, Franklin told *Sports Illustrated* that he believed that some of his listeners were "out-and-out morons who deserve to be treated as such. "It's all they have in life," he said. The rest of those in radioland, he added, were intelligent and seeking the "unvarnished truth."

Was he obnoxious, wondered *The Plain Dealer's* William Hickey? "That's totally ridiculous," Franklin said. "And only a real dummy, like yourself, would ask such a stupid question. I am not obnoxious. It's just that I'm a hard-hitting, aggressive reporter of the local sports scene and I know where all the bodies are buried and I tell it like it is, regardless of whose bones I trample on or whose careers I dash to pieces. What's wrong with that?"

Some other classic Franklin jabs:

> "What do you think this show is, kid? Sesame Street? You should be in bed by now."

> "You bore me, meat-head. What did you take, Tylenol for dinner?"

> "I love to talk to intelligent sports fans. The rest of you dummies, hop inside a mummy and sew yourself up."

Franklin's acerbic style probably turned off some folks, but for many, many Clevelanders, he struck a perfect chord. Young fan Gary Powers, who was 14 in the Summer of '74, certainly remembers listening to Franklin. "My brother had a new stereo and we'd sit there and listen to him," Powers recalls. "He was really stirring things up. It was more like the Jerry Springer show." Greg Nagy, also a fan, said he used to listen to Franklin constantly. "He sounded like he was from New York and he hated the Yankees. I loved it because I hated the Yankees. I hated the Yankees since I was tall enough to hate anything. He helped stir things up." Carol Yurmanovich, another young fan, listened, too, and Franklin was exactly what the City of Cleveland and its sports fans needed. "I can remember Pete Franklin building us up, building us up" ahead of Ten Cent Beer Night.[32]

---

32 It would have been wonderful to find recordings of precisely what Franklin said ahead of Ten Cent Beer Night, but this writer couldn't track down anything specific. Check out YouTube, though, for some of Franklin's interactions with callers: Pete Franklin Sample.

In the Spring of 1974, Franklin was fully entrenched in the hearts and minds of Indians fans, who listened to him in their cars, barber shops, garages, and homes. He was the master of his craft. So when the Texas Rangers brawled with Indians on May 29th in Arlington, Texas - *and* the Rangers were due to visit Cleveland less than a week later - it took very little for Franklin to spot an opportunity. Not only were the Indians disrespected in Arlington, but there was the small additional subplot that they were led by one of the most obnoxious former Yankees of all, a personality and loudmouth just as outspoken and grating as Pete Franklin: Manager Billy Martin.

Franklin's critical tone, albeit focused primarily on sports, fit in perfectly with an overall questioning of authority that had been building in the United States for many years. Protests calling for the end of the Vietnam War continued to underscore a lack of faith in leadership. On May 4, 1970, just 35 miles southeast of Cleveland, members of the Ohio National Guard fired on student protesters at Kent State University, killing four college students and wounding nine. America and the world were horrified.

The next day, in New York City, a thousand protesters met at the United Nations. The day after that, hundreds of student protesters gathered in Lower Manhattan, calling for an end of the war. A group of a couple hundred construction workers pushed past the "mostly indifferent police" and attacked the student protesters, injuring 70 of them. The incident became known as the Hard Hat Riot and President Nixon framed what had happened as an indication of support for the war.

Additionally, the early '70s were marked by an ever-increasing distrust in authority. In 1971, *The New York Times* published parts of "The Pentagon Papers," which had been obtained by two consultants, Danield Ellsberg and Anthony Russo. The Pentagon Papers basically showed that previous presidents Lyndon Johnson and John F. Kennedy had essentially lied to Congress and the American people about the Vietnam War. Initially Nixon and his administration were unconcerned, but then Secretary of State Henry Kissinger convinced Nixon that allowing the media access to such "secrets" set a bad precedent for his administration. White House Chief of Staff H.R. Haldemann explained it to President Nixon:

To the ordinary guy, all this is a bunch of gobbledygook. But out of the gobbledygook comes a very clear thing…You can't trust the government; you can't believe what they say; and you can't rely on their judgment; and the—the implicit infallibility of presidents, which has been an accepted thing in America, is badly hurt by this, because It (sic) shows that people do things the president wants to do even though it's wrong, and the president can be wrong.

Nixon and his administration took the *Times* to court, trying to suppress the publication of the documents, but they lost; the Supreme Court ruled in favor of the media. "Only a free and unrestrained press can effectively expose deception in government," wrote Justice Hugo Black. Ultimately 19 newspapers, including *The Washington Post*, published parts of The Pentagon Papers and used them for in-depth investigative journalism. The upshot was just as precisely what Haldemann had told Nixon: you can't trust the government.

From anger about the Vietnam War, confusion and disappointment with the President of the United States, to a growing criticism and over-analysis of professional sports, a general tone of frustration festered in early 1970s America. Perhaps it was only natural, then, that one of the ways people began to express their frustration was to simply take off all of their clothes and "streak" gleefully through public.

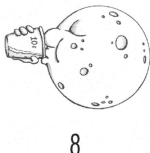

8

BOOGITY, BOOGITY!

"Get that streaker off the field - throw him in jail!"

— Ray Kroc, owner of the San Diego Padres to the crowd of 39,000 on Opening Day, 1974

Perhaps only God only knows who the first streaker was. Was it Adam, or was it Eve? Surely both ought to get equal credit. Completely stripping down then running naked through a public space, seemed to really flourish in 1973, particularly on warm-weather American college campuses.

The fad truly hit the front pages of the sports world in the Spring of 1974. Streaking scholars (who are a sordid and boisterous lot that you should probably do your best to avoid) generally credit Australian Michael O'Brien as the world's first sports event streaker. Manning up to a wager from "his mates", O'Brien was one of some 50,000 fans at an April 20, 1974 charity rugby match between England and France in Twickenham, England. Even one of the most popular royals of the day, 28-year-old Princess Alexandra of Kent, The Honourable Lady Ogilvy, was there to witness the moment.

O'Brien respectfully waited until the halftime whistle blew, stripped completely naked then bolted across the pitch in front of the raucous, unbelieving, and encouraging crowd. It was a moment which may not have been quite so special and almost unchronicled if not for Irishman Ian Bradshaw, who was there on behalf of *The Daily Mirror*, a British tabloid. While most of the other photographers had taken a break for tea and to warm themselves in the stadium's tunnels, Bradshaw had remained on the sidelines. As it happened, O'Brien captured one of the penultimate photos of his career and a streaking history icon: a series of photos that detailed three smiling "bobbies" as they gently coaxed a bearded and slightly relaxed O'Brien, flowing hair cascading behind his head, thus bearing a remarkable resemblance to Jesus Christ, off the pitch. One bobby graciously deigned to cover O'Brien's privates perfectly with the iconic policeman's "custodian's helmet," while a rugby official scurried behind O'Brien and the policeman ready to drape the streaking star with a trenchcoat. It was at once Biblical, raucous, and utterly hilarious.[33]

Princess Margaret actually witnessed streaking at *another* sports event when she attended, along with over 165,000 others, the 100th running of the Kentucky Derby later that spring. A year earlier, Secretariat had won the Derby on his way to the first Triple Crown in 25 years. In 1974, amidst a mass of people in the infield, streakers took turns shinnying up a flagpole as onlooking well-dressed fans sipped their mint juleps (and perhaps tried hard not look directly up the flagpole).

To some degree, it seemed that the popular 1968 rock musical *Hair*, celebrating hippie counterculture, helped to pave the way for the streaking craze. Before it hit the stage, the play's director and choreographer saw an opportunity to give Broadway audiences a shock that they hadn't seen before: completely naked actors and actresses. The nudity, inspired by Central Park protests, was meant to be an act of defiance and freedom and a celebration of the human body's beauty.

---

33 O'Brien reportedly won $25 (Australian dollars, perhaps?) and was reportedly fined $26 for the streak. But he lost his job as a London stock broker. Streaking scholars, however, celebrate Erika Roe as England's most famous streaker. Roe also chose Twickenham - what is it with Twickenham? - as the site of her January 2nd,1982 streak during an Australia v. England rugby match. Inspired by alcohol, Roe and a friend disrobed then ran gleefully down the field before they were corralled by authorities. Known now as "The Twickenham Streaker," it seems that Roe's 40-inch breasts may be what earned her such recognition. After the streak she headed to the pub to carry on drinking.

Six years later, people were streaking all over the world, prompting some members of the press to call it a "streaking epidemic." Cleveland stores offered "streaking packages." One local company sold army-style face masks for $1.50 and a $4 bag to hold clothes while you streaked. In New York, a man told police that he had paid $25 for a "streaking package" without checking to see what was in it. When he opened it he found that it contained absolutely nothing. And a New York toy company saw a surge in sales of naked plastic dolls called "Baby Streakers."

Charles Schulz's popular comic strip "Peanuts" parodied streaking as Snoopy's alter ego, Joe Cool, took off his collar and sunglasses, in order to be "naked" and streak. In March, just weeks before the opening of the '74 season, singer-songwriter and comedian Harold Ray Ragsdale, a.k.a. Ray Stevens, celebrated the craze in song with "The Streak." Naturally, Stevens's song streaked up the charts and spent three weeks at the *Billboard* #1 in May. It went a little bit like this:

> Oh, yes, they call him the Streak
> (Boogity, boogity)[34]
> Fastest thing on two feet
> (Boogity, boogity)
> He's just as proud as he can be
> Of his anatomy
> He goin' give us a peek…

And at the 1974 Academy Awards, just as host David Niven prepared to introduce Elizabeth Taylor (who would bring out the envelope for Best Picture[35]),

---

34 NASCAR announcer Darrel Waltrip actually rekindled the use of the word "boogity" in NASCAR telecasts for Fox. Someone had expressed to Waltrip that broadcasts needed more than simply "the green flag is up" at the start of a race. Waltrip, who had been friends with Stevens, happened to hear "The Streak" while prepping for a race in Darlington, South Carolina. "That's it, *that's it*," Waltrip reflected. "Of course, I added one — 'Boogity, boogity, boogity. Let's go racin', boys,' and it stuck. Did I think when I did that that 19 years later, I'd still be doing that?"

35 The nominees for 1974's Best Picture included "The Exorcist," "American Graffiti," "Cries and Whispers," "A Touch of Class", and "The Sting," which won

a streaker named Robert Opel jogged out from behind Niven, flashed a peace sign, then sprinted across the stage. The crowd roared, while the incredibly poised Niven waited patiently for the chaos to subside, then finally said, "Just think, the only laugh that man will ever get in his life is by stripping off his clothes and showing his shortcomings." Taylor eventually emerged from off the stage with the envelope. "That is a hard act to follow," she laughed then stumbled over her words. "I'm nervous," she laughed. "That really upset me. I think I'm jealous!"

Even world leaders acknowledged the craze. When asked about some gray hairs on his head, President Nixon joked, "They call that streaking." And even law enforcement dabbled in streaking. In Portsmouth, Rhode Island, more than two dozen policemen blitzed naked through the halls of a Ramada Inn the night before a parade. Parade organizers were happy they got it out of their system the previous evening.

Of course baseball stadiums featuring sparse security and their inviting verdant spaces were a perfect venue for streakers - and most of the games were played in relatively pleasant weather.[36] The '74 opener for the Chicago White Sox, however, was not played under gentle baseball conditions - but it did nothing to dissuade happy streakers. Over 30,000 fans turned out to see flamethrower Nolan Ryan and the California Angels against knuckleballer Wilbur Wood and the White Sox. It was 37 degrees, though probably much worse thanks to a predictably "biting wind" that whipped off the edge of Lake Michigan. For whatever reason - perhaps because some fans had been "overserved," according to press reports - numerous brawls broke out in the stands. Reporters observed one fan being carted away on a stretcher, while another reported, "strong young men choking each other" with their backs jammed up against the guard rail in

---

the Oscar. Opel appeared on several TV talk shows after his Oscar streak. In 1979, though, he was shot dead during a robbery-drug deal in his San Francisco sex shop.

36 In July of 1974 at a minor league game in Lakeland, Florida, a tanned "brown-haired miss" streaked naked to the mound, kissed pitcher Pat MacCormack, bolted past security and behind the batting cages where an accomplice waited with her clothes. The woman refused to give her name to reporters but claimed that the Lakeland GM had paid her $20 to streak, recreating a streak she made when the same two teams had played a week earlier. The GM and team president denied the claims.

the upper deck. In the 7th inning (given such an atmosphere), it didn't surprise those in attendance when a naked young man jumped onto the field wearing only a bright red batting helmet. After dancing around on the field, being completely ignored by extremely tolerant security officers, the streaker climbed back into the stands only to realize that he had left his red batting helmet on the field. So (naturally!), he clambered over the railing again, ran out onto the field, snagged his helmet then exited for a second time. As the game neared its merciful end, other fans, male and female, stripped down but opted to just simply remain in the stands. At one point one "aged half-streaker paraded through the outfield," apparently not fully confident enough to go completely naked, he wore just his underwear. "I was afraid for my wife and child up there in the stands," said White Sox pitcher Terry Forster, who was almost hit with a can of beer while warming up in the bullpen. "I never saw anything like it," said White Sox manager Chuck Tanner. White Sox player Ron Santo agreed. "I never saw a crowd that bad. It took a lot of concentration away from us. But I don't believe this will go on every day. Streaking is just a fad and will die out." Nolan Ryan walked a stunning 10 batters through 8 innings, but somehow yielded just two runs (on four hits) and the Angels won 4-2. The atmosphere in the stands on the White Sox's opening day was a portent of fan unrest that would pop up in New York, Cincinnati, and many other major league cities (and, of course, Cleveland).

But Santo was wrong - streaking was not just a fad. Somewhere in the Cleveland Indians fan base, dozens of streakers were either planning to race across the Municipal Stadium field on the evening of June 4, 1974 - or, more likely - caught up in the madness of the evening - would suddenly decide to do so that evening. Among them would be a young man who might have passed for an Olympic 10,000 meter runner. He would wear only a single dark sock as he dashed and dallied throughout the outfield - to the delight of the crowd and the frustration of the overmatched Cleveland police. The streakers were not part of the planned promotions for the 1974 season - just kind of an organic - enthusiastic - bonus.

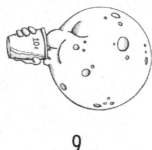

9

THE 1974 CLEVELAND INDIANS

"I have endeavored to retain a low profile in baseball. The organization has been more than helpful in that direction."

– John Lowenstein

Amidst the icy winter of '73 and into the spring of '74, the Cleveland Indians pondered the same questions as the Texas Rangers and every other professional ball club: How do we improve our pitching? How do we score more runs? How good of a team can we be? Could we actually compete? And, of course, how do we get more people to come to our games? The Rangers and Indians knew each other well, featuring players on both sides who had played against one another in the minor leagues, or who had at one time been on the same teams together, or who had even been swapped for one another. In November of 1973, Bonda reported to a gathering of Mileti and the other owners that they had lost slightly more than $1.5 million on the year. Overall, though, the gathering of bigwigs had a positive tone and no one seemed to express tremendous concern about the future. Bonda also reported that the team had rejected a Boston Red Sox trade offer for Gaylord Perry. The team, Bonda said, felt very good about getting back into the black, though, thanks to expected 1974 TV revenues (including a $400,000 advance) from WJW. And they seemed to be fairly happy with the squad they would field the next season. The 1974 Indians, like every other team in baseball, embraced hope eternal and dreamt of winning it all - or at least finishing above .500 for a change. And though they finished the '73 season 71-91, there were glimmers of hope. Perry, who was 19-19 in 1973, led the American League with 29 complete games. And in March of 1974, the Indians traded with the Tigers for his older brother, Jim. It was a homecoming for the older Perry - the Indians had drafted him in 1956. He came to the Indians after a 14-13 season with Detroit.

Heading into the '74 season, Perry was the subject of seemingly greater scrutiny than ever (and it certainly didn't help that he had teamed up with Sudyk to write and publish an autobiography called *Me and The Spitter*). But part of Perry's aura was simply the continual suspicion that he was *possibly* throwing a doctored ball. On the mound he would gesture, touch his shirt, touch his hat, touch his ears - touch just about everything he could - to simply make the opposition think he was up to no good. And it usually worked. In late June of '73, Yankees manager Ralph Houk, convinced that Perry was throwing a spitball, stormed out to the mound and snatched the hat from the suspect's hand. Afterwards, Perry (who wasn't "caught" with anything) laughed uproariously, spoke of the incident in a southern vernacular, and acted as if it was more satisfying than harvesting tobacco with his Dad and brother on a pleasant North Carolina evening. "Hey, now we're back on the beam," Perry declared. "The thing I want to know is what'd they wait so long for? I mean I haven't had this much fun since last season. When they came out to check me, I finally felt at home." A few months later, in the midst of the offseason, the rules committee announced that umpires could - suspecting a spitter - declare a pitch illegal. The first such declaration would result in a ball against the guilty pitcher and the next would result in ejection.

At the plate, the Indians had high hopes for the likes of power hitters Oscar Gamble, Charlie Spikes, and the mercurial and talented George Hendrick. The Indians had acquired Gamble in a trade with the Phillies in 1973. Although he had hit just eight home runs - and had not registered an overly impressive batting average - Gamble was young and extremely promising. He was, Leo Durocher had said a few years earlier, "the next Willie Mays." Above all, though, he made his mark when he showed up for the 1973 Indians Spring Training in Arizona with a remarkable, head-turning Afro, probably the greatest coiffure in baseball history. Duke Sims asked Gamble if he had stuck his finger in a light socket and said he kept expecting Briar Rabbit to jump out of his hair. Aspromonte and his "permissive policy" allowed players to have mustaches - and 14 of those in camp did - but the Afro, he said, would have to be cut down. Gamble simply said that he had hoped to get notice more via his hair (and he did), but he complied with Aspromonte's request, ultimately trimming 2 ½ inches off of his hair. After he did it, he said that he felt a couple of pounds lighter and that his hat size had instantly gone from a 7 ⅞ to a 7 ⅜.

Hendrick, drafted #1 by the talent-rich Oakland A's in the January 1968 draft. Competing with the likes of Reggie Jackson, Sal Bando, Bert Campaneris, Mike Epstein, Hendrick was a mostly reserve outfielder on the 1972 World Series Champions A's. But few could deny his potential. At 6'3", 200 pounds, many described the ball as "jumping off of his bat." He appeared to many to be a blossoming five-tool player.[37] At the dawn of the '73 season it appeared that Hendrick might be sent down to the minor leagues - a possibility he did not care for. In late March, shortly before the '73 season would begin, the A's traded Hendrick and catcher Dave Duncan to the Indians in exchange for catcher Ray Fosse and infielder Jack Heidemann. Aspromonte immediately used Hendrick as his primary starting center fielder in 1973. Hendrick performed reasonably well, batting .268 with 61 RBI and 21 home runs in 473 at bats. The highlight of the season almost certainly came on June 19th when Hendrick hit three home runs to give the Indians an 8-7 win over the visiting Tigers. He was still just 23-years-old and his career seemed limitless.

The members of the media, however, were rough on Hendrick. Frustrated with his lack of loquaciousness, they dubbed him "Silent George." Hendrick didn't care. "Man, I gave up caring about what the world thinks about George Hendrick a long time ago. The people only believe what they read and what they want to believe. I'm happy the way I am. I have my friends and family and that's the way it's going to stay." Even after the single game home run outburst,

---

37 A five-tool player hits for power, hits for a high average, can field well, can throw well, and can run with exceptional speed.

Hendrick wouldn't talk. "There are people who play until their stomachs sag and their hair falls out and they don't have a night like George Hendrick had at the stadium Tuesday," wrote Dan Coughlin. "In their dreams cowards fancy themselves heroes and heroes fancy themselves gods. What George Hendrick thinks of himself today will be left to your imagination because he isn't talking. Few players in the grand old game have been so heroic and less communicative. When badgering reporters finally did get Hendrick to speak about the performance, he would only say, "I got lucky." "Beyond that, he didn't have a word to say. The biggest mistake the Republicans made when they sneaked into the Watergate was not hiring Hendrick to do the job."

If Hendrick wouldn't speak to the media, at least they had the phlegmatic and hilarious John Lowenstein, who gushed Yogi-Berra-level quips. Lowenstein satirized fan clubs, bluntly declaring, "Fan clubs? What are they for? Does a player have to have one? I think they are a waste of people's time. A youngster should be out self-educating himself in other pursuits instead of running a fan club." And so, the Lowenstein Apathy Club, or "The LAC," was born in Cleveland. Thousands of fans would send Lowenstein letters detailing how disinterested they were about his career. Fans also unfurled a long banner from the upper that said, "Hey John…" then stretched out long and blank. At one point, after being on losing team after losing team, Lowenstein suggested that the only way to improve the heavy clubhouse atmosphere would be to hire Norman Vincent Peale, famous for *The Power of Positive Thinking*.

And if Gamble, Hendrick, Perry, and Lowenstein didn't provide enough copy, a few fans were drawn to the singular tale of pitchers Mike Kekich and Fritz Peterson. Kekich and Peterson, who were good friends - and whose wives were good friends - were both on the New York Yankees in 1973 when they decided to swap wives…and lives. According to several accounts, Kekich and Peterson and their better halves went to a party at legendary sportswriter Maury Allen's and somehow concluded at the end of the night that they would simply go home with each other's spouse. In ensuing weeks, then, they decided to swap families, cementing their status as absolute living legends of the 1970s.

On June 12, 1973, the Yankees traded Kekich to Cleveland for Lowell Palmer, who had last pitched two innings in a game in 1972, yielding two hits and one run. Palmer would never pitch again. But Kekich could never find his groove with the Indians. After struggling in spring training, the Indians finally cut him just before the '74 season was about to begin. Naturally, who picked him up a month later? Bingo. The Texas Rangers. Many pointed out that the Indians did not have a left-handed starter and considered this a problem as the season was about to begin. Peterson was a lefty and still with the Yankees…and still with Kekich's wife and family. But what would it take to get him?

When camp broke, the Indians would begin the season with an all right-handed rotation. In addition to the Perry brothers, another pitcher the Indians had high hopes for was Milt Wilcox, whom Sparky Anderson and the Reds traded to the Indians in 1972. Anderson had been disappointed in Wilcox's velocity, which certainly inspired Wilcox, at least according to *Sports Illustrated's* Ron Fimrite. "If there is anything a pitcher is sensitive about it is his velocity," Fimrite wrote about Wilcox in late May of 1972. "So the madder Wilcox gets, the harder he throws. He has now established quite a ferocity-velocity ratio."

The local media seemed to peg the Indians at no better than 5th in the American League East, a division which included the defending champ Baltimore Orioles, the New York Yankees, the Boston Red Sox, the Milwaukee Brewers, and the Detroit Tigers. Many predicted that the Red Sox, who had made some strong moves in the off season, would win the division. They had former Indians pitcher Luis Tiant, who was finally getting offensive support he hadn't gotten in Cleveland - he had gone 20-13 in '73. Even the diminutive Indians clubhouse attendant, Cy Bunyak, didn't see his team winning more than half of their games - though everyone agreed that an 81-81 season would be a sign of significant improvement. But, as they left spring training in late March of 1974 - like every other team in baseball - the Cleveland Indians were 0-0, and could dream big.

The Cleveland Indians pose for a 1974 team photo a few hours before Ten Cent Beer Night. Photo credit: Courtesy of The Cleveland Guardians

Nick Mileti (center) encourages Carl Fazio, left, and Kip Horsburgh, right. Photo credit: Courtesy of Kip Horsburgh Scrapbook

Bonita Gamble has some fun with baseball's greatest Afro, sported by husband Oscar Gamble. Photo credit: Paul Tepley (CSU/The Cleveland Press)

Indians Coach Joe Lutz and Manager Ken Aspromonte seek enlightenment from an AL umpire. Photo credit: Paul Tepley (CSU/The Cleveland Press)

The acquisition of lefty Fritz Peterson gave the Indians a bona fide starter and another character, although it came at the expense of future star Chris Chambliss. Photo credit: Paul Tepley (CSU/The Cleveland Press)

Even without the spitter (?), Gaylord Perry had one of the most dominant stretches of his career in the first half of 1974. Photo credit: Paul Tepley (CSU/ The Cleveland Press)

A reporter interviews one of the winners of the Texas Rangers '72 Hot Pants Night. Photo credit: SMU G. William Jones Film & Video Collection

Famous baseball clown Max Patkin pulls some hijinks in the Indians dugout. Photo credit: Paul Tepley (CSU/The Cleveland Press)

Even Ted Williams, the greatest hitter of alltime, couldn't fix the '72 Rangers.
Photo credit: Paul Tepley (CSU/The Cleveland Press)

Pitchers Jim and Gaylord Perry were the second winningest brother combo of all time (after Joe and Phil Niekro). Photo credit: Paul Tepley (CSU/The Cleveland Press)

Hugo Zacchini blasts out of a cannon on Opening Day '74 at Municipal Stadium. Photo credit: Paul Tepley (CSU/The Cleveland Press)

No one could fire up the fans or rip them apart like Pete Franklin. Photo credit: Paul Tepley (CSU/The Cleveland Press)

John Lowenstein always kept things light with Yogi Berralike wisdom.
Photo credit: Paul Tepley (CSU/The Cleveland Press)

Ted Bonda tries to hit a 5iron over the scoreboard while Charlie Sifford watches.
Neither were successful. Photo credit: Paul Tepley (CSU/The Cleveland Press)

Cleveland's Municipal Stadium, nestled along frequently chilly Lake Erie, seen here in the early '50s. Photo credit: Paul Tepley (CSU/The Cleveland Press)

TED BONDA
EXECUTIVE
VICE PRESIDENT

Alva T. "Ted" Bonda was born in Cleveland, Ohio on June 1, 1917. He graduated from Glenville High School and completed his military service in the U.S. Army in 1945. He and his wife Marie make their residence in Bratenahl, Ohio. They have three children: Penny Bonda Solomon, who is married and lives in Maryland. Bonda's sons Joel and Thomas both are residents of Cleveland.

For 28 years, Ted Bonda has been active in the transportation industry. In 1945, he joined in the formation of a car rental business in Cleveland. In 1949, Bonda along with his friend and partner, Howard Metzenbaum, founded Airport Parking Company of America (APCOA) which later became the largest parking concern in the country. He was President of that firm until 1968, and at that time, APCOA merged into ITT Corporation and Mr. Bonda was named Chairman of the Board of ITT Consumer Services Corporation.

From 1968 through 1972 he was Chairman of the Board of Avis. He is directly involved presently as Chairman of the Board of Penril Data Communications, Inc.—a Maryland corporation making computer modems. He is on the Board of Directors of W.R. Berkley Inc., Avis Rent A Car, Inc., The Society National Bank of Cleveland, Greater Cleveland Growth Association, the Jewish Community Federation of Cleveland and Mt. Sinai Hospital.

He has long been active in civic and philanthropic activities. He is active as a board member and officer in many organizations, some of which are . . . The American Cancer Society—Cuyahoga County and the Ohio Division and served as the 1972-73 Crusade Chairman. The Greater Cleveland Growth Association—Chairman in 1973, The National Conference of Christians and Jews, The Police Athletic League (1969 to Present), The Bellefaire Home and a Fellow of Brandeis University.

His great interest in sports helped to bring the Davis Cup to Cleveland. Soccer was a game of interest in 1967, and he brought into being the Cleveland Stokers. Unfortunately, the lack of public enthusiasm for the game finally forced the owners to abolish the team. He is a Director of the Cleveland Cavaliers Basketball Team, the Cleveland Crusaders Hockey Club, and a partner in the Indians.

On August 29, 1973, President Nick Mileti called upon Bonda to take the reins of the Tribe, and he was given the title of Executive Vice President of the Indians.

Enough bashing of the greatest city in the world! (or so said Captain Cleveland: the cover of the May 1974 issue of Cleveland Magazine. Photo credit: Cleveland State University Michael Schwartz Library

Jeff Burroughs swings and misses at Municipal Stadium. Burroughs would go on to be honored as the 1974 AL MVP but had a rough night on June 4th at the plate and in the field. Photo credit: Paul Tepley (CSU/The Cleveland Press

Legendary groundskeeper Marshall Bossard gave the Indians and his crew tried to help the home team. Pitcher Jim Kern, who also played for the Elmira Pioneers, tries to help. Photo credit: Paul Tepley (CSU/The Cleveland Press)

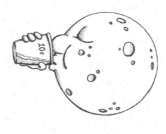

10

THE PROMOTIONS DEPARTMENT

"Life is on the wire. Everything else is just waiting."

— The Great Wallenda

It wasn't a bad crowd, considering the weather: temperatures in the 50s, a brisk Canadian-borne wind, and a light rain. But it certainly wasn't the crowd that Carl Fazio had hoped for. Fazio, former co-owner of the Magic Valley Cowboys and Elmira Pioneers, was now the Director of Sales and Marketing for the 1974 Cleveland Indians. He stood on the metal roof of Municipal Stadium, assessing the conditions and the crowd below. It was Friday, May 31, 1974, and Fazio shook his head slightly. "Wouldn't you know it?," he thought, "It just had to rain on *this* particular night, didn't it?" Fazio and his small but inspired Cleveland Indians Promotions Department harbored high hopes to fill many of the seats thanks to the post-game entertainment scheduled for the evening. They drew just over 15,000. Fazio didn't know much about walking on a high wire, but he definitely knew this much: it was a skilled and delicate art mastered by a handful of daring souls on the planet - something that was certainly not made any easier by wind and rain off of nearby Lake Erie.

Fazio stood on the roof with one of that elite - the Indians had scheduled the accomplished daredevil known as "The Great Wallenda." What was a little foul weather, wind, and a slightly wet wire to The Great Wallenda, "the remarkable funambulist"? Wallenda, the 69-year-old patriarch in a long line of entertainers, was poised to pocket $5,000 for his efforts for that evening - a significant sum for less than an hour of work - especially in 1974. Wallenda had essentially made similar walks many times before, too, for several other professional ball clubs. He had walked on a wire high above St. Louis's Busch Stadium and took a similar jaunt from roof-to-roof above Philadelphia's Veterans Stadium. During the latter, 22 months earlier, Wallenda hired 40 men to hold the wire taut for him. At one point, unhappy with the wire's tension, Wallenda sat down on it and motioned for the fans in the seats below to get out of the way because he was just about to plummet down amidst them. It was all part of the act. But he completed the walk and collected a nifty $3,000 for his feat. In one respect it was remarkable that he did it - just two weeks before, his son had fallen from a high wire and died.

Karl Wallenda hailed from a family of performers known as The Flying Wallendas. They had seen both triumph and tragedy over the five decades of performing high wire and circus acts. He had struck gold doing it at ballparks, though he was occasionally prohibited from doing so. The Baltimore Orioles hired Wallenda to try his walk in 1973. The Orioles had won the World Series in 1970, and had made it again in 1971 - but lost to Roberto Clemente and the Pittsburgh Pirates. Despite their success on the field, the Orioles also struggled with attendance, averaging about 11,000 fans per game, and prompting frustrated owner Jerry Hoffberger to threaten moving the team. But with Wallenda booked and just about ready to take his first step, Baltimore's "city fathers" stepped in, declaring that his act was simply too dangerous.

As Fazio and Wallenda stood on the exposed roof of Municipal Stadium, a light rain continued to mist upon Cleveland. It didn't exactly feel like summer was near thanks to a slightly the mid-50s temperature. Near Lake Erie, though, it often felt much cooler; it *almost always* felt cooler in Municipal Stadium. The Indians, perhaps still hung over from their road trip and a lusty brawl with the Rangers in Texas, had just lost 4-2 to the Kansas City Royals. But the 15,387 rapt fans stuck around, waiting to see Wallenda tiptoe along a 5/8-inch taut cable anchored to the Stadium's roof top light standards. The walk would take him 110 feet above the Municipal's playing field - roughly equivalent to being

8 stories above the earth and roughly over 2nd base where the wire would sag about 30 feet. Even the Indians and Royals players, some flanked by their families, popped back out of their clubhouses to watch the show.

Initially, the Indians suggested that Wallenda attempt his walk from Municipal's upper deck level, not the considerably higher roof. Wallenda reacted indignantly to this proposal. "Do you want to ruin my reputation?" Wallenda demanded. On Municipal's rooftop, Fazio felt compelled to offer a final chance. " 'You know, you don't have to go,' I told him," Fazio told him. "He looks at me like I'm crazy."

Wallenda's daughter Carla directed the event from the ground. The City of Cleveland's fathers, whoever they were, however, (unlike their colleagues in Baltimore) apparently had no concerns about The Great Wallenda and his aerial stroll. Larry "The Duker" Morrow, a WIXY radio DJ, silenced the crowd to help the daredevil concentrate. After a slow start, The Great Wallenda eased along the first of the 700 feet ahead of him, navigating a route that took him directly over 2nd base. But then, on cue, a crisis! "He goes and he does that thing where they make it look like, "Whoaaaaaa! - I'm gonna fall!' " recalled Fazio, adding that Wallenda went into a dramatic squat, wobbled a bit, then recovered.

It was all part of a well-rehearsed act, of course, as Wallenda completed the dangerous walk in just over 13 minutes. Afterwards, he drank cold champagne and chatted casually with reporters. Like Ali after a fight, he proclaimed victory. "It wasn't any more difficult than any other similar walks I have made. However, it's not the highest walk I've ever made."[38]

---

38 In 1970, Karl Wallenda tossed back his requisite two martinis then tightroped his way 821 feet along and some 750 above the Tallulah Gorge in northern Georgia. Guinness declared it a world record.

Before his walk above Municipal Stadium, *Plain Dealer* reporter Dan Coughlin spent time with Wallenda. "I've been 54 years on the wire and people ask me why I do it. It's my job. I can't walk away from it," Wallenda reflected. It's unclear if he meant that last line as a pun. "It gives me a chance to make money and care for my children. But if someone gave me more money to do something else, I wouldn't take it. I will do this kind of work as long as the Good Lord gives me strength. Is it not a nice feeling to know you are respected by the American public so much? You cannot buy this."

In 1974, over the course of 81 home games, Fazio and the Cleveland Indians' promotional department planned 37 events with the goal of bringing in at least one million fans. It was a nice, neat, sexy number - and reaching a million fans would put them in the vicinity of actually making money rather than losing it. Opening Day alone featured another daredevil, Hugo Zacchini, blasting out of a cannon some 180 feet through the air, a parade of unicyclists from St. Helen's Church in nearby Newbury, military color guards, marching bands from local high schools, and a first-pitch battery of Mayor Ralph J. Perk (yes, the mayor whose hair had caught on fire) on the mound with U.S. Senator Howard Metzenbaum crouched behind the plate. Ohio Governor John J. Gilligan mimed a swing and miss at the ceremonial first pitch. It was the first step towards an ambitious franchise goal: one million fans, a bold number in many respects. The previous year, a paltry 615,107 fans clicked through the turnstiles, relegating the Indians to last in the American League in attendance and 23rd out of 24 in the major leagues. In 1974, the Indians wanted to almost double their attendance figures from the previous year. Only the San Diego Padres, who were only in their fifth season of existence, had worse attendance in 1973.[39] To Fazio, executive vice

---

39 Finishing just ahead of the Padres gave some context to the depths of the Indians' attendance misery. Ray Kroc, who drove McDonalds to become a global icon, bought the Padres in 1974 for $12 million. The franchise had finished last (6th) in the NL West in every season of their five-year existence. But like any new owner, Kroc was very optimistic and excited about his new purchase - perhaps he thought he could figure out what was wrong with a struggling professional baseball squad and could energize the Padres in the same manner he revolutionized making hamburgers via an assembly line. On Opening Day, though, the Padres were losing 9-2 to the visiting Astros. Kroc couldn't take it. He barreled into the announcer's booth, grabbed the PA mic in an effort to commiserate with the fans. "Ladies and gentlemen," he said to the crowd of just over 39,000, "I suffer with you." At that moment, a streaker dashed across the field, prompting Kroc to bellow, "Get that streaker off the field - throw him in jail!" Kroc sort of settled himself then continued. "I have good news and bad news. The good news is that the Dodgers drew 31,000 for their opener and we've drawn 39,000 for ours. The bad news is that this is the most stupid baseball playing I've ever seen." The crowd loved it. The Padres, including future Hall of Famer Willie McCovey, did not care for Kroc lecturing and embarrassing them. Right after the game Kroc scurried off to Florida on

president Ted Bonda, and others in the front office, their mission was very clear - and important to downtown Cleveland.[40] For Fazio, the goal of a million fans was certainly a long way from the attendance goals that he and Horsburgh had in Twin Falls, Idaho and Elmira, New York. In Cleveland, though, he was also inspired by civic pride. "We were trying to save baseball in Cleveland," recalls Fazio. "Attendance was horrible. We were going to be very aggressive, put on a full court press and leave no stone unturned to save the franchise."

Since 1960, the Indians had recorded only three winning seasons out of thirteen and a malaise hung over the franchise like a persistent fog over the docks near Municipal. The city was in decline. There were constant rumors of the team relocating to another city, management had been ineffectual, the stadium was old, cold, and unattractive. The 75,000-seat capacity destroyed any reason for fans to buy tickets in advance. You could *always* get a seat.

The City of Cleveland performed only the minimum in maintaining the stadium. Finally, Browns owner Art Modell stepped in and agreed to invest $10 million in capital improvements in exchange for $1 annual rent. New suites were built under the upper deck and the revenue they generated was a positive development for the Browns and Indians. Other infrastructure and scoreboard improvements were made as Modell's commitment swelled to over $10 million. "There were real challenges, but if it were easy, it would have already been done," said Fazio.

The '74 Indians had just sixteen front office employees, plus support staff, located above Gate A of Municipal Stadium. The sixteen were Ted Bonda

---

a trip that he claimed he had previously planned (though many think he was trying to escape that he was suddenly in an unwanted spotlight). He later apologized and said he just believed in giving the customer value for their money. At one point Kroc reflected on owning the Padres: "I bought the team to have some fun. But it is proving to be about as enjoyable as a wake – your own."

40 Bonda and the Indians allotted a healthy $200,000 for promotions in 1974. The *Plain Dealer* noted the renewed effort of Fazio and the marketing department: "Beginning with Hugo Zacchini's portrayal of a 105 millimeter Howitzer round...the Indians will combine circus stunts with baseball for most of the 81-game home season. The club's owners believe the combined effect will be a season home attendance in excess of 1 million. Zacchini, last performing member of a family that began climbing down cannon barrels in 1922."

(executive vice president), Bun Blossom (treasurer), Art Pease (controller), Phil Seghi (general manager), Bob Quinn (farm director), Carl Fazio (director of sales and marketing), Dino Lucarelli (public relations director), Jackie York (promotions director), Rich Rollins (group sales director), Dan Zerbey (stadium operations director), Jack Gallagher (ticket manager), Frank Lohn (assistant ticket director), Bob Gill (traveling secretary), Randy Adamack (public relations assistant), Paul O'Day (scouting) and Joe Pavia (scouting).[41] "There was a door that opened from our office that you would take to a ramp and take you to the upper deck of Municipal," Fazio recalls. Despite their stark workplace, Fazio explains that they were also focused on urban salvation. "Everyone was on board. And what brought more people to the downtown than the Indians and Browns?"

Everyone who tried to do business in downtown Cleveland understood what was happening. From 1970 to 1980, Cleveland's "central city" lost nearly 25% of its population, shrinking from 750,902 to 573,822. Cleveland's challenges were no different than many other major cities nearby - Detroit, Buffalo, and Pittsburgh had the same problems, really just continuing a trend that had begun a couple of decades earlier. "You saw people that were moving out to the suburbs and they were migrating to other areas," said York. "The downtown areas started to take a pretty big hit. There was a cancer going on in all those cities. Urban sprawl. They were moving on out to the suburbs for the malls, the movies, the restaurants, housing, and everything else. Cleveland was very much like a lot of the other cities in our region. Yeah, we did catch a couple of bad breaks - our river did catch on fire," she laughs.

Fazio connected with marketing and promotional folks from other teams. "My whole thing is let's see what else is doing and take and apply what would work for us," he said. "Maybe massage it for Cleveland." To that end, Frank Sullivan of the Phillies was very helpful with ideas, as was Dick Hackett of the Brewers. And in December of 1973, Fazio and Bonda invited Ewing Kauffman, owner of the Kansas City Royals, to speak at The Stadium Club to a gathering of Cleveland leaders, baseball enthusiasts, and Indians front office personnel. Kauffman flat-out berated those in attendance for, well, attendance. The Indians,

---

41 Municipal Stadium offered four gates for fans: A, B, C, and D. The Browns' offices were by Gate B.

he pointed out, had fairly pathetic ticket sales, which impacted visiting teams like his. "We're partners," Kauffman told the crowd, referring to Major League Baseball's 1973 profit sharing structure. "You get 20 percent when you come to Kansas City. When we come to Cleveland, we get 20 percent. But we're not even making expenses when we come here." Kauffman turned, then, to financial losses and season tickets. "You lost $1.5 million last year. If you don't sell season tickets, you're going to lose another $1.5 million and you can't afford to lose that. You're going to lose your team."

Kauffman, who had made millions through Marion Laboratories, a phamaraceutical company he started out of his house in Kansas City, boasted about how he sold 1,700 season tickets in his first year. The Indians, he said, should lean on every one of its 50 owners to sell at least 200 season tickets to area business leaders, politicians, and anyone with a heartbeat. "If any owner does not sell 200 season tickets, get rid of him," Kauffman declared. He exhorted the owners and others there to pressure local business, accounting, and insurance firms, and "strongarm local banks" into buying boatloads of tickets.

Fazio recalls loving Kauffman's pep talk and his blunt speech that day inspired at least one audience member: former Cleveland Mayor Ralph Locher, who had since become a probate court judge. Locher was so fired up that he grabbed the microphone and piggybacked off of Kauffman. "The mayor should not only buy tickets, but he should be there every night - and he should invite the bishop," Locher said, then perhaps revealed too much. "During the five years that I was mayor, I not only bet on the results of the game, but I bet on the attendance."

The Indians were indeed ready. Fazio announced the formation of the "Chieftain's Club," something akin to Kauffman's "Lancer's Club" in Kansas City. The club, Fazio outlined, empowered fans to be recognized for either purchasing or contributing to the buying of season tickets. Selling (even to yourself) 10 season tickets got someone into the Chieftain's Club and opened the door to a private club (formerly called "The Wigwam") during home games. Selling 18 earned a VIP parking pass near Gate A of Municipal Stadium, selling 25 earned you a trip to Tucson for spring training, and selling 30 landed a weekend road trip with the team. The top 10 salesmen would also be taken to the All Star Game in Pittsburgh. All "salesmen" were also awarded with Tribe blazers.

Indians Executive Vice President Ted Bonda added that the team hoped to sell 5,000 season tickets before the start of the '74 season. And, he assured everyone that, despite Kauffman's comments, the Indians weren't moving anywhere. Throughout that winter and the spring of 1974, The *Plain Dealer* occasionally reported on season ticket sales. They were not exactly up to Kauffman-like standards, but they were up noticeably from previous years.

In the Indians' group sales department, Bonda's son Tom knew how hard it was to attract fans in '73, when he worked there. "It was very difficult. The team was terrible. I joke about the fact I'd call up a Catholic priest to try to get a large group of his parishioners to come to a game. He'd say, 'Are you out of your mind?' "

A few years earlier - on the eve of a new season in April of 1971 - several baseball executives noted how more competition from other pro sports had prompted their sport's brass to scramble for ways to attract fans via promotions and giveaways. "Years ago all baseball had to do was open the gates and people would flood in," reflected Charlie Finley, the owner of the Oakland A's. "But now, along with other businesses, we have competition and we've got to compete. Giveaways are just good sound promotion." Some teams gave away bats, balls, batting helmets, batting gloves, T-shirts, pennants and posters, cushions and cars, glasses and mugs, diamonds and scarves, pantyhose, and fertilizer. Other franchises were also even willing to give away the previously unthinkable: tickets. "When you start giving away your product, it's bad business," argued New York Mets Promotions Director Arthur Richman. "You can't turn the ballpark into a supermarket. Look what happened to the movies when television became popular. Movie houses were giving away dishes, glasses, and a lot of other junk. None of it helped. They were still closing down." Commissioner Baseball Bowie Kuhn wished baseball would "do without the giveaways." "At the same time," he said, "I think baseball has a different atmosphere than any other sport. There is a carnival feeling to baseball. It's a family affair and, in that, promotion fits in." Bowie added, "I think it comes down to this: If the promotion is done in good taste, then I'm for it. If not, then, the club should examine the event, correct its faults or plan on not holding it again."

Additionally complicating matters in terms of the average fan's discretionary spending, in late October of 1973, the Organization of Arab Petroleum Exporting Countries (OAPEC) declared an oil embargo on countries that had backed Israel in the Yom Kippur War, which had unfolded earlier that month. The initial targets for the embargo were Canada, Japan, Holland, and the United States. The embargo led to a 300% rise in oil prices worldwide by March of 1974. In the U.S., the average price of a gallon of gas rose from 38.5 cents in May of 1973 to 55.1 cents in June of 1974. Some states banned Christmas lights in December of 1973 and at one point President Nixon requested that gas stations not sell gas on Saturday evenings or at all on Sundays. Something in the range of 90% of gas stations followed his suggestion leading to some lengthy photo-worthy lines. Also, on January 2, 1974, Nixon signed the Emergency Highway Energy Conservation Act establishing a 55-mph speed limit nationwide - a feeble effort to encourage fuel efficiency. Most people ignored the law, though states were required to adopt it if they wanted federal funds for highway repairs. The bottom line, though, was that due to increased gas prices, some families had to carefully consider whether going to the ballpark was really worth it (and if the money they would spend on tickets should be reserved for gas). So, the Indians - and every team in Major League Baseball - did what they could to draw fans.

In 1974, beyond Opening Day, the Indians' promotions department planned a plethora of other special events intended to draw more fans to Municipal. They included two barnstorming softball acts, The Queen and Her Maids and The King and His Court, country and western singers George Jones and Tammy Wynette, an Up With People concert, and fireworks displays sprinkled throughout. Fazio and the Indians also scheduled College Night, Ladies Day, a Father-Son-Daughter Game, Poster Days, Grandstand Managers Night, Money Scramble Night, Home Run Derby Day, and Fan Appreciation Day. They gave away warm up jackets, T-shirts, bats, and balls. "The promotion department, over the years, tried every kind of giveaway," wrote Bob Sudyk, who covered the Indians for *The Cleveland Press* from 1962 to 1977. They included the giveaway of plastic horns that were apparently so annoying that stadium ushers were directed to wrestle them away from fans. Other promotions include a Mother's Day giveaway of spray deodorant as well as the giveaway of a pony, which no one claimed."

The 1974 Indians also planned to tap into the glory days by honoring the 20th anniversary of one of the greatest teams in franchise and baseball history, the 1954 Indians, with an old-timers game. The 1954 Indians won a major league record 111 wins and appeared poised for the franchise's 3rd World Series title - they needed only to neutralize a young Willie Mays and the New York Giants, who were no slouches with their 97 wins. In Game One at the Polo Grounds, the teams were tied 2-2 in the top of the 8th. The first two runners reached base. With Al Rosen on first base and Larry Doby on second, Vic Wertz stepped into the batter's box. Wertz demolished a ball into dead center, the most cavernous part of the oblong-shaped Polo Grounds. But Mays raced toward the centerfield wall and made one of the most iconic catches in baseball history, wheeling and firing back to the infield to hold the runners. Many estimate that Mays probably made the catch some 440 or more feet from home plate; in any other ball park, Wertz's blast would have resulted in a three-run homer. As it was, the catch helped the Giants escape the inning, win the game, and ultimately sweep the series. In hindsight, 1954 was the peak of a glorious stretch set in motion in the late 40s by Indians owner and promoter extraordinaire Bill Veeck. Bolstered by the likes of Larry Doby, the first African-American in the American League, Lou Boudreau, Al Rosen, and superstar Bob Feller, the Indians won the World Series in 1948. From 1947 to 1956 the franchise went 928-613-11, the winningest ten years in team history. Feller, who was 13 and 4 in 1954, pitched only two more seasons and won just four more games. The Indians did finish 2nd in the American League in both 1955 and 1956, but after that began "the bad old days."[42]

The 1974 Indians were certainly not alone regarding their promotional ambitions. Finley and his World Champion A's offered a "Hot Pants Day" for the ladies of Oakland. In the spring of 1973, Finley had also promised to introduce orange baseballs that he vowed would become standard equipment in the game.

---

42 Veeck sold his interest in the Indians in 1949. In 1951 he bought an 80% stake in the St. Louis Browns. On August 19, 1951 he brought the 3'7" Eddie Gaedel to the plate. Gaedel, who wore the uniform number ⅛, walked. It was arguably one of the most famous stunts in baseball history.

"The fans can see it better," he said. Finley actually convinced the Indians and A's (the latter maybe didn't have much choice in the matter) to try the orange balls in a spring training game, a 27-hit, 16-run affair. The game featured six home runs, three of them by Hendrick, who noted that he could not see the spin on the ball and that he got lucky. The balls were dyed orange - stitches and all - so many batters didn't care for Finley's diabolical creation. Aspro reported that his batters told him that they did not like it. Naturally, one Indian admitted that he didn't mind the orange balls too much. "I'm color blind," Lowenstein said.

In Cleveland, York and the Indians also marched out a promotion in 1974 that was already in play by Finley and others: ball girls. "A bevy of beauties," also known as the "Indianettes," graced the foul lines of Municipal Stadium, according to *The Plain Dealer*. Selected primarily from the Barbizon School of Modeling, York chose five "beautiful specimens" to corral foul balls or the occasional home run that bounced back into the field of play. "Spectators at the Tribe's home contests (especially the male gender) are now watching what happens along the left and right field foul lines as well as the action on the field, per se."

"Their first duty is promotion work," York told *The Plain Dealer*, "That includes looking pretty (it isn't hard for them to do) at business luncheons and passing out flyers and pamphlets on the Indians." The Indianettes were adorned in red, white, and blue outfits. "We want to see the girls be more active and hustle more not only in retrieving balls but also when they run out to brush off the bases during the middle half of the seventh inning," said York, adding that she would like to see the girls "show a little more sportsmanship" by occasionally dusting off a player's shoes or smacking an umpire's butt. *The Plain Dealer* also noted that "Miss York is quite an eyeful herself."

York had come from a baseball family: her father had pitched in the Red Sox organization but saw his career end when he injured his Achilles. Her great uncle had been the traveling secretary for the AAA Rochester Redwings. Her family knew Indians GM Gabe Paul personally, but York proudly states that she did not get her job because they knew Paul, but because she had graduated from Bowling Green University with a journalism degree and public relations. "The first job I had was working in the ticket office," she recalls. "Eventually I made my way upstairs." Literally. York knocked on Paul's office. "I was green behind the ears. He proceeded to tell me that I would never make it in baseball. That's the worst thing to tell me." Unfazed, she carried on and got her chance to do more than just sell tickets - an opportunity to promote the Cleveland Indians.

Before the '74 season, Fazio and York also decided they needed to liven up the mood at Municipal. "We went to a West Side Cleveland music store and bought an organ and asked the guy (at the store) who could play it. The key was that he understood baseball and understood the timing," said Fazio.

They followed a trail of musical notes to the house of Art Broze, a 52-year-old local musician, to audition him for the role as a ballpark organist. They asked Broze to play the "The Star Spangled Banner," "Deep In The Heart of Texas," and "Take Me Out to the Ball Game." Fazio and York hired him. Broze said he had always dreamed of making it to the major leagues. He finally did, just not as an outfielder as he had once hoped.

Broze's organ sat between home plate and first base in Section 17 in the last row of the lower deck of Municipal Stadium. Throughout the course of a typical ball game, Broze would play upwards of - or part of - 70 songs. Like many ballpark organists, he would attach specific, perhaps cheeky, perhaps clever, songs to certain players. Charlie Spikes got "I've Been Working On The Railroad." John Ellis would stride to the plate with "Oh, Johnny, Oh," an old ditty by The Andrew's Sisters. ("Oh, Johnny, oh, Johnny, how can you love?/ Oh, Johnny, oh, Johnny, Heaven's above/ You make my sad heart jump with joy.../What makes me love you so?").

Not all of the fans loved Municipal's new addition. In July, with the Indians mired in a losing streak, *The Plain Dealer* published a short missive from North Canton's John Thompson: "The perpetual playing of the organ at Indians' games is bush league garbage. Enough of this musical mish-mash which diminishes the inherent drama of the games and annoys the real fans. How about an organ transplant? From Cleveland to, say, Tierra del Fuego?" [43]

---

43 Throughout baseball history, stadium organists have been celebrated, bemoaned, and even ejected. In 1974 Cardinals Manager Red Schoendienst, listening to the Pirates organist before a game, said, "Something ought to be done about these guys who pound that organ so nobody can hear himself think." Captain Moss Bunker of Brookfield, Connecticut took time to write to

In general, as the NFL and NBA grew in popularity, professional baseball teams were vying to compete for the attention and dollars of the American sports fans. In 1974 the NFL implemented a number of rule changes to add "action and tempo" to games. Paul Brown, a member of the league's Competition Committee, said that the changes were intended to encourage teams to win by scoring touchdowns rather than by kicking field goals. New rules included moving the goalposts from the goal lines to the end lines and instrumenting a sudden-death overtime. The NFL also expanded the 1974 season from 14 to 16 games. Ultimately, it all added up to record attendance for the NFL, which edged over 12 million fans for the season. Meanwhile, the young Cleveland Cavaliers, only four years old in 1974, had just 164,520 in the '73-74 season, then more than doubled that total the next winter.[44]

Dan Epstein, who celebrates 1970s baseball in *Big Hair and Plastic Grass*, marvels at the decade. "The 70s were weird. It was kind of like it just didn't fit in with the nostalgic Ken Burns treatment. And out of that chaos came the promotions. It was like the Wild West era of baseball promotions. You would

---

The Sporting News in 1974: "Now that Bowie Kuhn has been reelected (as Commissioner), let him get those organs in the various parks to pipe down. They distract us from the game." Another ballpark organist, Lambert Bartak, began playing a Hammond organ for the College World Series in 1947. Bartak, the son of a Czech immigrant, credited his accordion-playing father with instilling in him the love of music and in getting him started. Bartak's father sold 20 pigs to buy him his first accordion. Bartak also played the organ for the Omaha Royals from 1972 to 2002. In 1988, umpires ejected Bartak from a game because he played the theme from *The Mickey Mouse Club* in the midst of a heated argument between an umpire and manager. "The truth is," recalled Bartak's son Jim Bartak, "Dad didn't know why he was being ejected. He was not a sports fan, and he had no idea what a Mickey Mouse call was. He said, 'I was just playing 'Mickey Mouse' for the kids.' "

44 Baseball also considered interleague play during this era as a way to inject something new and different to the sport. In 1973, the American League wanted interleague play, while the National League voted against it. Kuhn, as commissioner, had the power to cast a deciding vote to make it happen. He supported the concept, but opted instead to establish a commission to study the idea, which subsequently foundered for two decades like some sort of Congressional bill languishing but never getting signed. As such, interleague play did not begin until 1997.

never have a wet T-shirt night at a major league baseball game today - and for good reason. Now it's very codified and more predictable. The minor leagues today are *much* more imaginative and much more creative."

In Arlington, Texas, Kip Horsburgh and an overworked Rangers staff also focused on getting fans through the turnstiles, peppering their home schedule with promotions. They offered Farm & Ranch Night (the first 10,000 fans got a certificate they could redeem for a free bag of fertilizer) and a cow milking contest between coaches (an exhibition of udder nonsense, wrote Shropshire). In previous years, the Rangers had hosted Hot Pants Night, which featured dozens of scantily clad women in "itty bitty shorts," admitted to the ballpark for free, parading around the infield after the game. Fans - mostly male - stood to admire the proceedings and even the Rangers players popped up the dugout steps to watch the parade. Winners included a 72-year-old honoree. "I don't like it - my husband made me," she told a reporter. According to Shropshire, the contestants outnumbered the fans.

In Seasons From Hell, Shropshire noted the team's efforts, prior to Horsburgh's arrival, were ineffective: "Promotions like 'Cough Syrup Night' were not filling the seats in Arlington. The owner was getting desperate. Rumor had it that during the last home stand, someone called the stadium ticket office asking what time the game started and was told, 'What time can you be here?' "

In Cleveland, the small but determined Indians' front office staff kept chugging along - between promotions, group sales, and walk ups, the franchise continued on their march toward their ambitious goal, one home game at a time. And of course it should be noted that amidst the planned 37 promotional events in 1974, the Indians scheduled *four* Ten Cent Beer Nights, set for June 4, July 18, August 20, and September 12.

Regarding those, The *Plain Dealer* added with a considerable sense of humor and unknowing irony: "Baseball games are also scheduled as part of each (beer night) promotion."

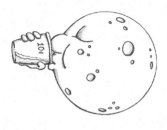

11

THE TEXAS BRAWL:
THE MOSTLY UNTOLD STORY OF BEER
NIGHT

"Take care of him, will ya? The guy's got a big mouth."

— Gaylord Perry to Milt Wilcox

The 1974 Indians lost their first five games, the fifth one in front of a home crowd that the Elmira Pioneers would have been disappointed in: a measly 1,910 fans. Also in that game, public address announcer Bob Keefer got hit in the side of the head with a paring knife. "Fortunately the handle struck Keefer," *The Plain Dealer* noted. Aspromonte noted that the meager turnout discouraged him and the team. "Don't get me wrong, I'm not blaming the fans, but when there is nobody in the stands, it is tough on a ball club. That's not why we're losing, of course."

But on April 26th, Seghi who had just had kidney stone surgery and was lying in bed at home, pulled off a significant trade, sending '71 American League Rookie of the Year, Chris Chambliss, Cecil Upshaw, and pitcher Dick Tidrow from the Indians to the New York Yankees for four pitchers: righties Steve Kline, Fred Beene, and Tom Buskey, and lefty Fritz Peterson. Seghi declared that the Indians now had "a hell of a pitching staff" and that, with the addition of Peterson, they had fulfilled something they had been "aching" to get: a left-handed starter. The *Plain Dealer* did note that Peterson had been involved in the famous wife/family swapping episode with pitcher Mike Kekich, who had just been released by the Indians in spring training. But most seemed to be excited about the addition of a quality lefty. Some, though, recognized the potential blunder in trading the sweet-swinging Chambliss, who appeared destined for greatness. The day after the trade, fans hung a banner in the upper reaches of Municipal. It read, "We Want Chris Back."[45]

In April, Perry conducted what must have been sort of slightly comical bull-pen gatherings: informational sessions for umpires to observe his various pitches (but certainly not the spitter!) in order to see how they behaved. Perry wanted the umps to carefully study his sinker and his forkball. On Saturday, April 20th, Perry hosted several umps and Dick Butler, the supervisor of American League umpires, in the Fenway Park bullpen for such a session. The *Plain Dealer* cleverly dubbed Perry's session "a dry run" and an AP photographer armed with a tele-photo lens stood atop the Fenway roof to hone in on the alleged trickster. "There was nothing wrong with what he threw today," Butler told reporters later. "But that's not to say he doesn't throw something else on occasion." In some respect it was a hilarious gathering as Perry obviously wouldn't lube up a ball for all to see. Instead, he wanted to show them his forkball and sinker. Aspro said they had "accomplished what they set out to do." "Gaylord proved that he has a better than average forkball and that the umpires ought to be alert for it." Perry said that veteran umpire Nestor Chylak was the most helpful as he explained some of Perry's pitches to the others. "See, look at that tumbling motion," Chylak reportedly said about one of Perry's forkballs. After the demonstration, Perry talked with the umpires and told them that he was doing his best to break "old habit of going to (his) neck and ear and hat before every pitch." The umps agreed that this would do nothing but improve upon their continued skepticism. How sincere he actually was about this is anybody's guess. Umpire Hank Soar, who watched Perry's bullpen, said that he knew what a forkball looked like and that

---

45 It should be noted that former Indians GM Gabe Paul was now with the Yankees and not only got the better end of this deal, but also other trades between the Yankees and Indians.

he knew how, comparatively, a spitter behaved. "It's very possible that his forkball could be mistaken for a spitter, but he didn't fool me," Soar said, explaining that a spitter comes in on a hitter and drops down like a ball that is rolled off a table."

In late April and into early May, though, the Indians finally began to click, completing a 7-2 West Coast road trip. New pitcher Kline noted that even the normally demure Gaylord Perry was excited. Dino Lucarelli, in charge of Indians PR, reported that there was electricity in the air and that the phone had been "ringing off the hook." Unfortunately, Lucarelli noted, the electricity had not translated to robust ticket sales. But there was some optimism that as the cold spring gave way to summer, the fans would come. Since the big trade, the Indians were 9-2 and the baseball world seemed to think the Seghi's additions had been precisely what the team needed - amazingly, it appeared that the Indians had maybe even gotten the better end of the deal (but it was certainly too soon to make such a conclusion). The 35-year-old Perry showed no signs of slowing down and on his way to a dominant season. After losing the opener, Perry began a stunning streak of wins (or no decisions) that would run into early July. After winning on July 2nd, he would stand at 15-1. It was a streak that included an incredible 16 complete games (!) and three shutouts.[46] In early May, Bonda flew "Mother Perry," aka Ruby, the mom of Gaylord and Jim, to Cleveland for Mother's Day. Mother Perry described how a blind neighbor in Williamston, North Carolina had "about 20 radios" and could pull in an Indians game. She would listen to the games then call the farmhouse of Ruby and Evan Perry to give them a full report - sometimes at 6 a.m. It was a joy, then, to watch her boys in person.

In Arlington, the Texas Rangers had a tough assignment to begin the '74 season, although Billy Martin probably wouldn't have wanted it any other way. To wit, they welcomed the 1973 World Series-winning Oakland A's to Arlington Stadium for a three-game series. And despite winning it all the year before, the A's actually had a new manager: former Cleveland skipper Al Dark. Dark and the A's, who were loaded with talent, were in the midst of "the good old days" - at least on the field. In the clubhouse, though, they were a team renowned for

---

46 It took the eventual World Series champ Oakland A's to finally hand Perry his second loss of the season on July 8. In that contest at Municipal, though, Perry threw 9 ⅔ innings and struck out 13, but was a hard-luck loser.

brawling with one another. The Rangers' first game against the champs was a clunker as they made two defensive errors and managed just six hits off of the talented James Augustus "Catfish" Hunter. The A's hammered Jim Bibby for six earned runs and Reggie Jackson churned out a four-for-five day, including a home run off of Rangers reliever Steve Hargan. But the next day, the Rangers gave a small glimpse of what they perhaps could be in 1974. Fergie Jenkins showed precisely why he was one of the best pitchers in either league, tossing a complete game one-hit shutout, striking out 10 Oakland A's. He pitched, according to Shropshire, "like a mean kid pulling the wings off of flies."

The Rangers immediately proved that they were a different squad than in '72 and '73, going 13-8 in April of '74 and putting them 2 1/2 games up in the difficult AL West. They struggled at the start of May, though, lowlighted by a 6 game losing streak and a horrific collision between Randle and former Indian Dave Nelson. Two of the quicker men in baseball, they were both in pursuit of a "Texas leaguer"[47] - Nelson from his spot at second base and Randle from center. They hurtled toward the ball and each other at full speed. "There was a sickening thud, a collective gasp from the fans in Arlington Stadium, then silence, except for Randle's moans." The collision broke Nelson's nose, gave him whiplash and knocked him out for 10 minutes - he finally awoke in an ambulance. "I still can't remember it happening. All I know about it is what they told me happened," he said later. Randle took his bumps and bruises and kept playing, while Nelson was out for several weeks.

After the Randle/Nelson collision - and some other outfield wrecks and near crashes - Martin armed center fielder Cesar Tovar with a whistle and told him to "blow the shit out of it" (if calling for a ball). "I blow the whistle because I do

---

47 "Texas Leaguer" refers to a weakly hit pop up that barely gets over an infielder but falls safely in front of an outfielder. On May 21, 1892, Houston Mudcats Ollie Pickering had seven such singles, seemingly leading to the creation of the idiom that is still used today. Less than ten years later, Pickering led off for the Cleveland Blues on April 24, 1901, which gave him the honor as the first-ever batter in the American League (and the first-ever batter for the Cleveland franchise).

not want to collide with Mr. America," Tovar told reporters, referencing stout right fielder Burroughs.[48]

In the third week of May of '74, the Indians embarked on a nine-game road trip: three in Baltimore, three in Detroit, three in Texas. The tilt began poorly with two losses to the Orioles, but the Indians won the third game against Baltimore, then topped the Tigers in the first of three in Detroit. On the morning of Saturday, May 25, 1974, they were 21-20 and had every reason to be optimistic: a quarter of the way through the season, they were just one game out of first place in the American League East.

That afternoon, Bob "Wolf Man" Johnson took to the mound at Tiger Stadium and pitched wonderfully, scattering just six hits and giving up just one run over six innings. The Indians offense reciprocated, scoring two in the eighth to give Wolf Man a 4-2 lead. In the bottom of the 8th, Aspro turned to reliever Fred Beene, who had stymied the Tigers the previous weekend in Cleveland. This time, though, Beene just didn't have his magic beans. Mickey Stanley singled. Al Kaline did the same. Then slugger Willie Horton, who would later play for the Indians, promptly blasted a three-run bomb into the lower deck of left field. The Tribe failed to score in their half of the ninth, and - just like that - found themselves on the wrong end of a 5-4 result. It was simply one of those games, Aspromonte told reporters, "that got away."

After the game, Johnson, who had turned in a quality start and watched a potential win evaporate like the morning mist over the Detroit River, retreated to the trainer's room, while Beene sat and stared sullenly at his locker. The Indians eventually returned to their hotel and then the bars of Detroit. The next day, the Indians lost another one-run affair. Slightly dejected and now 2-4 on the road trip, they made their way to the Detroit airport to catch a flight to Texas where they would have their season's first encounter with - insert John Adams drum roll - Billy Martin and the Texas Rangers.

---

48 Tovar, aka Pepi, by the way, was another Martin favorite and allegedly married to three different women in three different Latin countries. In 1968, while playing for the Twins, Tovar played all nine positions in one game. He began the stunt as a pitcher, throwing a scoreless inning in which he struck out Reggie Jackson (who may have been laughing a little bit as he faced Tovar).

Perhaps what happened that Sunday evening and into Monday morning could be attributed to the frustration of seeing wins that were virtually in-hand just slip away in the late innings. Or perhaps it was simply the stress of playing professional baseball combined with the rigors of travel. The Tigers closed out the Indians at about 3:40 p.m. After showers and a few interviews, the Indians arrived at the Detroit airport at 5:30 p.m., ready to fly to Texas.. But their flight was delayed, so they waited. In the meantime, Johnson (and several teammates) passed the time by getting, in his estimation, "snockered" in an airport bar. Then, just as they boarded at 10:45 p.m., American Airlines deemed their plane unfit to fly due to mechanical reasons and scrambled to prep another plane. Finally, at 11:30 p.m, the plane took off. Somewhere, then, in the sky south of Detroit, a blitzed Johnson cornered Indians travel secretary Bob Quinn on the plane and excoriated him over travel frustrations. The plane stopped in Indianapolis about midnight, adding a few more passengers, and forcing some of the Indians players to move seats. At this point Johnson completely lost it with a steward-ess and simply decided to just walk off the plane. On his way past a sleeping Aspromonte, he apologized. "I apologized for the language I used, but that's all," he later told reporters. The Indians made it to their hotel in Texas about 3:30 a.m., due to play that evening at Arlington Stadium. To probably no one's surprise, the boys from Cleveland were completely flat for that evening's game against Jim Bibby and the Rangers. Bibby threw a complete-game 3-hit shutout against the Indians, easily beating Jim Perry. Johnson, meanwhile, caught up with the Indians via a later flight.

The next day, though, Gaylord Perry was due to pitch and in a good mood. "You guys better score some runs," an unshaven Perry (no shaving before a start) half-joked while driving to Arlington Stadium. He said, too, that his phone was ringing off the hook with media requests about his book, *Me and The Spitter*. "I didn't know there were that many radio stations in Dallas," Perry laughed. Teammate Wilcox told him that he could switch rooms with him as no one ever called him.

Perry and Martin were old enemies. The Texas manager had been after Perry for his "greaseballin' ways" for many years - they had crossed paths many times when the Indians played the Tigers or Twins. Perry sarcastically loved to refer to Martin in his book as his "good friend." In his previous start, Perry had shut down the Orioles with a complete game three-hit shutout. The Indians had scored just 11 runs over their previous 7 games, but Aspromonte was understandably confident with Perry, who was in one of the most dominant stretches of his career, taking the rubber. Still, Aspromonte acknowledged the offensive struggles. "Gaylord will hold 'em for us...the only trouble is how do we win zero to zero?"

It turned out that Aspromonte didn't need to worry. Perry dominated the Rangers, throwing yet another complete game shutout. He struck out six, gave up just five hits (but walked five), while the Indians pounded out 12 hits. They won 8-0 and now stood at 22-23. The Rangers fell to 22-24. The win set the stage for a rubber match game on Wednesday, May 29th. The Perry win was the kind of game that infuriated Martin, who always believed that the old "greaser" was cheating, which was precisely what Perry wanted. Perry used the mere hint of ball doctoring to his advantage. Meanwhile, Randle had one of the five hits off of Perry. After the game, according to Milt Wilcox, Randle said something to the press about Perry's decline and that he was "all washed up." Perry read the news story and approached Wilcox, who was due to start the third game of the series, in the locker room. "Gaylord walked over to me and said, 'Take care of him will you? The guy's got a big mouth.' " Wilcox added, "I played with Lenny Randle later and I liked him. But when you played against him, you hated him." Perry, too, had activated one of the secret bat signals[49] in baseball: back up your teammates. Additionally, Wilcox called Perry his mentor. Ten years his elder, Perry and Wilcox spent lots of time together talking when they weren't pitching. Perry also taught Wilcox during spring training that they weren't throwing batting practice to Indians pitchers - rather, it was "pitching practice" for them. "He was trying to hit the corners and the guys would get a little mad at him," Wilcox recalls. And Perry also made an impression on Wilcox as simply a pure competitor. "He just wanted to win so bad. I kind of took that mentality." As for Perry's pre-game request to shut Randle up? Wilcox received the elder Perry's directive. "That's just how baseball was played," Wilcox recalled. "I didn't think anything of it."

---

49 Pun intended!

As the game unfolded, tension rose on the field. In the fourth inning Randle slid hard into second base and slammed his shoulder into Brohamer. "It was a cheap shot, totally uncalled for," Brohamer said later, "Randle is a hot dog and he hit me dirty," Brohamer later said, adding that he didn't have any chance to turn a triple play.[50] Peterson had started the game, then gave way to Johnson, then Hilgendorf. Then, thanks to the baseball gods, Aspromonte made the call to the bullpen to bring in Wilcox in the bottom of the 7th. Now he had his chance to fulfill Perry's request. Wilcox yielded a single to Burroughs then got Grieve to ground into a double play. Lenny Randle, batting 6th, strode to the plate and dug in the box. Wilcox toed the rubber, wound up, and sailed a fast ball behind Randle's head. Randle put his hands on his hips and stared out at Wilcox. He turned to Indians' catcher Dave Duncan for clarification. "What's going on?" he asked Duncan. "The pitch just slipped, I guess," Duncan replied. Randle didn't buy it.

In the age-old duel between hurler and hitter, the pitcher is given the obvious advantage, particularly if there is any ill-will. Satchel Paige liked to call his purpose pitch, ideally whistling under a batter's chin, "a bow tie" and passed that idea along to the game's all-time strikeout leader, Nolan Ryan. That approach could have almost applied in this situation, apart from the fact that the pitch rocketed several inches behind Randle's head and not under his chin. Randle stood briefly and stared out at Wilcox. After his brief conversation with Duncan, he dug back in then attempted a revenge tactic that rarely works for the hitter: a bunt along the first baseline intended to draw the pitcher in close enough to enable proximity. Or, in Randle's case, a bunt along the first baseline that might allow him to revisit his old Arizona State football days – with Milt Wilcox as his opponent. Such a bunt would have to be almost perfectly placed - forcing the pitcher to field it and putting him in a less-than-defensive position while he did. Randle's bunt was perfectly placed. Wilcox fielded it and Randle veered left onto the infield grass, and lowered his arms as if trying to bust through collegiate gridiron defenders. He made a beeline for Wilcox, hammering him with his forearm and launching him into the air. Amazingly, Wilcox, who was 6'2" and 185 pounds, somehow held on to the baseball, and sprang back up to proudly show

---

50 The hard slide Brohamer refers to is also on YouTube via G. William Jones Film Collection at SMU: Indians @ Rangers Footage.

the umps that he had done so. He spiked the ball and sprinted toward Randle, who was already beneath the loving embrace of Indians first baseman John Ellis, who was listed at 6'2 and 225 pounds. Home plate umpire Dave Phillips signaled that Randle had been tagged out then retreated a few steps while the benches and bullpens emptied. First base umpire Bill Deegan waved his arms as if to say, "Let 'em have at it…they don't pay me enough to get into this." All hell broke loose or, as they might say in Texas, "Someone tipped over the outhouse." The bullpens emptied. Someone sucker punched the already targeted Jack Brohamer. Duncan wrestled with someone just beyond first base. Martin was out there in the mix. Randle later called the bunt his "bump and run." "You gotta protect your family, your jewels and your stuff," he said years later. "None of that was my fault - it was his fault. If John Ellis hadn't tackled me, it wouldn'ta been a brawl. He (Wilcox) threw the ball away."

During the melee, Rangers first baseman Mike Hargrove - heeding Martin's directive to get into the mix - tackled Brohamer from behind. "I ran toward him (Wilcox) and got tackled from behind - blindsided," Brohamer said. "I had no idea what that was about until the next day when I saw the newspaper and saw that it was Hargrove.[51] The 5'9" Brohamer said that the six-foot Hargrove punching down on him was equivalent to him punching down on the diminutive Indians clubhouse attendant, Cy Bunyak. When order was finally restored, the Indians returned to their dugout where they were greeted by a raucous crowd. Ranger fans, who were snot-slingin' drunk, united to form a sort of fire brigade - but with beer - passing down cups of brew to a middle-aged man

---

51 In 1980, Brohamer was playing for the White Sox while Hargrove had become a mainstay in Cleveland. Brohamer said he walked into a locker room at Municipal and saw a smiling Hargrove standing there waving a white towel. As for brawling, Brohamer agrees with Wilcox that it was just kind of the way baseball was played in 1974. And it's no surprise that Martin was right in the middle of it. "He was just one of those old-school managers…he and Earl Weaver. In Chicago I played for Bob Lemon and he was more of a 'Go out and play' manager and didn't get that mad, but Martin and Weaver were fiery." Brohamer added that when he played for the White Sox they found themselves brawling with Weaver and Orioles. Bart Johnson, one of Weaver's teammates, took a shot at Weaver, who didn't know initially who had done it. "But Weaver found out through the papers - sort of like I did - and he said, 'Bart, I will get you - even if I have to trade for you - I will get you.' "

positioned by the Cleveland dugout.[52] He showered the Indians, including Aspromonte, with the frothy stuff. One local fan wearing a shirt that said, "Eat More Possum," poured beer on Duncan and sought to test his pugilistic skills against him. Duncan was more than willing to oblige, attempting to scale the roof of the dugout to get to him, but half of the Indians' dugout pulled him down. Eventually the three policemen, with hands on their guns, arrived and hauled the troublemaker off and eventually fined him $27.50.[53]

After the game, Aspromonte said he didn't condone fighting, but - just as Martin expected of his players - that if one did break out, he expected to see his entire team out there. They weren't. "Not all of them did, and I'm not very proud of those who held back," he said. His reflections, and those of reporters covering the series, were prophetic. Aspromonte thought about the Rangers fans around the dugout. "Those people were like animals in a zoo," he said of the Rangers fans. Little did Aspromonte know how prescient the words he had just uttered would be. The same could be said for the report of *Plain Dealer* writer Russell Schneider, who wrote that he had been astounded by the brawl, particularly the lack of security. "Nobody appeared to quell the near-riot at the dugout for more than five minutes. Somebody, fan or player, could have been severely injured."

As for Wilcox's attention-grabbing pitch, few people in Arlington Stadium thought the ball slipped. But 44 years later Indians manager Ken Aspromonte

---

52 Some have maintained that the Rangers were actually hosting a "beer night special" that evening, but there is no record of that.

53 The Rangers' ushering/security staff was completely unprepared for the quick build-up of angry fans during the brawl on the field in the first few rows behind the dugout. Standing at the top of the lower box seats and yet untrained in such growing kinds of fan misbehavior, they were unable to even reach the front row before fans threw beer at the Indians players returning to the third base dugout. As a direct result of this moment, security protocols were changed the next night to have security personnel standing at the front rows near the dugout and field between each inning, standing with their backs to the field and facing toward the fans in stands, to show "security presence" *before* such problems even started. This new protocol soon spread to most other major league stadiums and later into other sports venues, all in the aftermath of this beer-throwing event.

said the same thing. The ball had simply slipped. "It was a misunderstanding," Aspromonte said. "Wilcox told me the ball slipped out of his hand. It's hard for the other team to understand that. I tried to talk to Billy at the time and he understood." Randle claimed he was simply trying to bunt his way on and not "laying an ambush" for Wilcox (and Martin seconded his player's emotions). Martin also claimed that Randle didn't veer. "I don't know if they were throwing at Lenny or not," Martin said. "But he never got out of the baseline in the collision with Wilcox." Randle maintained the same line of defense. "I don't know if he was trying to hit me," Randle told *The Fort Worth Press*. "I was just trying to get on base and I didn't think they would be expecting a bunt with two outs. I didn't try to hit Wilcox. We just sort of collided while I was running to first," he said with an angelic grin.

The sequence of events - the Brohamer/Randle play at second, the purpose pitch, the bunt, and the brawl - were filmed and are available through SMU's G. Williams Jones Film Collection and on YouTube - unusual for footage of a midweek game in 1974 to have been captured. In any court of law - baseball or otherwise - Martin and Randle would have a tough time presenting a solid counter argument as the video shows that Randle clearly veered from the baseline and directly into Wilcox.[54]

Duncan said he always thought of Randle as a "pretty nice guy." "It's too bad he had to do something like that," Duncan added about Randle's beeline toward Wilcox. "There was nothing between me and him and the goal line." Peterson, though, did not speak highly of Randle. "He's a (censored). He wouldn't do that on the road." And Brohamer alleged that Randle had a history of violating some of baseball's unwritten rules. "In the minor leagues, he stole third base on us and his team had a 12-run lead. That's the kind of guy he was. It was a cheap shot. I didn't have a chance for a triple play." Brohamer added that Randle was "stupid."

---

54 Video footage of Randle's veering tackle of Wilcox is on YouTube under "WFAA Film of A Great Baseball Fight - Rangers vs Indians 1974". It is a fine slice of early to mid-70s baseball. Check it out through SMU's G. William Jones Collection. You'll see Martin in the melee and an angry Duncan in the dugout. Also, pause it around the 42 second mark to see Gamble tomahawk a bat into the crowd, dangerously close to a little girl in the stands: Indians @ Rangers Brawl.

"He's a good ball player, but he's got to learn something upstairs. He's a pop off, he argues everything, a real hot dog." Aspromonte avoided writers by repeatedly going to take a shower. "I have nothing to say," was all he would, well, say.

Martin pointed out that he was in the midst of the melee in an effort to aid the peacemakers. He said he was knocked down twice, but didn't throw any punches. He also said that he wasn't quite what he used to be in terms of such baseball dust ups. "I'm slowing up getting out there. Me? I was going after my pitching coach, Art Fowler. I was trying to make sure that somebody who might be trying to break up a fight didn't get popped. Those are the guys who usually get hurt. I got knocked down twice. First time my uniform's been dirty all year. This was my kind of game, though. Good base running. Good pitching. Some defensive plays. Those fans in Cleveland will really be on my back when we get up there next week. Anytime there's a fight, people always think I started it."

The Rangers won the game 3-0 to put them at 23-24. They were very pleased with the pitching performance of Jackie Brown, who gave up just three hits on his way to a shutout and who apparently hung back from the fray. "Press box observers credited him with a no-hitter in the brawl." Brown said the fight "jacked him up" and allowed him to finish the shutout. Randle claimed he was just trying to get on base. Shropshire recapped the night with this lead for *The Star Telegram* that turned out to foreshadow what would transpire the following week: "A quietly routine evening at the ball yard exploded into a scene reminiscent of nickel beer night at Harold's Cave Creek Saloon."

Both teams would play one another in six days, but Martin told a group of reporters that he was unconcerned about retribution. Reporters then delighted in telling him that the Indians had planned to host a Ten Cent Beer Night promotion. "I couldn't give a (expletive deleted)," Martin snapped. Meanwhile, several of the Indians were pleased, anticipating that the combination would lead to greater intensity. "It's a break we hadn't counted on," joked Duncan. But the nitpicking and diatribe certainly mattered, setting a definite tone for the media to latch onto, not to mention greasing the wheels for the next meeting between the two teams.

A few days after the Indians brawly trip to Arlington, United Press International reporter Milton Richman wrote, "Finally, inevitably, the sludge from Watergate has spilled over and begun to contaminate baseball." Richman cited the Arlington incidents, along with others, as an indication that the American people were confused about Nixon's impeachment. He compared POTUS to a baseball manager who has lost control of his team but assures everyone that the squad will bounce back.

"The lawmakers in this country aren't at all sure he (Nixon) will. Much more important, the people aren't sure. They're confused, alarmed and anguished over what happened at Watergate. They have difficulty distinguishing right from wrong anymore and few places has their general despair become more evident than at the baseball parks. Baseball fans have taken to verbalizing their dismay and it comes out in a terrible Exorcist[55] form of raw abuse upon the ballplayers. Fan abuse and rowdyism aren't really anything new, but they now seem to be reaching unprecedented proportions."

When asked to analyze fan behavior, psychologist Dr. Lucille Blum said she could see how the general mood in the world could manifest itself in the stands. "Everybody is quite apprehensive," Blum said. "The uncertainty of the future is a little more intensified now because of our national condition, and whatever resentment people have, the ballpark is a very compatible atmosphere in which to show it. This is a form of aggressive or immature behavior with them. The words these people are using are ones they are normally prohibited from saying. Throwing beer is also a child-like action which fits into the general pattern of repression."

In Lorain, just west of Cleveland, sportswriter Hank Kozloski disagreed with Richman regarding the Watergate connection. "I think he's off base," Kozkloski wrote in his June 2nd, 1974 column, "Koz's Korner," a Sunday feature in *The Morning Journal*. "It seems to me he was merely trying to come up with a 'column angle' the other columnists hadn't already used. Kozloski also covered the Indians on a regular basis and saw the potential for trouble. "One reason the 'beer brawl' took place in Arlington was because the Rangers did not furnish adequate police protection inside the stadium…That's what makes this Tuesday's game in Cleveland's Municipal Stadium a potential powder keg. The Indians

---

55 The Exorcist, released on December 26, 1973, was the highest Christmas-week grossing film of all-time until *Titanic* passed it in 1997.

are just as guilty as the Rangers with regards to police protection." Kozloski proceeded with prescience: "But the potential does exist for Tuesday's game. If the Indians are alert to the situation, they will see to it that additional policemen are stationed in and around the Rangers' dugout…how's that saying go: (sic) To be forewarned is to be forearmed."

Around Cleveland, though, a simple and enticing red-lettered poster adorned the walls outside of bars and restaurants, on the columns upholding highway overpasses, and pretty much everywhere and anywhere such a poster could be plastered.

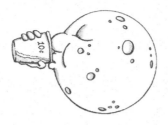

12

TEN CENT BEER NIGHT

Reporters: "Are you going to take your armor to Cleveland, Billy?"

Billy Martin: "Naw," Martin smiled. "They won't have enough fans there to worry about."

Such were Billy Martin's taunting, post-brawl comments in Arlington, Texas. The media then proceeded to tell Martin that the next time the two teams would see each other - six days hence - that the Indians would be hosting a previously planned promotion:"Ten Cent Beer Night." Then he pondered a little more about various elements. "You're kidding," Martin responded. "Oh-oh. They'll be on me. Every time a fight starts, those fans say Martin started it. Well, I'll see you in Cleveland. Bring your beer." He also said, "Oh, shit."

After the brawl in Arlington, the Indians caught a flight to Cleveland while the Rangers stayed put, awaiting the visiting Baltimore Orioles. Both squads had Thursday, May 30th off. On Friday, May 31st, the Great Wallenda did his thing in Cleveland and the Indians won two out of three in their weekend series against the Royals. The Saturday game, played in chilly 50-degree weather, saw a measly 4,205 fans click through the turnstiles.

In Arlington, the Rangers won two out of three against the Orioles, which was no small feat.[56] On Saturday evening, thanks to Bat Night, over 39,000 fans showed up and the game had to be delayed by 15 minutes due to traffic choking the highways. One of the Whiz Kids, Horsburgh, remembers it with amazement. "It was a real 'flash crowd' - Rangers baseball was beginning to show signs of life. We were all there and we all felt it. 39,000 people coming out to a game in the middle of the season - it was shocking - our first sellout since the David Clyde debut." In Arlington, Horsburgh found himself being run ragged in the Rangers front office. He was doing everything - from helping to execute something like the bat night promotion, to calling the Rangers affiliates so that he could hand-write out all of Rangers' minor league player statistics. As for Bat Night, the Rangers had to issue coupons for many children to get theirs. Also, it was so successful that at the end of each inning the Rangers public address announcer would rattle off a list of "missing children," requesting that they report to the box office so that their parents could claim them. The annoying quality of thousands of children beating on the metal bleachers with their bats also made the Rangers rethink the promotion - in the future, they decided, they would hand out the bats to kids upon exit. Still, they were thrilled with the turnout. When Short had agreed to move to Texas, he had set up a fantastic deal (for the Rangers) with the City of Arlington: the Rangers would rent Arlington Stadium for one dollar as long as the season attendance stayed under a million fans. After the million mark, though, an escalating rate would kick in, allowing the city to take some of the ticket sales. It hadn't been a concern in '72 or '73, but suddenly, in '74, it seemed as if it would come into play. After bat day, the Rangers - amazingly - had eclipsed the 400,000 fan mark, and it was only early June. Both teams had Monday, June 3rd off.

On the morning of June 4, 1974 - with Ten Cent Beer Night looming like a mid-week fraternity party - the sun shone gently on downtown Cleveland. The weather forecast called for sunshine and a high of 78 degrees. And once the sun had done its job, somewhere around 8:56 p.m., a full moon would light up the sky. The big news story of the morning involved a close Nixon aide, Charles Colson, pleading guilty to obstruction of justice in the case of Daniel

---

56 The Orioles, who had won the AL East in 1973, would go on to win it again in '74 with a 91-71 record.

Ellsberg, who had leaked The Pentagon Papers. More notable, though, was the additional story that Colson, who had once called himself the "chief ass-kicker of the White House" and a guy who would "walk over his own grandmother to help re-elect Nixon," would cooperate with Watergate prosecutors in their investigation of the president. Sprinkled throughout the newspaper were ads for Father's Day presents: Pulsar watches, handsome recliners from Higbee's, golf shoes at Halle's, "swagger slacks" from Rogoff Bros. in Shaker Heights, a Donegal matching leisure suit at May Co., ("Be A Sport For Dad".) Meanwhile, the sports pages advertised Cruex medicated sports powder ("Jock itch? Chafing? Rash? Cruex."). The National Steel Corporation proudly reported that it had declared a dividend for the 2nd quarter of 1974 and would pay out 62.5 cents per share on June 14. It was, they said, their 178th consecutive quarterly dividend (a span of over 44 years).

That morning's *Plain Dealer* sports section highlighted Wickliffe High School's dramatic 6-5 win over Cincinnati Princeton for the Ohio AAA baseball title. It also featured a cartoon of a muscular and shirtless Chief Wahoo holding a baseball glove in his right hand and dangling a pair of boxing gloves in his left: "So - play ball…" the dialogue box declared on one side, and on the other, "But be ready for anything." Next to the cartoon, Indians beat writer Russell Schneider previewed the series in a short article: "The last time the Indians and the Texas Rangers saw each other, six days ago in Arlington, Tex., they were throwing punches and shouting epithets."

Schneider went on to list the pitching matchups and featured comments from Aspromonte. "I don't anticipate any trouble, at least not on our part," Aspromonte said. "What happened in Texas was a misunderstanding…it was just one of those things. We had it out, and that's it. We're not going to back down from anything, but we won't be antagonizing them either." Martin struck an equally indifferent and ostensibly professional tone. "I don't expect anything more to develop," he said. "Of course there's some chance some trouble might come up, but I don't think so. As far as I'm concerned, I don't blame anybody for what happened when we played the Indians last time. What happened is all part of the game." Randle concluded that what happened in Arlington was water under the bridge. "You forgive and forget. I didn't think nothing of it. I'm from

Compton, CA - we're happy to play," he said later. "We grew up hard, tough and rough - and gentlemen." Seghi claimed, though, that the Indians would have extra security on hand that evening. *The Cleveland Press* also fired up the troops a bit: "Rinse your stein and get in line. Billy the Kid and his Texas gang are in town and it's 10-cent beer night at the ballpark."

"Players don't get into the promotion," Randle said in 2019. "We didn't know it was 10 Cent Beer Night. Players just shut up, show up, and play the game. We looked around and said, 'Wow, are we in Cleveland?' We were so confused. We saw that river - what's its name? - and then we said, 'Oh, we must be in Cleveland!' " Although Randle also recognized that Cleveland fans and players might target him. *The Dallas Morning News* reported that Corbett asked him how many security guards he would personally need. "I told him not less than 600." He added that he would be wary but was not going to go up there with his "head up in the air acting like Hercules."

The Lorain Journal quoted Brohamer that if the Indians harbored any thoughts of revenge they should reconsider exacting it because two of their stoutest players were injured (and presumably unable to brawl). "With Bell and Ellis out right now really isn't a good time to get in a fight." Martin wasn't naive. "Oh, they hate me in Cleveland, in fact I'm sure they blame the whole thing down in Texas on me. They can draw a crowd of 300 for a game and 200 will be threatinin' to kill me. I've never exactly been a big favorite here."[57]

In Texas on June 4, 1974, *The Fort Worth Press* published a feature about budding superstar Jeff Burroughs and his stature in the Dallas-Fort Worth area. Writer Tommy Love noted that Burrough was not exactly comfortable with it all: "Jeff Burroughs, quite simply, has become an idol. The view from the pedestal, however, doesn't do much for him. In an area hungry for sports heroes to worship, Burroughs is the first bonafide home run hitter (outside of a brief glimpse at a fast-fading Frank Howard) baseball fans have had since Duke Snider was warping bats at LaGrave Field. It was love at first sight. Fathers are naming babies after him, which is bound to displease some girls when they grow up, people are

---

57 Martin actually played 73 games for the Indians in 1959, batting .260. The Indians traded Martin to the Reds in December of that year.

comparing him to Jimmie Foxx; and higher ups have even altered the dimensions of the ball park for him."

Yet Burroughs, who was not looking to simply appease the public, openly declared his goals: "I'm not playing baseball because it's fun. The only two goals I have are to be financially stable and to do as good a job as I can. It's hard to get the first without the latter, though." Burroughs acknowledged the need for reporters to highlight someone. "The media is prone to exaggeration. They need someone they can write larger-than-life stories about and I guess I fit the bill. It doesn't bother me one way or the other." Heading into Ten Cent Beer Night Burroughs had hit 12 home runs, a league-leading 53 RBI, and was clipping along at a fantastic .333. At some point in the afternoon, semi-refreshed by a precious and rare off day on Monday, the Indians sauntered into Municipal Stadium for a team photo. The squad donned their cherry red tops and white pants.[58]

Late in the afternoon, nearly forty miles south of Cleveland, a dozen members of Akron University's Phi Delta Theta fraternity crammed into several cars. They were fired up for some cheap beer. Knowing that Billy Martin would be there, they had also stuffed their pockets with tennis balls. They were ready for "low-powered brew and high-powered goings on," according to the *Akron Beacon Journal.*

Throughout Municipal Stadium Fazio, York, and others were busy preparing for what they thought would be a bigger crowd for Ten Cent Beer Night. Around 5:30 p.m., the fans began to stream in. York recalls noticing two unusual elements: the weather and the fans. It was oddly hot and downright sultry for early June - the rainy and blustery front that Fazio and Wallenda had experienced on Municipal's rooftop days earlier had definitely blown through.

"That stadium never got warm until July. That night it was hot," recalls York. She and other members of the Indians organization also noticed a different vibe

---

58 In later years they would go all red, prompting Boog Powell to famously compare himself to a blood clot. Others compared Powell to a red fire engine, while others said he looked like the World's Biggest Bloody Mary. The red color was not coincidental - it was the same as the uniforms by the Magic Valley Cowboys and the Elmira Pioneers. The all red uniform was proudly displayed afterwards at the Baseball Hall of Fame in Cooperstown for several years.

and looked at the crowd streaming into Municipal Stadium. "I remember walking around the concourse saying 'I don't know who these people are coming in' - it was a different audience." *Press* photographer Paul Tepley also recalled the weather - and the vibe. "It was a stinkin' hot, humid night, and you just kind of had a feeling things weren't going to be good."

Patrons began flooding into the ballpark. Some of them wore bell-bottom jeans and tight fitting t-shirts. Some donned shirts with big - "tapered" - collars. Some of the women wore their hot pants and halter tops. Some of them came in having had a few drinks already. Some of them had smoked a little pot. As they entered the stadium, everyone of age was presented with six red tickets, each redeemable for a cup of beer. Fan Gary Powers, though, disagrees with the "of age" part. "They look just like raffle tickets and you got two double rows. I'm 14 and they're red. Everyone that wasn't a mother holding a baby in their arms got one. You walk in and the tickets are all over the floor."

Bill Konyha was 25-years-old at the time and described himself and his friends as "legitimate fans." We were legit baseball fans and used to crowds of 5 or 6000, not 25,000," Konyha laughs, "The only 10 cent beer we had that night got poured down our backs. We went to get 10¢ beers, but the lines were so long that if we had stayed there we'd have missed the game." Fans Rich Foulk and his pal Dave Szabo were among the crowd filing into the stadium. "We drank beer like water then. It was part of being 20 and 21 and being dumb. We took turns going down (to get the beer). I probably had a dozen. A lot of people went there just to drink."

Behind the home run fence and in front of the bleachers, the beer was flowing; fans flocked to a beer truck manned by two young college girls who at first patiently accepted the tickets and doled out beer into plastic cups - as well as any other containers given to them. Creative fans smuggled in their own alcohol and containers. Some were empty and some were not. And some would *soon be empty* to make room for beer.

Thus, fans - or a good percentage of the 25,134 attendance figure that would later be posted - began consuming massive amounts of Stroh's[59] "3.2 beer," a

---

59 TCBN scholars debate which beer was served that evening. It would make sense that it was Genesee Beer, which hailed from Rochester, New York, and

lower-than-usual brew that had its origins in the 1930s. It was beer that was "3.2 by weight (ABW)" or "4% by volume (ABV)." Also dubbed "three-two beer," "light beer", or "low-point beer", the rationale was simple: less alcohol, less drunk. On April 7, 1933[60] President Franklin D. Roosevelt signed the Cullen-Harrison Act, legalizing the sale of 3.2 % beer. After signing, Roosevelt famously said, "I think this would be a good time for a beer." It was around this time that a leading academic, Anton Julius Carlson, the chairman of the University of Chicago Physiology Department, weighed in - literally. Carlson announced that in his estimation 3.2 ABW was the "standard of non-intoxication." In other words, an individual could drink 3.2 ABW beer and still walk a straight line. Also pertinent to Ten Cent Beer Night, in 1971 Congress passed the 26th Amendment which lowered the national drinking age from 21 to 18.[61]

But not everyone wanted to drink the 3.2 beer, Foulk recalls. "There was an elderly guy in front of us - probably 75 or 80. He was there with his grandson and had a big cooler with him and he said, 'I'm not gonna drink that stuff' and started pulling malt liquors out of there."

---

who had teamed up with the Indians for several years. Throughout the '70s, pocket-sized schedules, featuring a green Chief Wahoo (to match the primary color of Genesee), listed the Channel 8 viewing schedule. The 1972 schedule proclaimed, "See the Indians on TV....(sic) Channel 8. So good...Genesee Beer (insert pic of glass mug) it's out of sight." Also, Genesee offered a low alcohol beer. Almost a year to the day after Ten Cent Beer Night, though, the Indians had another Beer Night and *The Plain Dealer* reported on it in a sports page article: "Royals supply punch for Beer Night '75." Coughlin reported, "A mostly somnolent crowd of 7,043 watched on this Beer Night and, because of a new coupon method for allocating 15 cent beers, consumed far less than a year ago. A representative from the Stroh's distributorship said 350 barrels were dispensed a year ago, when Cleveland made national news for its inability to hold its alcohol. Tuesday night the distributor man said between 50 and 60 barrels were sold." Perhaps it was Genesee distributed by the Stroh's distributorship? Perhaps not. Later, dear reader, beer lovin' Billy Martin will refer to Stroh's. Whatever the case, it was cold, yellow, and it was beer. 350 barrels of beer is a lot of beer, no?

60 April 7 is still celebrated as National Beer Day. On National Beer Day of 1974 the Indians lost 7-1 to the Yankees.

61 Congress ratified the 21st Amendment, repealing Prohibition, in December of 1933.

On the field, Randle remembers noticing how plastered the fans were before the game even began. "At batting practice everyone was drunk," he said. "We hadn't even put on our uniforms and everybody was drunk," adding that the fans began heckling them. "We never got heckled during batting practice."

As game time approached, Martin popped out of the dugout. He turned to face the crowd, who showered him with lusty boos. With his lineup card in hand, Martin smiled and blew kisses toward them then walked over to home plate where he met Aspromonte, Umpire Nestor Chylak, who would serve as the crew chief, and the three other umpires: Larry McCoy (home plate), Joe Brinkman[62] at 1st base, Nick Bremigan at 2nd base. Chylak would ump at 3rd base. Chylak, the son of Ukranian parents, grew up Olyphant, Pennsylvania, a small town outside of Scranton. He had enrolled in the University of Scranton, but had his academic endeavors interrupted by World War II. In the winter of 1944, United States Army Sergeant Chylak found himself snowed in as a member of the 99th Infantry in the dense Forest of Ardennes along with hundreds of thousands of other American troops. It was there, at the Battle of the Bulge, that the Americans repelled the German Army in one of the most pivotal clashes of the war. All told, nearly 20,000 Americans died and over 62,000 were injured. Among them was Chylak, as an exploded shell propelled shrapnel into his face, blinding him. He lay in a hospital bed, his eyes bandaged, for ten days. Fortunately and dramatically, when the bandages were removed, he could see again. (Yes, for a short time an umpire was actually blind.) Chylak rarely spoke of the trauma of World War II and was thought of as incredibly kind and generous, a result (his son would later say) from the friends he had lost on the battlefield. Chylak, most agreed,

---

62 Nine years after Ten Cent Beer Night, Brinkman was involved in another infamous Billy Martin contest when he managed the Yankees: "The Pine Tar Game." After Kansas City's George Brett hit a crucial home run against the Yankees in the 9th, Martin - upon the urging of old Elmira Pioneer Don Zimmer - convinced the umpires that Brett had violated a rule by applying beyond the allowed 18 inches to his bat handle. Brett stormed out of the dugout towards the umpires and was then thrown out of the game, which was suspended based on a protest by the Royals. Lee MacPhail, who we will hear more from later in this book, agreed with the Royals and upheld the protest. The game was eventually resumed several weeks later with the Royals winning 5-4. The "resumed game" took less than 10 minutes to play.

was a fantastic veteran umpire, described frequently as "no nonsense," "fair," and "not wishy washy about anything." McCoy would serve as the home plate ump. He had been an AL umpire since 1970, but was surprised that evening. "When we walked out on the field that night there was a smoky haze that night that looked like fog. I didn't know anything about dope or anything. I asked one of the guys I said what in the world is that sweet sticky smell. Nick Bremigan, who is now deceased, told me 'Rock, you never smelled marijuana before?' I said, 'No, I never have.' So there was already a layer of marijuana covering the ballpark."

Martin and Aspromonte presented their lineups to Chylak and his crew:

The Texas Rangers

1. Cesar Tovar - CF
2. Lenny Randle - 2B
3. Alex Johnson - LF
4. Jeff Burroughs - RF
5. Tom Grieve - DH
6. Jim Fregosi - 1B
7. Toby Harrah - SS
8. Leo Cardenas - 3B
9. Jim Sundberg - C

   Fergie Jenkins - SP

The Cleveland Indians

1. John Lowenstein - 3B
2. Jack Brohamer - 2B
3. Leron Lee - LF
4. Charlie Spikes - RF
5. Oscar Gamble - DH
6. George Hendricks - CF
7. Ossie Blanco - 1B
8. Dave Duncan - C
9. Frank Duffy - SS

   Fritz Peterson - SP

Peterson, due to start for the Indians, was just five weeks removed from the huge trade that brought him to Cleveland. He was 3-3 with the Indians during that stretch and had struggled against the Rangers in Arlington in the brawl-marked game, giving up four hits and one run over two innings. Jenkins was 7-5 with a 2.76 ERA.

As "The Star-Spangled Banner," echoed through Municipal, both squads, the umpires, and some of the fans honored America by standing at attention, caps off, hands on hearts. But in the stands, an ill omen bubbled up: a fan who had spilled his beer began brawling with a vendor.

Warmup before first pitch: Rangers 0, Indians 0
Beer vendor: 1
Fan: 0

The first inning was probably the quietest of the evening. Peterson got Tovar to ground the ball to Lowenstein, who threw him out at first. He then walked Lenny Randle. Alex Johnson dug in. Randle tried to steal only to get thrown out by Dave Duncan. Brohamer made the tag, which must have been slightly satisfying given their interactions from the previous week. Johnson flew out to end the inning. The bottom half of the inning went very much the same for the Indians - Leron Lee singled but Jenkins escaped without any trouble. Fans continued to drink.

End of 1st: Rangers 0, Indians 0

Peterson struck out Burroughs to begin the 2nd inning. Then Grieve dug in and promptly blasted a home run to center field. But, as Grieve trotted around the bases, a "large female fan" staggered toward the on deck circle. The crowd bristled with anticipation. The woman raised her shirt and exposed her breasts to the crowd.

Middle of the 2nd: Rangers 1, Indians 0
Bare Bosoms: 1

The Indians failed to score in the bottom of the 2nd. In the third inning, Jim Sundberg and Tovar smacked back-to-back doubles in the 3rd inning to pick up another run for the Rangers. Randle says he was at the plate (naturally) for what happened next. AAccording to Randle, while he stood in the batter's box, another large-bosomed woman dallied out onto the field then ambled toward home plate and smiled. "Who wants me?" Randle said the woman inquired of him, home plate umpire Chylak, and catcher Dave Duncan. Then Chylak (according to Randle) said, "I haven't been kissed since the end of World War II - I'm about due for some." [63] [64] A policeman escorted the woman off of the field as the crowd roared their approval.

End of the 3rd: Rangers 2, Indians 0
Flashers: 1
Smoochers: 1

In the top of the 4th, Dick Bosman replaced Peterson. Grieve welcomed the new pitcher by launching his 2nd home run of the game to give the Rangers

---

63 Many Ten Cent Beer Night storytellers (whom I like to think of as sitting around a crackling fire) have suggested that Morganna, the infamous "Kissing Bandit," was the woman who dallied out onto the field to kiss Chylak, but all indications are that the woman who did that was *not* Morganna (though perhaps certainly inspired by her?). For several decades - from roughly 1969 to 1999 - Morganna Roberts, a busty, blonde and green-eyed exotic dancer, gained massive notoriety by sprinting onto the baseball field and kissing superstars. Over the years she kissed Pete Rose, Steve Garvey, George Brett, Len Barker, Cal Ripken Jr., Nolan Ryan and many others. She also smooched Kareem Abdul-Jabbar on court. Morganna estimated that she kissed 37 MLB players. On April 9, 1985, after she kissed Ryan, who got down on his knees to welcome her, Morganna had to appear in a Houston court. Lawyer Richard "Racehorse" Haynes argued that Morganna had no intention of trespassing on the field, but that she leaned over the railing and her bosom's gravity did the rest. Eventually, the Houston Sports Association, which ran the Astrodome, dropped the charges against her and she was spared the potential sentence of six months in jail and a $1,000 fine. Morganna has Ohio connections as she married an accountant from Columbus in 1999 and, as of 2019, lived in Ohio.

64 Some say that the kissing woman incident happened in the 2nd inning. But if the baseball gods wanted anyone to be up to bat when it happened, it *had* to be Lenny Randle, who would later be called "Baseball's Most Interesting Man" because of some Forrest Gump-like moments. Randle was up to bat at Shea Stadium when the lights went out in a massive 1977 NYC blackout. He is also famous for getting down on his hands and knees along the Seattle Kingdome's third baseline to blow a fair ball foul. Umpires had never seen it and were very confused but ultimately decided that Randle was not allowed to do that. As for Ten Cent Beer Night, Randle was up in the 1st, 3rd, 5th, 7th, and 9th.

a 3-0 advantage. In the midst of Grieve's home run trot, a streaker bolted onto the field and slid into second base before Grieve reached it. Sliding and streaking scholars believe the streaker chose the traditional feet-first slide rather than the Pete Rose head-first version. Had he chosen the latter, though, it surely would have been a Hall of Fame moment. As more and more streakers bolted across the field, Adamack was watching it all in the leftfield stands with a group of college friends. They were seated near a group of nuns. "They were watching what was happening and I could hear them saying, 'Oh my.' It was pretty amazing to watch all this happen."

Middle of the 4th, Rangers 3, Indians 0
Streakers: 5
Horrified ("Can't You See This Woman's a Nun!?"[65]) Nuns: 4

In the bottom half of the inning, Leron Lee launched a missile into Jenkins' stomach. Approving fans in the upper deck loved it and began chanting, "Hit 'em again! Hit 'em again! Harder! Harder!" "A torrent" of tennis balls began to rain down on the field and with little police enforcement fans began to feel like they could do whatever they wanted without repercussions. Gamble singled, moving Lee to third then Charlie Spikes singled to score him. Also, a naked man sprinted around the bases and slid into second base. At some point in the early innings, a reporter caught up with Bonda and asked him about the wisdom of having a discounted beer night. "We plan to have them," he said. "These are young people. They are our fans. Where have they been? I'm not going to chase them away."

Beer lines grew longer and some of the young fans Bonda had praised grew impatient. One enterprising man, who had some beers in his hands and an obvious sense of humor, worked his way down the line trying to sell beer for 5¢. Another patron chose the Samaritan route, receiving beers at the front of the line and shuttling them backwards. Then, when he finally tried to get some for himself, he was denied. He argued with those dispensing the beer and finally won his case. With six beers in hand he began heading toward the stands when a teenager bashed into him, causing all of his beers to crash to the ground. "That's when the guy started beating on this kid," recalled fraternity man Ford. "He hit

---

65 Nacho Libre (2006)

him on the head three times. The kid was crying and he went down. The guy was so mad he bent over, took two dollars out of the kids pocket and went on his way."

End of 4: Rangers 3, Indians 1
Streakers: 10

Sliding streakers: 2
Beaten Teenagers: 1

In the 5th inning, a father and son duo sprinted out to the infield, assumed their positions, then mooned the crowd. Equally emboldened, a handful of kids jogged out to right field and approached Indians right fielder Charlie Spikes who gave them high fives and patted them on the head before conveying a sense to the kids that, as one fan later recalled, "you gotta go." So they did, simply climbing back into the stands. Stadium public address announcer Bob Keefer, located near the visitor's third base dugout, requested that fans not throw anything onto the playing field. The fans responded with loud booing and by throwing objects at Keefer.

End of the 5th: Rangers 3, Indians 1
Full Moons: 3

In the 6th inning, Bosman got Johnson to pop out and Burroughs to ground out. But then Grieve continued to lead the Rangers' offense, singling to left field. Fregosi followed with a double. The Rangers had runners on 2nd and 3rd with two outs. Harrah tripled and drove them both in to give the Rangers a 5-1 lead. Despite the shenanigans throughout the ballpark, it appeared that the Rangers were in full command of the game. In the bottom of the inning, though, Brohamer smacked a ground rule double. Lee reached on an error by Hargrove and Brohamer scrambled around to score. After Spikes lined out, Gamble grounded the ball to first base. Lee hustled toward third, sliding and promptly spiked Jenkins, who had sprinted over to cover the base, in the leg. Martin had seen his lanky ace suffer enough and replaced him with rightie Steve Foucault. Hendrick singled, scoring Lee. In the meantime, the Indians informed everyone in the press box that, for the safety of all, they had removed the fireworks from the outfield, so if the home team managed to hit a home run, they would not see the traditional pyrotechnics. Meanwhile, in the left field stands, fans began to tug at the padding along the wall. Members of the ground crew ran out in an effort to stop them and a tug-of-war the padding ensued. Fans continued to bombard the Rangers dugout with smoke bombs and bottles encased in paper cups. They would also light strings of firecrackers and dangle them into the dugout. Martin emerged from the dugout and thumbed his nose at the crowd.[66] Ford and his Akron fraternity buddies rained tennis balls down on Martin, who responded by scooping up handfuls of gravel, and spraying it into the crowd. The Rangers bullpen, more exposed than the players in the dugout, was also under attack with firecrackers and smoke bombs.

End of the 6th: Rangers 5, Indians 3
Thumbed nose: 1

What happened next seems burned into the memory of most who were there - one of the most notable of the evening's streakers: a fit and naked young man - perhaps in his late teens or early 20's - descended the bleachers, scaled the centerfield fence then landed like a cat on the warning track. He carefully deposited his clothes at the base of the wall. Then, like a well-conditioned and confident cross country runner warming up before a race, he dashed around the outfield accelerating at will and generally dallying about. What was partly notable, other than his impressive gait and agility, was that he was still wearing one piece of clothing: a single dark sock adorned his right foot. Was it a political statement? Was it a bold and desperate message directed toward the stocking industry? Or perhaps just a rookie mistake? The world may never know. A handful of Cleveland police officers pursued the young man in vain, establishing a kind of Keystone Cops effect. Or, Randle recalled, it appeared that Laurel and Hardy were chasing him. The crowd roared as the young man maneuvered and evaded the police. "He had better moves than Jim Brown!" recalled famed drummer John Adams.

The one-socked bandit ran at will, dallying around the verdant Bossard-beatified outfield, then finally bolted towards the centerfield wall from whence he had come. The crowd spurred him on but also seemed to be trying to tell

---

66 Thumbing one's nose is a classic expression of derision. The thumb is placed on the nose and the rest of the fingers above it are wiggled slightly. It is also known as "cocking a snook" in England. It is a delicate art and should only be attempted by professionals or under the supervision of a trained nose thumbing expert.

him something. In the bleachers, Adams also saw what was happening. A small but determined string of Cleveland police were waiting for him on the other side. He tried to clamber up the wall and began to go over it, but the pursuing Cleveland police officers had caught up to him. Meanwhile, officers had congregated on the other side of the fence. Straddled on top, both contingents claimed him and began to pull. The crowd's hero was essentially castrated on the home run fence. "The guy is screaming, 'They got me! They got me! They got me!' " Adams recalls with a hearty laugh. "It must have seemed like an eternity." When police finally pulled him down on the bleacher side, cops covered up his vital parts with a garbage bag and marched him off in front of the roaring throngs.

Top of the 7th: Rangers 5, Indians 3
Cleveland Police: 1
Outfield Wall: 2 (balls)
One Socked Bandit: 0

On the field, Indians reliever Tom Buskey walked catcher Jim Sundberg and Cesar Tovar to start the 7th inning. With their most productive hitters up next, the Rangers were poised to add on to their lead. But Buskey managed to get Lenny Randle to pop out then Alex Johnson to hit into a fielder's choice but walked Burroughs. The bases were loaded with the red-hot Grieve up next. Aspromonte called on Wilcox. Grieve nearly blew the game wide open with a grand slam (to notch one of the best game's of his career) by hammering a ball to deep centerfield, but Hendrick ran it down and the Indians escaped.

Middle of the 7th: Rangers 5, Indians 3

As Fazio reported later, "In the middle of the 7th, this situation got out of hand as approximately 50 fans started sprinting across the outfield from foul pole to foul pole." Most of these fans, Fazio observed, were between the ages of 14 and 21. "They were not on the field to cause harm to any players or fans. But rather for the sheer excitement of setting foot on a major league field. Many stopped to shake hands with the outfielders on their way by. At no time did any fan interrupt play by coming onto the field while an inning was in progress."

Someone in the Rangers dugout picked up the phone (probably Martin or pitching coach Art Fowler) to call down to the bullpen and tell the pitchers to abandon their bullpen. The pitchers grabbed their stuff and jogged toward the safety of the Rangers dugout, avoiding many of the frolicking fans and an Indianette who was heading out to sweep off the bases. Indians first base coach Larry Doby, ready for the bottom of the 7th, stood and watched. Aspromonte sent word to Martin that he should feel free to take as long as he likes to warm up any relief pitchers coming into the game. Chylak agreed - if he needed to warm up a pitcher, what with the bullpen abandoned, Martin could do it for as long as he liked on the mound.

At some stage, the long lines at the beer truck were too much for the two college girls dispensing the suds; they simply gave up and walked away. Thirsty yeast-craving fans pushed aside the tables that blocked the trucks and began helping themselves, some putting their mouths directly below the taps. In the stands, though, Akron University student Ford said there were numerous fights. "There were so many fights in the crowd," he said. "Everybody was so drunk. What happened was guys would turn around, say something to someone and wham, wham, …wham. That was it. I must've seen 10 fights." Foucault struck out three Indians - Brohamer, Lee, and Spikes - to quickly take care of the Indians in the 7th.

End of the 7th: Rangers 5, Indians 3
Fans: 1
Beer Truck: 0

Rookie sensation Hargrove pinch hit for Jim Fregosi in the top of the 8th inning. In the bottom of the inning, Hargrove took over at first base when a Thunderbird wine jug suddenly landed about 15 feet behind him. Hargrove went over to it and kicked the bottle aside, expecting a grounds crew member to retrieve it. But they didn't. Instead, a fan jumped out of the stands, sprinted over to the bottle, grabbed the glass jug, then returned to the stands. Naturally.[67]

---

67 Thunderbird was also dubbed "The American Classic" and considered a fortified wine. The 1957 radio ad for it went like this: "What's the word? How's it sold? Good and cold. What's the jive? Bird's alive. What's the price? Thirty twice?" (in other words, 60 cents a bottle).

Middle of the 9th: Rangers 5, Indians 3
Random Fans Sprinting About: 50-plus
Thunderbird Wine Bottle Collectors: 1
Grounds Crew: 0

In the 9th inning, the crowd seemed to have found a fresh supply of ammunition to hurl at the Rangers, firing bottles, batteries, hotdogs, and tennis balls at them. Also, as if in some kind of battle where territory mattered, fans advanced and occupied - like a gang out of the cult film *The Warriors* - atop the Rangers' dugout. They stood defiantly on top of it and let the Rangers know they were there, stomping their feet and dangling and detonating firecrackers into the dugout below. Martin snatched a bat, busted it against the dugout rooftop, then retreated. He and the other Rangers stood in the safety of the dugout with bats in their hands. Martin's looked like a maligned walking stick.

Had the Rangers scored three quick outs, perhaps the infamy of the evening may have never fully transpired, everyone would have left - some to bars, some to their homes. The full moon would have transitioned to the meridian at midnight and ultimately disappeared from view in the west. The game would have ended in a 5-3 victory for the Rangers and perhaps not achieved as much notoriety as it has today. The magnificently mustachioed Foucault, who would later become a police officer in Arlington, had sailed through the 7th and 8th innings and got Gamble to ground out to begin the 9th. But Hendrick, who had singled off of Foucault in the 6th, laced a double into left field. The crowd rumbled with delight. Aspromonte then called upon three straight pinch hitters. It worked. Ed Crosby pinch hit for Ossie Blanco, promptly singling to right field and scoring Hendrick. Next, Rusty Torres, batting for Dave Duncan, hammered a single into center field, moving Crosby up to second base. Alan Ashby then stood in for Frank Duffy and managed an infield single. The bases were loaded with Cleveland Indians.

Bottom of the 9th, 1 Out: Rangers 5, Indians 4
Rabid fans: 25,134

The crowd reached a fever pitch, stomping their feet and shouting. Broze played on. Lead off hitter Lowenstein, who was 0-4 on the night, strode to the plate. Of his baseball abilities Lowenstein once said, "I've always considered myself as an intangible asset to my team. Perhaps because the tangible assets of my career are not so impressive." On such a peculiar evening as this one, was there anyone better to have at the plate at that particular moment? On June 4, 1974, somewhere in the vicinity of 10 p.m., intangible asset John Lowenstein proved himself. After he worked the count full, Foucault toed the rubber, eyed the sign from Fregosi, checked on the runners and fired. Lowenstein lifted a high fly ball to his counterpart in quirkiness - Randle, who caught the fly ball in center, but could not prevent Crosby from hustling home. The game, which had been so close to slipping gently into that good night, was now suddenly knotted at five runs apiece. The drunken and ecstatic crowd lifted off into an orbit of delirium.

Bottom of the 9th, 1 out: Rangers 5, Indians 5

"That's the first time I ever hit a sacrifice fly and raced for the dugout," Lowenstein said after the game. As Lowenstein headed to the dugout, three fans in the right field stands couldn't suppress their enthusiasm. One of them was Terry Yerkic, the 1973 A/AA state wrestling champion at 183 pounds. Yerkic had just finished his freshman year at Cleveland State University and had come to the game with his Richmond Heights High School buddies. After drinking beer throughout the game, he concluded that he wanted one thing: Jeff Burroughs's hat. Yerkic and his pals dropped down out of the right field stands and advanced toward an unsuspecting Burroughs. When they reached him, Yerkic snatched the hat off of the rightfielder's head. "I felt it in my hand and then I slipped. I looked at him and I said, 'Oh...*shit*.' " Burroughs kicked him in the thigh. "He left perfect spike marks. Then Burroughs slipped. The incident sparked the riot. From their dugout, the Rangers saw what had happened. Some say that the crown of the field contributed to a sense that Burroughs was in trouble. Others say Burroughs wasn't in any danger. "That's all Billy Martin needed," said Fazio, who was watching it all from near the Indians dugout. "Billy Martin was not going to lose a game that he was leading 5-1 a couple of innings ago. He strategically led his players onto the field, bats in hand. He knew exactly what he was doing, looking for a forfeit."

Martin and the Rangers, bats in hand, charged out the dugout toward right field. Randle said later that they needed the bats. "It was self defense. We held our bats like bayonets," said Randle. "We didn't want to hurt anyone." Yerkic got to his feet. "I just took off. I got up and started running - I ran through center and they (the Rangers) were chasing me. I was really in good shape. I was running in left field just on the other side and ran through the gate. I got back up in the bleachers. Burroughs also slipped and from the dugout, the Rangers lost sight of him." From his 2nd base position, Randle said he turned to see what was happening behind him. "Jeff goes, ' Lenny, Lenny, help, help' and I said, 'What's going on?' One guy's trying to take his glove. One guy (Yerkic) is sprinting out toward center." The Indians were quick to follow (though not wielding bats) and came running out of their dugout. Hundreds of other fans, in the lower reaches, began to clamber over the railings along the right field line, the left field line and any line. Some fans scooped up gravel from the warning track and began spraying it toward the oncoming players.

Fazio later noted, "Three Rangers players caught a fan before he could climb into the stands and began pummeling him with punches." Hargrove turned around at 1st base and saw Yerkic attempt to snatch the hat off of Burroughs. He also saw the ensuing scuffle and then a flood of fans coming out of right field. "It just looked like a wall. I kind of thought maybe this is what Custer felt like and the melee started at the mound," Hargrove said. Hundreds of blitzed fans poured onto the field. "They were drunk," recalled Randle. "They weren't even speaking English."

As various mini battles ensued on the field, fans continued to throw whatever they could find from the upper deck. On the field, *Press* photographer Tepley later recalled a chair landing near him.[68] Another chair thumped Indians pitcher Tom Hilgendorf on his head. Some fans, stunned by what they were witnessing, did stay in their seats. The malt liquor-drinking old man in front of Foulk and Szabo approved of at least one part of the melee he saw. "He shouts, 'Kill those motherfucking cops!' Then he looks down at his grandson and I think he realized what he was saying - then he says, 'I just hate those cops.' "

Chylak tried to restore order, imploring fans near the Indians' dugout. Eventually he and his crew gathered near second base. Chylak would later say, "We were trying to figure out the lines of least resistance. But there was no place

---

68 Tepley told *Ohio Magazine* that the chair had come from the upper deck, though Fazio says there were no chairs up there.

to go, really." They finally concluded they would head toward the umpire's locker room underneath the stadium. As they made their way behind enemy lines, Chylak got thumped on the head with a missile - it was a bottle encased in a paper cup.

Oddly enough, perhaps oblivious to the abject danger all around, or perhaps drunk, a father lowered his four-year-old son onto the field near the Indians dugout and told him to "Go ahead!" - this was his golden chance to run the bases. However, at some point fans stole the bases - hopefully the 4-year-old made his dash before that happened.

Above the field, Shropshire bristled with joy. "From my safe haven in the press box I was delighted by the entire spectacle since my dispatch to the newspaper back in Texas would offer something out of the ordinary and I figured that players' post game quotes might not be as cliche as usual."

After 10 minutes, somehow, players and police on hand managed to restore some order and, as Schneider wrote, "apparently the game was going to continue." The Rangers, accompanied by the Indians as a sort of security phalanx, began to walk toward the infield then an additional fracas started at the pitcher's mound as Hargrove and the others began fighting with a young man.

Throughout the City of Cleveland, various police officers on duty were listening to the radio broadcast and assessment by Tait and Score that a riot was underway. Some went on their own to help while the dispatcher rallied 20 cars from the "tactical and impact units" from the 3rd, 4th, and 5th districts to the Stadium. Jim Herron, a Cleveland policeman from 1967 to 1994, was there. "We had riot sticks with us. We had to swing 'em," Herron recalled. "We had to use force sometimes."

The umpires finally made their way into the dark recesses of the Stadium's underbelly. As they walked along the dark hallways, a frustrated Chylak took his heavy mask and methodically smashed out light bulbs along the way. He was a great and well-respected umpire and he had survived the Battle of the Bulge, but he simply couldn't control what had just gone down in Municipal Stadium.

The Indians bullpen emptied and made their way from behind the left field wall toward the infield. As they approached, the throngs of crowds opened up a corridor to Gaylord Perry as if he were some kind of deity. "Lord, it was literally like God was parting the Red Sea," laughs David Clyde. "They let Gaylord walk through and the Lord closed the sea up. If you wanted to be totally safe, just stick to Gaylord."

Wilcox popped out of the dugout and into the fray when he was suddenly surrounded by his own Italian security detail. They were friends of his from Nascala, a Richmond Heights restaurant that Wilcox and several Indians frequented. The group was led by Carmen Piunno Jr., the owner of Nascala, located on Wilson Mills Road in Hilltop Plaza. "Carmen was a big backer of the team. I started toward right field and four or five of them circled me and said, 'Nobody's gonna touch you.' " Fans ran up to players and tried to shake their hands. Others ran around the bases. Others stole the bases. In another act of defiance, emboldened fans tried to snatch the hats off of policemen's heads and the badges off of security guards.

All the while, Broze continued to play his organ - perhaps in an effort to normalize the bizarre scene or perhaps to satirize the events that were unfolding (and slightly oblivious to the danger). Some have said that at one point he played a beer jingle - and at another point, the ol' classic: "Take Me Out to the Ball Game." Responding to a letter to the editor later, a team spokesman would say that he played some "charge" songs that are part of his repertoire and he just had some bad timing in playing while the riot ensued. Keefer gave up trying to announce for the fans to clear the field. The Indians management turned off Municipal's lights. The Cleveland police detonated a series of tear gas canisters and the crowd finally began to disperse.

In the umpire's locker room underneath Municipal Stadium, Chylak and the umpires made a decision, declaring that the game would not be resumed. He declared the game a forfeit in favor of the Texas Rangers and sent word to Keefer to make the announcement.

Game Over: Texas Rangers 9 Cleveland Indians 0 (via forfeit)

An exasperated Chylak spoke angrily to the media. "They were uncontrolled beasts," he said, displaying a bloody hand. "I've never seen anything like it except in a zoo." He also showed reporters one of the many "missiles" (particularly the one that had thumped him). He added that he saw two knives brandished in the crowd. He praised the Cleveland players for protecting the Rangers and the umpires. "The Cleveland players were super, great, coming out there to try to quiet the fans. And so were the police. You can't hold back animals. Animals. Animals. Have I ever seen this before? Yes, in the zoo. The (beeping) zoo. The (beeping) zoo. How can the cops stop them? It was 2,500 animals per cop."

In the Indians locker room, Aspromonte - "choked with anger, disgust, and frustration" - sat and couldn't speak for ten minutes. Finally, he spoke softly to reporters. "Those people were like animals. But it's not just the society we live in. Nobody seems to care about anything. We complained about their people in Arlington last week when they threw beer on us and taunted us to fight. But look at our people. They are worse. I don't know if it was just the beer, I don't know what it was, and I don't know who to blame, but I'm scared."

Aspromonte's phone rang and he picked it up. It was Martin, who was thankful for the help of the Indians. "Billy feels as badly as we do, but he was grateful we helped," Aspromonte told reporters. Dazed Indians pitcher Steve Kline, partly in uniform, confirmed as much and philosophized a little while sitting on a stool in the locker room. "What I can't understand is their motivation. They were hitting everybody, it didn't matter who. We had to protect their players, we couldn't let 'em down. Who knows, we might be in their shoes some time. I sure would have wanted some help."

In the Rangers locker room, Martin praised the Indians for helping to protect the Rangers while bashing the fan base. "They came out like champions. That Dave Duncan was great," Martin said. "There was Rusty Torres, Ken Aspromonte and all of them. The fans showed the worst sportsmanship in the history of baseball but the Cleveland players were great." Martin added that he thought Burroughs might be "destroyed" in right field. Others believe that Burroughs was in no real danger and that Martin was just trying to secure a forfeit. "I guess these fans just can't handle good beer," Martin quipped as he doubled down on his comments and downed a beer of his own as he spoke to reporters. "I've been in this game 25 years and I've never had an experience like this. People were acting like idiots. Was it the beer? I don't know. They were on something. All it proves is this town can't handle good Stroh's."

Hargrove later recalled that he was never really scared while out in the midst of the melee, but as he neared the dugout and proceeded to go down the steps the gravity of the situation began to weigh on him. "When I got into the club-house it hit me how dangerous it was." Burroughs admitted that he was fright-ened. "Scared? I had nothing to protect myself. It was an insane situation." But he also threw out a joke. "I guess this was the first time you could say the Indians saved the Rangers." He walked over to Shropshire and inquired whether or not the stats would count.

Even members of the media weren't safe. Coughlin, a young beat reporter for *The Plain Dealer*, wrote in the third person about himself as victim: "A truculent youth standing in a mob on top of the Texas Rangers' dugout punched a newspa-per reporter in the side of the head several minutes after the riot at the Stadium had apparently subsided." Coughlin later told ESPN, "He punched like a girl."

Indians players were angry because the riot cost them the game. Dick Bosman had been at the last recorded Major League forfeit - the final game of the Senators in Washington. "The fans in Washington were not mean…they were only looking for mementos. This was a mean, ugly, frightening crowd." In the locker room, though, Perry provided some mirth. "Hey Ken," Perry called out to struggling Indians pitcher Ken Sanders, "You know, you take the loss in the forfeit!" The locker room erupted in laughter. Sanders had the team's worst ERA and a 0-1 record at that point. He hadn't even pitched in the game.

Actually, to answer Burroughs's question to Shropshire and piggyback off of Perry's joke, the offensive stats from the game did count but the pitching stats did not - and no pitcher was credited with a win or loss. Shropshire described the evening like this: "Woodstock had become Kent State." Tovar compared the crowd to those in Venezuela. "These people are different. Very different," "Got no respect for the police. Of course they'd shoot the people who tried that at home."

Al Frielander, the head of Municipal Stadium concessions, marveled at the notion that so many people got drunk off of 3.2 alcohol beer - even if they were pounding six of them at a time. Frielander said that the crowd consumed about 65,000 cups of beer.[69] Catcher Dave Duncan said he got hit with something

---

69 Because people apparently brought in their own alcohol and their own containers, it's difficult to measure precisely how blitzed fans were. Also, once

in the posterior. He reached back and realized it had been a water balloon that had soaked his butt. What ultimately seemed to quell the situation was tear gas, turning off most of the lights, and one other dramatic arrival. The outfield gates opened up and several mounted police units charged onto the field.

Post Game
Mounted Police: 1
Rioters: 0

Both teams and the umpires were held in their respective locker rooms for quite a while then escorted out by security. The Indians headed to their cars, some of them armed with bats that had been leftover from a recent souvenir Little League bat day giveaway. The Rangers boarded a bus that took them to the Hollenden House, a hotel on the corner of Superior Avenue and E. 6th Street.[70] Security guards were posted on each floor that the Rangers occupied and they were instructed to not go out in downtown Cleveland. But not everyone followed the mandate, according to pitcher Don Stanhouse.

"My roommate - Pete Broberg - and I, snuck out and went to a club right next to the hotel," Broberg laughed. "Oscar Gamble's wife[71] was singing there.

---

the beer truck taps were abandoned, it's not hard to imagine fans putting their mouths under the source and imbibing straight from the tap.

70 The Rangers and other visiting teams typically stayed at the Hollenden House, a 400-room hotel built in 1965. The original Hollenden Hotel, which sat at the same location, had opened in 1885 and was one of the most luxurious and glorious places to stay in downtown Cleveland. It had 1000 rooms and was the home to some permanent residents as well as folks passing through the city. It featured electric lights, 100 private baths, intricately paneled walls, redwood and mahogany fittings, and crystal chandeliers. Over the years, five presidents stayed there. The original hotel was demolished to give way to the smaller version. In 1989 the Hollenden House was demolished and replaced by a 32-story office building.

71 Gamble's wife Bonita and former Indians pitcher and TV broadcaster Jim "Mudcat" Grant were apparently regular performers in local clubs (and the players from both teams would often go support them). Grant was the first black pitcher to win 20 games in the American League (in 1965). He pitched for the Indians from 1958 to 1964.

There were a lot of Indians players there - and a lot of Rangers players...It was just like nothing happened."

In the next day's *Plain Dealer*, Indians beat writer Schneider concluded simply, "It was a bad day for baseball in Cleveland." Another newspaper noted with a tone of utter shock: "Even a woman had to be apprehended by the police, and she was wobbling, too."

Indians pitcher Milt Wilcox respected his elders, particularly ace Gaylord Perry.
Photo credit: Paul Tepley (CSU/The Cleveland Press)

Billy Martin pleads about something on the during Ten Cent Beer Night. Photo
credit: Paul Tepley (CSU/The Cleveland Press)

Unlike many of the previous years, Indians fans did show up in 1974 (including this game from July of '74). Photo credit: Paul Tepley (CSU/The Cleveland Press)

The batwielding Rangers cavalry help escort right fielder Jeff Burroughs off the field after all hell breaks loose. Photo credit: Paul Tepley (CSU/The Cleveland Press)

Bewildered and bloodied umpire Nestor Chylak leads his crew to safety after the riot. Photo credit: Paul Tepley (CSU/The Cleveland Press)

1973 Ohio wrestling champ Terry Yerkic poses in his singlet. Photo courtesy of Terry Yerkic

The Texas Rangers abandon their bullpen in the 7th inning. Photo credit: Paul Tepley (CSU/The Cleveland Press)

Police help Indians pitcher Tom Hilgendorf, who got hit in the head with a chair, off of the field. Hilgendorf pitched great the next night, though. Photo credit: Paul Tepley (CSU/The Cleveland Press)

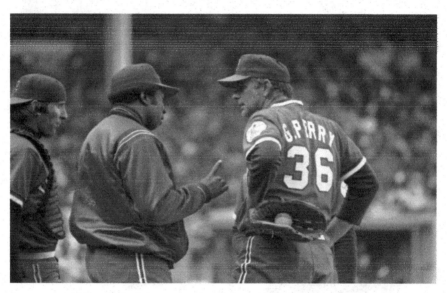

Manager Frank Robinson and pitcher Gaylord Perry try to figure things out together in '75. Photo credit: Paul Tepley (CSU/The Cleveland Press)

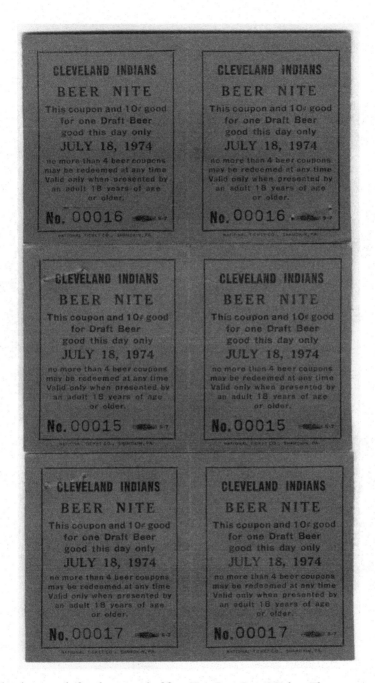

Red ticket panels for the second of four Ten Cent Beer Nights. The same type of tickets were used for the infamous night. Courtesy of Tom Bonda

A bloodied fan gets slowed down. Photo credit: Paul Tepley (CSU/The Cleveland Press)

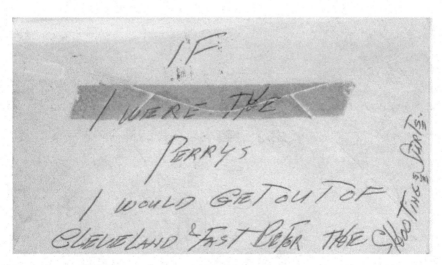

Just after TCBN, an anonymous angry fan from California wrote a semi-threatening note to Bonda. l

Fans frolic in right field in the 7th inning as Indians 1st base coach Larry Doby watches. Paul Tepley (CSU/The Cleveland Press)

The author and Cleveland superfan John Adams, who was at Ten Cent Beer Night but was not beating on his drum during the riot. Like many, he was simply a stunned observer.

Rare video footage shows Umpire Nestor Chylak trying to calm the crowd atop the dugout.

Rare video footage showing right field after all hell broke loose

Rare video footage of the dustup involving Hargrove and a fan. Cleveland Press photographer Paul Tepley is there (bottom left) to snap a pic

Rare video footage shows Mike Hargrove administering a beating to a fan.

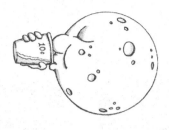

13

THE HANGOVER

"They were all drunk and they were drunk all over the place."

– Frank Ferrone, Municipal Stadium Head of Security

Just as it had the day before, the sun shone the sun shone gently on downtown Cleveland. But, after what had happened just hours before, the mood in Municipal Stadium felt oddly different. Indians employees, including Bonda, streamed into their offices near Gate A. Bonda called for a morning meeting. York, the Director of Promotions, walked on eggshells as she entered the stadium, fearing the worst and pretty much assuming that Bonda would fire her. Instead, Bonda was true to his character and belief in his marketing team - and the overall mission to save baseball in Cleveland. Instead, Bonda, true to his character and belief in his marketing team - and the overall mission to save baseball in Cleveland. He informed York and Fazio that he wanted them to go to Milwaukee. "They're having a beer night," he said. "Figure out how they do it!" [72] [73] The Brewers, however, had experienced their own trouble with Ten Cent Beer Night three years earlier. In just their second year of existence and struggling with attendance issues, the Brewers welcomed just over 27,000 fans for a mid-June ten cent beer promotion. What followed were numerous "weird contests" among fans, brawls, and massive consumption. One man ordered 130 beers, which his group downed by the sixth inning. The fights were typically against the police and brawlers were carried away then released without any charges. The Brewers had actually expected 40,000 that evening, but rain and cool weather had discouraged a larger crowd.

On June 5, 1974, *The Plain Dealer's* top-of-the-fold headline read, "Stadium Beer Night Fans Riot, Ending Indians' Rally in Forfeit." And a small article noted that American League President Lee MacPhail, reached by phone at his home in Scarsdale, New York, declared that the Indians would not be allowed to have any beer nights "for the foreseeable future." Bonda and Seghi wired an official protest to the American League Office in New York, asking MacPhail, who had assumed that role in January of 1974, to negate the forfeit and resume the game. It was perhaps a little bit like *Animal House's* Delta Tau Chi requesting that Dean Wormer and Faber College reinstate their charter. Seghi even admitted that the protest didn't have "a tinker's damn chance of holding up," but that he wanted to get his views on record. According to Seghi, John Stevens, a supervisor of American League umpires, was actually at the game. "John said that at no time did he feel the game had reached a point where it should have been called off,"

---

72 On June 6, two nights after Ten Cent Beer Night in Cleveland, the Houston Astros implemented a beer promotion but forgot to tell the park's vendors about it. In the fourth inning, on a full count, Lee May hammered a home run into the stands, prompting hundreds of fans to immediately get up and head for the beer stands. It was "Foamer Night" in the Astrodome, which meant that if an Astros player hit a home run and the time was at an even number, fans could go get a free beer. In May's case, the time was 8:42 p.m. The beer vendors were extremely confused and unprepared for masses of people coming after them and demanding free beer, but calmly dealt with the situation and no riot transpired.

73 The Brewers hosted their Ten Cent Beer Night on June 21st. Unconcerned about any trouble, Bud Selig said, "The Cleveland affair is not germane to the Milwaukee situation," adding that customers would be limited to two beers apiece.

said Seghi. Bonda and Seghi also blamed Chylak and his crew: "The umpires," Seghi wrote, "Should have made a more concerted effort to have policemen clear the field so the game could be resumed." Rather than call a forfeit, they said, Chylak and his crew should have suspended the game and should have made clear announcements that the crowd's behavior could lead to a forfeit. The Indians allegedly had 48 policemen - 16 more than usual - on duty.

Dick Butler, also an umpire supervisor, visited Cleveland a few days later to take stock of what had happened. He met with Seghi, who continued to assert that the game should have been suspended and that forfeit had been too extreme. But Butler said there wasn't any provision in the rules for what had transpired. "There are set rules for suspended games but none fit what happened in Cleveland the other night," Butler said.

And true to his don't-panic nature, Bonda was unwilling to cave into the massive criticism of the promotion and kept referring to what happened as "an incident," not "a riot."[74] Bonda blamed the umpires for letting the situation get out of control and made light of the many fans who ran across the field during the ball game. "It gives me an idea for a new promotion. If you don't mind that I inject a bit of levity." Bonda suggested that Indians could "...let anyone who wants to run across the outfield, before the game of course, and give a prize to the one who can do it the fastest."

Bonda added that he looked up the definition of a "riot." "And yes, more than 12 people were involved, you could call what happened a riot. But this was a public demonstration, that's all. It said a riot is any disturbance involving 12 or more people. I'd rather think of it as an incident," Bonda said. "We firmly feel that in the 9th inning, it should be kept in mind, that both the Cleveland Indians and the Texas Rangers ball club had gone back to the dugout unmolested. And that the umpire should have made a more concerted effort to have our policemen clear the field so that a game could be resumed. This is to lodge a formal protest for the game of June 4th with the Cleveland Indians playing the Texas Rangers in Cleveland, which was forfeited to the Texas Rangers. While we deplore the

---

74 Indians broadcaster Joe Tait said that Bonda wanted to fire him for referring to it as a riot but that Mileti intervened, interviewing Tait and others and concluding that "riot" was a pretty darn accurate term for what happened.

incidents that led to the forfeiture, we also feel that there was no warning given to the fans during the course of the game by the umpires that any continuation of interruption of play would lead to a forfeiture of the game."

At 2 p.m. that afternoon, Bonda and Seghi sat in front of dozens of reporters - a much larger than normal group for a Wednesday afternoon press conference in the midst of an early June series between two teams struggling to stay above .500. The lights were described as "hot" as Bonda and Seghi referred to "an incident…a happening" at the previous night's game and that they "deplored" what had happened. Bonda said that he walked through the stands in the 7th and 8th innings and didn't see anything too worrisome. Both confirmed that they had not stuck around to see the end-of-the-game chaos. Seghi, who had been weakened by surgery, had been in the habit of leaving games in the late innings. Also, the media later noted that Seghi's wife had been sick. Mileti was not at the game. Bonda added that his "gut reaction" was to put a microphone on Gaylord Perry to plead with the crowd to stop. But he didn't. "I wish now I had done it, but that's hindsight. I talked to someone and he talked me out of it." Bonda did not identify who the "someone" was.

"There are a host of circumstances," Bonda told the media, "And I might even add that there was a full moon last night."[75] Bonda also cautioned the media "not to give beer a bad name" and struck an optimistic tone about future promotions involving beer. "We can see we should have done a lot of things differently in hindsight," Bonda said. "We're investigating all aspects now, including the selling of beer to minors and people bringing beer and liquor into the games."

---

75 Whether the moon impacts human behavior or not has been a matter of debate for centuries. The Cleveland Clinic points out that the word "lunacy" dates back to the 15th century and that folklore, mythology, and religion are full of anecdotes suggesting that the moon's cycles can affect people. Many scientists say there is no connection. Yet, in 2018 a well-respected study published in the *The Journal of Translational Psychology* suggested that there was a link between bipolar disorders and lunar cycles. "In a small study of 17 people, researchers learned that their patients cycled rapidly between depression and mania and that these cycles weren't random, but instead in sync with the lunar cycle."

Additionally, Bonda resisted the notion of canceling future Ten Cent Beer Nights. Instead, he said he would, "Vote 'yes' for beer nights" - and added that he loved seeing the young fans. "I'm not going to turn them away."

According to the *Akron Beacon Journal*, Bonda and Seghi fielded questions for about 30 minutes and that the media were a tough crowd and didn't respond much to Bonda's attempts at humor. For example, Bonda joked about an additional promotional idea borne out of the previous evening: "We can have a contest, see who can jump the left field fence, run across right field, and make it over the right field fence the quickest. The fastest one will win a prize."

The *Beacon Journal* reporter - and others - didn't bite: "Bonda was going for levity, but all he got was silence,"

In private, Bonda was forlorn and described as having a sleepless night. "I deplore the whole thing. It was a very difficult experience for us as an organization," he told Bob Sudyk of *The Cleveland Press*. "Here we're trying to build fan interest and when we get it something like this happens. If it isn't one problem with the Indians, two more take its place."

Perhaps a letter addressed to Bonda didn't help, either. The anonymous correspondent had clipped out and sent an article titled, "Bonda: Beer Not to Blame" and wrote under it, "What kind of nut are you?" They also scrawled, "Decent people will not be found at beer games and driving is dangerous." Also, "Watch your step, Mr. Bonda."

Another anonymous critic wrote and sent correspondence dated June 6, 1974 from the Bay Area. In the spot where the return address would normally be, the individual wrote, "Do We Assume The Mafia Runs/Owns the Cleveland Indians? Looks like it." And on the other side, "IF I WERE THE PERRYS I WOULD GET OUT OF CLEVELAND FAST BEFORE THE SHOOTING STARTS." Yet, Bonda also said that he had received several letters encouraging the front office to "not give up." Inside were clippings of the riot from *The San Francisco Chronicle's Sporting Green*. On them, someone had written "TOTAL DISGRACE TO BASEBALL" and "Is it safe to go to a ball game?" and "HIPS (hippies?), DOPE OR LIQUOR POISON ENY (sic) SPORT" and "SHOULD FIRE WHO ORGANIZED THIS STUPID MESS."

Downtown, The Wahoo Club luncheon at The City Club had scheduled none other than Billy Martin as their featured speaker. Martin made the short trip from the Hollenden House to show up as planned. He bluntly told the gathering that he was "ashamed" of Cleveland's fans, but he retracted a comment in which he blamed the media, and laughed at the notion of Bonda and Seghi filing a protest, calling that "ridiculous." Martin again emphasized that the Rangers were extremely grateful for the help of the Indians and that the Rangers planned to honor them in some kind of "appreciation day" when Aspromonte and his team came back to Arlington.[76] He added that he was sickened and saddened by the fans cheering when a line drive drilled Fergie Jenkins.

"They should do what President Nixon didn't do," Martin said of Bonda and Seghi. "Just come out and admit they made some mistakes and they will do everything to prevent it from happening again." He added that he didn't know Bonda, but that he could tell that he was "not a baseball man." Martin added that Bonda should return to whatever he was doing before he got into baseball. "They're just trying to save face," Martin declared. He also scoffed at his own role in the riot.

According to *The Cleveland Press*, police arrested nine people the night before. Eight of the nine were adults and appeared at Cleveland Municipal Court the day after Ten Cent Beer Night to face Judge Edward F. Feighan. Four of them pleaded innocent and were given hearing dates for later in the summer. Four pleaded guilty and were fined $33.65 and ordered to serve three days in the Cleveland Workhouse.[77] The judge lectured the four. "You have made a laughingstock of Cleveland. And I'm not going to let you make a laughingstock of this court." Euclid's Terry Winston, 27, was one of those sentenced. He called

---

76 There is no record that the Rangers ever had any kind of "Indians Appreciation Day" (or Night). Perhaps they should on the 50th anniversary?

77 The Cleveland Workhouse at Cooley Farms was located in Warrensville Township. It provided an outlet for courts to "aid in the rehabilitation and/or recuperation of those city dwellers suffering from the evils of urban dwelling." Some of those sentenced there were required to care for the farms, gardens, and orchards. The grounds also hosted a blacksmith shop, piggery, cannery, and sawmill. Established at this location in 1912, the buildings and grounds were in pretty bad shape by 1974.

his arrest "ridiculous.""I went to the aid of some young kids who were being beaten by the Rangers right fielder. I was struck by one of the players," he told *The Cleveland Press*.Lakewood's Valerie Sullian, 27, initially pleaded not guilty then somehow changed her plea an hour later. "I'm just an enthusiastic fan. I walked onto the field and raised up my hands and they arrested me. One policeman accused me of hugging an umpire - and I wouldn't do that." The juvenile, according to the Cleveland Press, would appear in another court. The Indians reported that only two fans reported to the "...police room for first aid. One was a man who slipped on the concourse at 7:45 PM, and the other was the large lady who was escorted off the field earlier."

Overnight, like an oily sheen atop the Cuyahoga River, news of the Cleveland Indians' disastrous Ten Cent Beer Night spread across the nation's news services. On NBC's *The Tonight Show*, enormously famous host Johnny Carson swung and connected on a comedic fastball right over the middle of the plate (and was lucky to have a more receptive audience in front of him than poor Bonda had in front of the media). Perhaps, Carson joked, everyone rioted in Cleveland because the Indians had "forgotten to unlock the restrooms."

The Wall Street Journal lampooned the Indians in their "Pepper...and Salt" cartoon. A group of tourists stood near what appears to be the dilapidated Roman Colosseum as one man says, "They must have had fans here a lot like those Cleveland Indians' supporters." *The New York Daily News* also had some fun at the Indians' expense via a cartoon showing a moat between the stands and the playing field. In the stands a vendor is selling beer for 10¢ and a fan leaning over the railing, examining the moat and pondering, "Are piranhas in that water?"

Nationwide, the media weighed in – and unsurprisingly not too favorably for the Indians. Some of them ignored that their local teams had hosted or would host a Ten Cent Beer Night. What happened in Cleveland was also, many sports writers decided, a chance to examine larger societal trends. In Chicago, *Tribune* sports editor Cooper Rollow wrote a column called, "Murder Next In Mudville?" "It is deplorable, disgusting and degrading to all sports fans," he wrote, "It is also, to carry the alliteration farther, damned dangerous. Do not scoff at the word 'murderer,' sports reader, because that's where it could all end up. If the trend toward unabated, undisciplined and unpenalized fan demonstrations at athletic events is permitted, that is what we will eventually have indeed - murder at the ballpark."

Buffalo Evening News writer Steve Weller cheekily called upon the legend of Veeck and one the most famous baseball promotions of all time: "Ever since Bill Veeck hired Eddie Gaedel as a pinch-hitter for the St. Louis Browns, baseball's leaders have frowned on the employment of midgets. They ought to be just as concerned about mental giants." Weller went on to write that one of Bonda's better press conferences "pearls" involved his jokes about beer related contests. "Terrific. One of the prizes could be the chance to repeat the trip and take a swing at the left fielder while doing so. The next logical step would be a missile throwing contest for accuracy. Bonda could have several categories - full bottles of beer (for the big spenders), no deposit-no return (for the thrifty), eggs (small, medium, large, and instant fracture), vegetables (homegrown and supermarket divisions), and freestyle (golf balls, shot-puts, tire irons and old encyclopedias).

Bonda must have taken particular offense in Weller's column and wrote to him. Then Weller wrote back, lacing his letter with sarcasm and cutting remarks:

June 24, 1974

Mr. Ted Bonda

Cleveland Indians

Cleveland, Ohio

I am overwhelmed by this unexpected honor, receipt of your first-ever letter to a newspaper. I would be remiss if I did not thank all those who made it possible - the many writers, who, in the week or so between the forfeit and MacPhail's decision, got aghast in print about the crowd, the promotion, and the "Problem? What Problem?" reaction of Cleveland front office types.

Admittedly, few of us were there. But then, I understand you weren't either.

I could spend a little time arguing a number of points in your letter, but I rather doubt I could convince you I'm right and you are wrong. But I will stand on my contention that 200-300 fans on a field are 200-300 too many, that when bats are being swung by players and chairs by fans (or was Chylak joking about that?) then park security has completely broken down. Since I have yet to see an umpire agile enough to keep one or two teeny boppers in the stands at any time I guess I have to blame the home club. So, too, did everyone else but the home club. Thanks again for your letter, even though I detected an effort to savage me with calm reasonableness. Please call if you come to Buffalo. We can go dutch for a beer.

Sincerely,

Steve Weller

New York Daily News writer Dick Young blamed Indians management. "Hungry for customers, they decided to sell beer, not baseball. They lure people into the park by offering a beer giveaway, 10 cents a cup. So, crowds go there to tank up, not to watch baseball. What do the Lords of Baseball expect?" Joe O'Day, also from *The New York Daily News*, wrote that baseball had awoken the day after with a "monumental hangover...and like any morning after there was all sorts of recrimination with the parties involved pointing the finger at each other."

The Atlanta Constitution's Wayne Minshew weighed in as follows: "Beer Night. How utterly stupid. How insane. How disgusting. If that isn't asking for trouble, then Leo Durocher loved umpires. Hank Aaron never hit a home run. What the heck is going on? What has gotten into people that they not only have to fight each other, but climb barriers to take a poke at players and umpires as well? Are things that dull? I wonder how these animals, these idiots, these young punks who can't hold their liquids, find their way to the ball park?"

Yet many writers felt like a raucous event like Ten Cent Beer Night could easily go down in their cities. "What is alarming," wrote Sam Blair in *The Dallas Morning News*, "is that a lot of people must have felt the urge to do something wild when they walked into the stadium and you seriously have to ask if it's part of a trend...realistically no one should be surprised to see it happen again."

The *Pittsburgh Post-Gazette* editorial said that the "riot...was a disgrace." "Are we coming to a time when we'll have to construct moats around the playing field as is necessary in soccer stadiums in Latin America?" Sports management was to blame for trying anything to get fans into the stadium, but also, the *Post-Gazette* argued, a general trend toward violence in sports is extremely troublesome. "Sports management may be inviting misery in another way. Increasingly the emphasis is on violence, whether in football or in hockey. Putting the opposing quarterback in the hospital seems to be a standard strategy. Hang sportsmanship!"

Fan reaction was generally also one of shock and disappointment. "(T)he owners of all major league baseball teams had better wake up!" wrote Norman, Oklahoma's John Gage in a letter to the *Akron Beacon Journal*. "How can they expect a man to take his wife and children to a baseball game with hundreds of cursing drunks in the stands?" Akron's Terry Modory was a "stunned witness" to the game. "We Indians fans are still in shock, figuring that these types of incidents only happen elsewhere." He worried that the nation would begin to think the rowdyism would make people think that Municipal Stadium was "full of violence."

Mrs. David Case of Parma wrote in to *The Plain Dealer*, saying the riot had altered their lives: "He was assaulted and beaten while we were trying to leave the Stadium. His injuries are substantial. The beer sellers are not going to pay his medical bills. We are. They are not going to miss final exams. They did not have to watch helplessly while he was beaten and kicked by three very large drunks. We are, after all, only the victims. The victim, true to form, is unnoticed. The victim always pays."

Berea's John Spooner said that his young son had just recently shown an interest in sports but that he had concluded he couldn't take him to Cleveland sporting events, citing Ten Cent Beer Night and a Cleveland Crusaders (hockey) game where he saw boys his son's age spitting on the visiting Toronto Toros as they came out of the locker room. "Where do they get the idea this is appropriate behavior? Is it a sign of the times? Can we blame it on Watergate? Is it their parents' fault? In my mind there is no excuse for it in any case."

Brunswick's Diana Miner was outraged as she summed up her experience with a passionate letter to *The Plain Dealer* (with references that Chylak might have agreed with): "An open letter to the persons responsible: I am sick, angry, ashamed, and frightened. Had I wanted to see destruction of property, violence, and nudity, and hear vile, obscene language I would have attended an unrated film. Instead I went to the baseball game (formerly known as family entertainment) expecting to see an interesting and challenging contest between two fine ball clubs. Thanks to you this was not possible. You made it impossible for thousands of people who had spent good money to enjoy one of America's best-loved sports. You made it impossible for all the fine athletes in both clubs to do their jobs. You harassed, threatened, and caused danger to fellow human beings. Your actions were not human. They were barbaric and animalistic. The Indians stand a good chance of winning a pennant this year. This will never happen if the games are handed to other teams, courtesy of the so-called fans. Real fans don't want you. The Indians don't want you. You know who you are - so do us all a favor - STAY HOME!!!"

Stan Parulis, who lived on W. 86th, agreed with Chylak's assessment that many of the fans were "like animals rioting in a zoo." "Well, I never saw animals rioting in a zoo, but those beered up hooligans belonged in one. A people's zoo, that is, with the animals on the outside looking in and saying 'people is the craziest monkeys.' " Meanwhile, Robert Dell of Cleveland Heights referenced the Bible: "To 'sportsmen' who might offer some perverted mitigation or rationalization of such animal behavior might apply the teaching of the Book of Job: 'If I justify myself, my own mouth shall condemn me.' "

In *The Sporting News*, Bob Broenig asserted that the promotion was "unwise on at least two counts." "First, it was held with the Rangers as the opposition. Just a week previous, the Indians and the Rangers had engaged in a donnybrook on the Rangers' field. Cleveland officials would have been smart to reschedule beer night against a foe less likely to trigger an excuse for a fan uprising. Second, the Indians put no limit on the amount of beer each customer could buy. The Twins employ a more realistic approach to their beer night promotion, giving each adult two chips, each good for one five-cent beer. The Brewers follow a similar policy. If the Indians hold another beer bust, they'd better adopt such a restraint. Meanwhile, blaming the umps and the Rangers changes nothing."[78]

---

78 It makes no sense to say we should have scheduled it later - we scheduled it six months earlier," said Fazio. "No limit on the amount of beer - that's completely wrong. We did limit each customer to six beers, but this shows the careless nature of reporting that followed the game."

Deep in the heart of Texas, Bob Lindley of Fort Worth's *Star Telegram* used the riot to bash where it happened as well as a number of other northern cities - and the people that lived there. Lindley struck a condescending (edging toward racist?) tone: "Unless you've lived in sinkholes like Newark, N.J., New York City, Detroit, Chicago, or Cleveland, it might be difficult to understand the chemistry that transformed Tuesday night's baseball crowd into a howling, destructive mob."

To him, the riot symbolized a "sick society." Alcohol, inadequate security and Billy Martin fanning the flames were certainly all to blame, he argued, but what happened in Cleveland would not have happened in someplace, say, like Anaheim.

"People who live in the shadow of Disneyland bear no resemblance to the great unwashed horde of tenement dwellers who inhabit the jungles of our major cities," wrote Lindley. "When you're living in squalor and your future is bleak and the only mark you're likely to make in this world is with a crayon on the restroom wall, you've got frustrations. It's a problem beyond the realm of baseball commissioner Bowie Kuhn. He can legislate against beer dime night, but that's like fighting terminal cancer with aspirin."

The Fort Worth Press led its recap with hyperbole (Special to the Press)[79]: "A fatal mixture of cheap booze and Cleveland Indian fans has toppled cancer off the list of the most dangerous killers known to man. An ugly incident that may go a long way in changing the national pastime's image to an event more savage than South American soccer resulted in numerous injuries to players, fans and umpires last night at the Texas Rangers were handed a 9-0 forfeit. The event was Dime Beer night in Municipal Stadium. It is destined to take its place alongside such other festivities as The Boston Massacre and Bull Run."

In *The New York Times*, Dave Anderson wrote that, "Once the grass of a major league ballpark was a sacred preserve. But the cameras influenced teenagers to run on the field, hoping they'd be seen. Even though TV no longer shows the showoffs, the fad has persisted. And in Cleveland they ran in packs." Anderson goes on to note security problems throughout professional baseball but

---

79 *The Fort Worth Press* story did not have a byline but sounded like Shropshire's work.

a strange lack of willingness by owners to act upon the deficiency. "The owners keep talking about more security. But the extra security never materializes until *after* an incident. The primary problem is that ballpark security policemen don't do their job. Not because they don't want to, but because they are intimidated by the thought of being involved in a possible court case. It's easier for them to let people run wild or let them yell anything they want than it is to stop them. The atmosphere has to be changed. And banning 10¢ beer won't do it."

The Rangers, meanwhile, gave mixed messages about the future of beer nights at Arlington Stadium. Rangers promotional director Oscar Molomot[80] confidently claimed. "No ten cent beer night is scheduled for this year or was ever scheduled. It was decided last year that we wouldn't have a beer night, a hot pants night, or a panty hose night." But the *Dallas Morning News* reported that Rangers owner Brad Corbett was actually at Cleveland's Ten Cent Beer Night and that Corbett had said, "Only Sunday our executive committee had voted for us to have a dime beer night, but now we'll certainly have to review that decision. I know they haven't had any trouble at our place in the last two years but something like what happened tonight scares me."[81]

In truth, the Rangers had indeed hosted several Ten Cent Beer Nights in the past and, "according to rumors, action in the cheap seats had resembled an old Clint Eastwood spaghetti western by the seventh inning."

In a June 6 editorial *The Fort Worth Press* urged, "Next time, Billy, march team off." "We don't think the players should be exposed to a bunch of rowdies tanked-up on beer, trying to certify their manhood (or womanhood in the case of the one woman demonstrator) by drawing knives and running nude and throwing chairs." They acknowledged that the resulting forfeit was "bitter medicine" for the Indians and the City of Cleveland, but that it was the only recourse umpires had. "A cool cup or two of beer always has gone hand in hand

---

80 In a 1981 story for *D Magazine*, Shropshire wrote, "The person in charge of the Ranger public relations and promotions that season was Oscar Molomot, a hyperactive character who could walk under the coffee table in your living room without bending over. Oscar ignored the conventional avenues for effective public relations campaigns since he didn't know what they were."

81 *The Dallas Morning News* reported that Corbett was there, but Fazio doesn't think he was. "If he had been there, we'd have known about it," he said.

with baseball. But the Cleveland incident questions the wisdom of Ten Cent Beer Night promotion. Apparently 10-cent beer may attract 10-cent brains… Don't let it happen here."

The next day, Martin recapped the end of the ball game like the commander who had managed to lead his troops safely through a life-threatening situation, but also acknowledged the casualties. "Uh, I stayed away from it as much as possible. We seen guys out there with knives last night. Uh, people were carrying chairs on the field and hittin' our players with chairs. I got a pitching coach with one eye (Fowler) - they hit him in the good eye. And Brian Zembley[82] - he fell down the steps and almost broke his arm. I got one pitcher right now that's in the, uh, at the doctor's and we're worried about *his* eye. I had to pull my players out of the bullpen because guys were throwing firecrackers on a string…so they were right in their face over the dugout and they were poppin' 'em in their face. They were throwin' cartons with beer bottles in 'em, uh, filled with rocks and throwin' 'em at 'em. It was probably the worst thing I've ever seen in my whole life in baseball."

Fazio shakes his head in bewilderment. "This is completely Billy Martin exaggeration," said Fazio in 2024. "The only true thing is that they had firecrackers. Guys with knives - no, no, no. Mischievous Martin was prone to exaggeration." Immediately after, the Rangers continued to praise the Indians for coming to their rescue, though Martin still criticized Bonda. "Our club knew it was not the good fans who did that. We don't mind the fans who boo us on the road - but they should have booed the other fans. They had plenty of police out here tonight to have handled anything. It's too bad they didn't have more last night. That vice president that pops off should have thought of that."

Duncan said that the Indians were "down" after the events of Tuesday. "We just tried to forget about what happened the night before and play baseball. It was just an unfortunate happening, one that I hope never occurs again." Aspromonte said that by the end of the year there would probably be four or five brawls among teams. "But the other thing, we resent what happened and we're sorry about it. But it's a new day, the sun is shining, and you just play the ball game."

---

82 It's difficult to verify who Martin is talking about here.

Unruly fans surfaced at other Major League Baseball games in the Summer of '74. In *Sports Illustrated*, Ron Fimrite wrote that team owners and commissioners would be forced to take long soul-searching looks: "They must begin to wonder if it is even possible now, in an age of free expression and at a time when violent action and reaction are everyday facts of life, to assemble large numbers of people in one place, excite them, and expect them to behave themselves. The question seems wholly legitimate in light of some sorry recent occurrences."

In Cincinnati, Astros outfielder Bob Watson, pursued a fly ball, crashed into the Riverfront Stadium fence and lay stunned on the warning track. At first, a dozen fans peered curiously down on Watson, then promptly opted to rain beer, ice, and crushed paper cups down on him. In various cities - New York, L.A., San Francisco, and San Diego, fans threw ice, batteries, and food at superstar Pete Rose. In San Francisco, a fan threw an orange at Hank Aaron, plunking the home run champ on the head. In Boston, a fan threw a cherry bomb into a dugout, slightly injuring several players and coming very close to pitcher Ray Corbin's eye. Fearing for their safety, some ball players actually began to wear batting helmets while in the outfield.

Fimrite cited reprehensible fan behavior in other sports, including professional hockey, auto racing, and horse racing. But he wasn't under an illusion that sports were part of some austere, church-like atmosphere.

"Not that organized sport in this country has ever contributed significantly to public civility. The baseball fan at the beginning of the century—free of the possibly inhibiting influence of women spectators and close enough to the playing field in those tiny ball parks to take immediate action against erring players or umpires—was, by all accounts, an abysmal churl."

He added that as stadiums grew larger, players became less familiar and vulnerable. "From afar, they looked like heroes, and for at least 30 years or more there was a general trend toward spectator conformity. The ball diamond was a sanctuary not to be broken into by Philistines. Then, too, there was no television to tantalize the show-offs...But for the most part, ballplayers were regarded with respect, even awe, and if the fans were not always orderly, they were at least cheerful. That can scarcely be said of the mob in Cleveland."

Fimrite agreed that the bad behavior was a reflection of the anti-establishment times. He also notes increased alienation between player and fan. Whereas players used to be held in high regard as heroes, in 1974 there was a greater sense that when snubbed by players, the fans didn't take their "rebuffs lightly" and that when a star player like Dick Allen[83] said that baseball was just a job to him, the fan begins to question whether his own loyalty has not been misplaced."

The next day, *The Cleveland Press* took Indians management and the radio announcers to task:

> The first thing to be said about the riot at the stadium last night is that only good luck saved the situation from being more serious than it was.
>
> Indian pitcher Tom Hilgendorf and umpire Nester Chylack (sic) were injured - as were a couple of fans. But it could have been worse, much worse. As a hurt, bitter Chylak put it, some of the fans acted like animals. The ingredients were there for an explosion. Last week the Texas Rangers and the Indians mixed it up in Texas and fans there poured beer on some Tribesmen.
>
> Unfortunately some dimwitted radio broadcasters (Pete Franklin and Joe Tait[84]) have hyped up the situation by intimating during the week that trouble could be brewing with the Rangers coming to Cleveland on Ten-Cent Beer Night. The Indians management could have put a stop to leering insinuations that maybe the Rangers deserved some trouble.

---

83 Jim Sundberg, also a 1974 All Star, was amazed at the nonchalant nature of Allen, who was due to start at 1st base in the '74 All Star Game at Three River Stadium. Allen skipped the workout the day before the game, skipped the meetings, and showed up just a couple of minutes before 7 p.m. in a suit. AL Manager Dick Williams said something to Allen in front of all of the players - essentially this - didn't he know about the 7:30 p.m. start time? Allen replied with some sense of surprise: wow, he asked, he actually had over 30 minutes to get ready for the game? Allen singled in the game scoring Rod Carew but the American League lost 7-2. Also for the AL, Gaylord Perry struck out four batters but gave up a run and three hits over three innings.

84 Fazio said that the media didn't intentionally try to "create a tsunami."

With several incidents early in the game, the situation was at a flash-fire point when a couple of spectators rushed on the field in the ninth inning to try to grab the cap of a Ranger outfielder. Then all hell broke loose.

To their credit, the Indians closed ranks and tried to protect the Rangers. It was the fans, many beer-sotted, who were responsible for the disgusting melee, not the players.

The Indian management must share part of the blame. Although hindsight is better than foresight, the Indians could have called off the Ten-Cent Beer promotion in view of the feeling building up. Or American League President Lee MacPhail could have made that decision. He should have been aware of the possibilities for mayhem.

Finally, according to many reports, the security seemed inadequate. The Indians must beef up their police force and quit offering cheap beer from now on if they want to take a chance on coming to the stadium.

Because of the riot, the Indians forfeited a game they might have won. That's unfortunate, but more important is that scores of fans might have been injured seriously. It must not be allowed to happen again.

In another opinion *Press* piece, Bob August said that it was giving fans too much credit to link the brawl in Arlington the week before to the riot at Ten Cent Beer Night.

"I think it was inconsequential. To assume those people charged onto the field because of an intense partisan feeling, however misdirected, gives them even a small credit they don't deserve."

A few days after, resolute organist Art Broze wrote to *The Plain Dealer* with a slightly different take on it all, echoing the notion that Martin knew precisely what he was up to: "The kids who were running around the outfield and disrupting the baseball game Tuesday night at the Stadium were not beer-drinking lush heads. They were 12-and 13-year-old kids who decided to act kooky, just because a couple of them already had got away with it. The beer drinkers were in the stands enjoying the beer and the ball game. The Texas right fielder, Jeff Burroughs, was in no danger whatsoever in the ninth inning. The kids around him were the 12-and 13-year-olds, no adults were included. When the score became 5 to 5, that's when Billy Martin and his team came charging out of the dugout with bats in hand; and they were coming on as fast as they could. They began kicking and shoving the kids around (not that they didn't deserve it). I don't think any of the kids were hurt. No one was helping the kids. That's when the adults got into the act. The Texas Rangers had no authority at all to come out of their dugout and attack the young fans. In another minute those fans would have walked off by themselves."

Broze lionized the Indians and made some bold assessments: "If it weren't for the Cleveland baseball players, the Texas Rangers would never have gotten back to their dugout, which they should have left in the first place. The game should have been forfeited to the Cleveland Indians, because of the Texas team taking the law into its own hands. They promoted the riot. Billy Martin wanted to win that game by forfeit, and he also wanted to show up our fine police department. If the Texas Rangers get away with this scot-free, there is no justice. I think we all remember Billy Martin and his shenanigans from last year. He doesn't seem to care how he wins, as long as he wins, regardless of what he says on TV."

Broze then revealed what he had played during the riot: "Until the adults got in the act, the tune I was playing during the juvenile disruption was 'Kids' from the show 'Bye, Bye Birdie.' That piece didn't cause any hostility during the musical, and I don't think it caused any hostility at the Stadium. I could have tried the Star Spangled Banner after the adults came on the scene, but I didn't think of it at the time and for this I apologize." Some have said that during the riot Broze also played "Take Me Out to the Ball Game " and an advertising jingle for Stroh's.

Lebovitz acknowledged that the media had fanned the flames and wrote that he had intended to pen a column called "Please Postpone Beer Night," and regrets that he didn't. "Whether my words would have carried any weight is doubtful and that's why I didn't write it. On the other hand it might have made a difference. I didn't make the effort, so I'm guilty."

Harry Reasoner ended the national broadcast of the *ABC News* with a commentary called "Baseball Bums," somehow connecting the events in Cleveland with the famous civil rights demonstrations in Montgomery, Alabama.

In it, Reasoner highlighted how brutal and bestial it was for police to hit a small black woman on the head with a billyclub, yet suggested that authorities in Cleveland simply needed to assert themselves more:

> The late Grover Cleveland Hall was in the 1950s editor of the *Montgomery Advertiser*, a fine writer and a strong defender of segregation. In one of those years there was a downtown demonstration by some blacks trying to desegregate eating places and out of it came a famous picture published around the world of a riot-helmeted Montgomery policeman cracking a small black woman on the head with his billy club. Hall wrote a great editorial: "No one believes more than I in the South and our principles," he said. "But I never thought I would live to see the day when our Southern traditions would be defended on the streets of Montgomery by apes in uniform. Well, I don't suppose to feel as strongly about baseball as Mr. Hall felt about the South, but I never thought I'd live to see the day when the national pastime was corrupted by Cleveland apes in T-shirts. The riot on Tuesday night was sickening. It could, of course, have been tragic and it is only the worst of a whole lot of behavior that has been a sort of fad in ballparks in recent years: throw things at Pete Rose, shout obscenities, rip up the field after either great victory or defeat. There are a number of things to do about it and the ball clubs had better do them or this sport and others will eventually be played in locked parks, the stands empty except for the television cameras. The most obvious thing to do is to increase security forces and, once in a while, arrest somebody. A few jail terms or fines for assault or theft would make throwing bottles at Pete Rose or taking first base home for a souvenir a lot less attractive. Then, too, perhaps someone could explain to the Cleveland management about

beer. It's intoxicating, fellas, especially when you're having more than one. It's got to be done. The green fields of the summer game have to be kept safe from the apes.

And with that ABC Anchorman Howard K. Smith ended the broadcast: "Thank you, Harry. That's today's news. I'm Howard K. Smith. Goodnight."

Shropshire led his next day's missive like this: "A robustly overweight woman wearing an Ohio State Buckeyes sweatshirt shoved her way into the outskirts of the police vanguard mustered to return the Texas Rangers to their hotel. Someone said it was a former Miss Cleveland. 'Please - please tell all the Texas players that not all the Cleveland fans are that vicious. I'm going to write the team a letter and apologize, on the behalf of the people who were sickened by the whole scene.' "

As for the frat guys from Akron U? They loved it! At least Bill Ford did: he proudly said that he had poured one of his beers directly down on a cop's head. Ford also noted an escalation of onfield mischief throughout the game: "People were running all over the place, and after a while people just got sick of simply seeing people run around. So they started doing somersaults and streaking and two guys dropped their pants. It was the best thing I've ever seen. They have another beer night and I'll be there. We'll be at all of them."

Twenty four hours after Ten Cent Beer Night, the Indians and Rangers shuffled into the ballpark. The atmosphere was decidedly different. Players and coaches patiently conducted interviews about the previous evening's madness. As the Rangers took batting practice, Indians pitcher Ken Sanders joked with the Rangers players, "Hey guys, get ready. Tonight's Whiskey Night."

Part of that evening's gate receipts were dedicated to fundraising for American Cancer Society and the Indians hoped for a better-than-usual crowd for a weeknight. But just over 8,100 showed up. Chief concessionaire Al Frielander added up the totals and reported that 5,492 beers were sold at 60 cents apiece - a decided contrast to the 65,000 cups Frieldander estimated were drunk the previous evening. (And that's not even counting the bring-your-own-containers that were filled.)

The Indians beat the Rangers 9-3 as Johnson, buoyed by three-run homers by Gamble and Duncan, picked up the win. After the game the curly, wild-haired

Johnson was slightly sullen but accepting. "It was a smaller crowd, but I liked it better," Wolf Man said. "The crowd was kinda quiet." Aspromonte agreed. "You resent what happened but you just have to put up with it and carry on. I liked the crowd tonight, especially when they stood up and applauded when the guys hit the home runs. There are the fans we want to come out to the ball park and enjoy our success with us. The others I don't want to see again."

Amazingly, Hilgendorf, who very likely suffered a concussion from the previous night, came into the game to relieve Johnson and pitched wonderfully - hurling two innings of hitless, scoreless baseball. He struck out three Rangers. A reporter wondered, "Did the cerebral clout sharpen his control?" Hilgendorf smiled. "Could be," he said, "Honestly, this is the best I've felt this year."

Before the game, Keefer warned the crowd that anyone who came onto the field would be arrested and subject to a fine. The crowd cheered.

The Cleveland Press all but queued up the song about the difference a day makes:

> The Stadium First Aid room had two injuries. A man fell down and a girl was hit by a foul ball. There was only a three-mile-per-hour breeze, they didn't even boo Lenny Randle, manager Billy Martin was charmingly silent, nobody tried to kill the umpire and the players played the game of baseball as if it were made of Steuben Glass.[85] Even a parent spanked his youngster on disrespect and a guy in a crew cut and suit said hello to a young hippie. Why, it could have been played at St. John's Cathedral.

Regarding the forfeit, Lowenstein summed it up in his classic fashion: "We have won 25 games and lost 26 and the Cleveland fans are 1-0. They lead the league."

After the game, Aspromonte walked into his manager's office to find a bottle of high-quality Scotch on his desk, a gift from Alfred Manuel "Billy" Martin Jr., a token of gratitude for the night the Indians saved the Rangers.

---

85 Steuben Glass was a high-end art/crystal from Corning, New York (Steuben County).

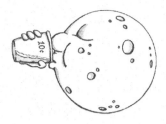

14

HAIR OF THE DOG

"There was no question that beer played a role in the riot."

— Lee MacPhail, American League President

The president rejected the Cleveland Indians' protest regarding the forfeit of the June 4th game against the Texas Rangers. Not Nixon, he was very busy defending himself regarding Watergate, the other president - Lee MacPhail, ruler of the American League. Seghi and Bonda even flew to New York to meet with MacPhail and tried to impress upon him that there was a 1939 precedent in which a forfeited game was overturned.[86]

The Indians did manage to put together a fantastic June, compiling a 16-9 record. They were just two games out of first place on July 1st and on an upward trajectory. On Sunday July 7, 1974, led by Jim Perry, they beat the Anaheim Angels 6-2. Ellis, Hendrick, and Gamble all homered. Aspro and his squad were 45-35 and, amazingly, in first place in the AL East, 1 ½ games ahead of the Boston Red Sox and two games ahead of the Baltimore Orioles. *The Plain Dealer's*

---

86 On September 3, 1939, thanks to a curfew rule and some unruly Red Sox fans, umpires called a game in favor of the Yankees. AL President William Harridge later overturned it and declared the game a tie and deemed it should be replayed, but it never was.

front page reported the happy news to northeast Ohio with a top-of-the-fold headline and story. Aspromonte gushed. "They're like a bunch of winners - which is what they are," he said. "The thing that pleases me so much is the attitude on the club. Everyone is chattering and talking to each other all the time." To get there, the Indians had won 12 of their last 14 games. The only problem was that they were headed next to Oakland for a severe test. Unfortunately, the series went as poorly as it could go as the A's swept the Indians in three straight. The Indians scurried off to Minnesota where they lost 2 out of 3 there then limped back to Cleveland. Still, they were just a game back in a division in which no one was playing that well. They were 46-40.

As of July 18, the team had lost five in a row and eight of their last nine and, unfortunately, the Oakland A's were now reciprocating, stopping for four games in Cleveland. The first game matched Gaylord Perry up with Catfish Hunter again. And, drum roll, that evening was also the second planned Ten Cent Beer Night. Understandably, there had been considerable debate about whether or not to proceed with any additional beer nights. Shortly after June 4, Bing Blossom, one of the 50 owners, urged Fazio and Bonda to *not* have any additional Ten Cent Beer Nights - because of the impact it could have on the team. Blossom had even checked the lunar cycles.

> June 7, 1974
>
> Carl Fazio, Jr.
>
> The Cleveland Indians
>
> Cleveland Stadium
>
> Cleveland, Ohio 44114
>
> Dear Carl:
>
> The moon will not be full on future dates planned as 10¢ beer nights, and I agree with virtually all Ted said about the first 10¢ beer night; i.e., beer got a bad rap, if the Rangers had not left the dugout, etc.
>
> And while I would hope to see many real fans at the stadium regardless of the league standings, I do feel the best publicity and fan attraction is the Indians as contenders for first place.

In this regard, the debates thus far have overlooked the impact of future beer nights on the performance of the team. Such performance would suffer at least during the few days prior to the next beer night, as attention would be drawn away from the game at hand, as memories and fears of forfeiture take hold.

I therefore am opposed to future beer nights; perhaps as an alternative we could show our appreciation to the Indians as good sportsmen and reduce ticket prices to a minimum on at least July 18. I would urge such an announcement be made as the Indians return to Cleveland on June 14.

My best regards,

C. Bingham Blossom

CC: Mr. Alva T. Bonda

MacPhail and the American League eventually relented and approved another discounted beer night. Bonda, Fazio, and York implemented some definite changes to their approach:

1) The team did not sell tickets to the first several rows of bleachers and near the bullpens, reasoning that these areas were especially prone to chaos.

2) Each ticket holder (apparently not in the bleachers or near the bullpens) were given two red tickets entitling them to two 10-cent beers. After that, beers were 65 cents apiece.

3) Staff searched bags at the gate and confiscated any incoming alcohol or containers - with the noble promise to politely return the contraband to the owners upon their exit.

The second largest home crowd of the season to that point - 41,848 fans - showed up. Everyone, including *The Plain Dealer*, deemed the promotion a success: "Sanity Reigns at Beer Night II" and (subheadline): "Fans sip in dignity as Tribe skids." "Beer Night II has come and gone and Cleveland baseball fans have shed the black eye they earned last month at Beer Night I."

After the game fans parked near the stadium walked outside to find a nifty present from the Cleveland Police, almost certainly a small retaliation for the disrespect and embarrassment that fans caused them on June 4: some 200-plus cars had been decorated with parking tickets.

On the field, Gaylord Perry pitched fairly well, but gave up nine hits and three runs. Hunter edged him yet again as the A's topped the Indians 3-2. The team had now lost six straight, yet somehow remained just two games out of first in the AL East. Aspromonte remained calm. "We've got to get back to being a cheering club, rah-rah baseball, pulling for each other, talking to one another," said Aspromonte, who conducted a team meeting to try to refocus the team.

It must have worked - at least with Dick Bosman. The next evening, Bosman pitched the game of his career, no-hitting the Oakland A's. Bosman threw just 79 pitches and very nearly pitched a perfect game - if not for a throwing error made by himself on a Sal Bando dribbler. Bosman's father George, who would typically go to one game a year, was in the audience. The 24,302 fans went nuts.

And so it went for the next several weeks - the Indians, almost impossibly, stayed in touch with first place in the AL East. On the morning of August 8, 1974, they were three games back. The date was significant for other reasons, though. Assuming that he would be impeached, President Richard Nixon addressed the nation and world, quoting from former President Theodore Roosevelt's 1910 speech, "Citizenship in a Republic." It sounded a little like Judge Smails's speech when christening the boat in *Caddyshack*.[87]

> Sometimes I have succeeded and sometimes I have failed, but
> always I have taken heart from what Theodore Roosevelt once
> said about the man in the arena, 'whose face is marred by dust
> and sweat and blood, who strives valiantly, who errs and comes
> up short again and again.' Because there is not effort without
> error and shortcoming, but who does actually strive to do the
> deed, who knows the great enthusiasms, the great devotions,
> who spends himself in a worthy cause, who at the best knows

---

87 It's easy to grin/ When your ship comes in / And you've the stock market beat./ But the man worthwhile,/ Is the man who can smile,/ When his shorts aren't too tight in the seat.

in the end the triumphs of high achievements and who at the worst, if he fails, at least fails while daring greatly.

And with that, Richard Nixon resigned. The 37th President of the United States was apparently discussing his embattled term, but is it possible that his words could have also applied to Ten Cent Beer Night? Had the Cleveland Indians dared greatly? Had they strove valiantly? Had men's faces been marred by dust and sweat and blood? Indeed.

Seventy-three days after uncontrollable beasts rampaged in Municipal Stadium and the City of Cleveland made unwanted national headlines, the Indians promotions department and the civic leaders mobilized again. The Rangers were coming back to town - for the first time since early June - and Bonda, Fazio, and the Greater Cleveland Growth Association decided the return of Martin and his crew would be a fantastic chance to celebrate the City of Cleveland and show the world how great the city and region were.

Organizers called it "Rally Around Cleveland," scheduled for August 16, 1974. All kinds of pomp and musical circumstance and general good vibes were piped into downtown Cleveland. The rally - a kind of wandering parade throughout Cleveland - began at noon as Trevor Guy's 8-piece Dixieland band accompanied vintage cars into the downtown. The procession stopped at Chester Commons where Gene Riddles and his orchestra serenaded them. From there they were off to Huron Mall where Judy Strauss and her jazz band waited. Then it was off to Public Square for Joe Bellini and his orchestra. Finally Chuck McKinney and his band waited at Hanna Mall where vendors presented food from around the world. Before the game, thousands gathered for the Party in the Park at Hanna Fountains where they once again listened to Trevor Guy and his band as well as Jimmy Lander's Rock Band. Manager Ken Aspromonte made a special appearance

The day and evening's motto featured the tag line, "The best things in life are here!"- which was also impressed upon keychains for the first several thousand fans that streamed into the ballpark. Ultimately 42,171 fans arrived, feeling very good about their city and Northeastern Ohio. Go-go dancers pranced atop the dugout and Evel Knievel performed a stunt.[88] The Rangers agreed with the whole affair - the best things in life were in Cleveland, specifically wins. They beat the Indians 7-3 and took two out of three from them that weekend.

For Fazio, though, it had been a valuable mini lesson. "I learned so much from Ted, most importantly how to make a positive out of a negative." Even Shropshire was excited about coming to Cleveland. In his preview of the series, he shed his critical tone and called the Indians and the Rangers "two of the American League's genuinely fun teams." He actually now relished the idea of returning to Cleveland. "Both teams can't help but be filled by fond memories of the Rangers' last visit to the mammoth ball yard in Cleveland. The exact date was June 4, 1974, a day that lives in infamy...Fans of all shapes and descriptions flooded the field carrying everything but torches and pitchforks in the acrid climax to the 10-cent beer night fiasco which stained the image of most beer drinkers all across this great land."

As August gave way to September, though, the Indians began to lose hope of winning the AL East. Aspromonte continued to project an image of positivity and fight and ignore criticism. On September 1st, the Indians were just 6 ½ games out of first but the month began with one more series in Arlington where the Rangers again took two out of three from them. On the season, the Rangers were 8-4 against Cleveland. The fans, though, were hard on Aspromonte.

Westlake's Mimi Houlehan was not happy: "Last Wednesday I went to *The Plain Dealer* Grandstand Manager's Game. I was thoroughly disgusted with the way the 'fans' were booing Ken Aspromonte and making dirty signs at him when he came out to make a pitching change. I couldn't believe some of the four-letter words I heard directed to him. I say give the man a break. I'd like

---

88 Knievel, who attempted to jump (on his motorcycle) the fountains Caesars Palace and a tank full of sharks, famously attempted to jump the Snake River Canyon not all that far from Fazio and Horsburgh's favorite town in Idaho: Twin Falls. On September 8, 1974 Knievel's "skycycle" malfunctioned upon take-off causing his parachute to deploy prematurely. Knievel floated down and landed in the canyon, dangerously close to the Snake River itself, where he said he would have drowned due to harness malfunctions. The entire event was broadcast live on ABC Sports.

to see some of these so-called smart-aleck 'fans' go out and take over Ken's job without a single mistake."

The team responded with a four-game win streak to put them just five back of the Orioles and a respectable 71-70 as of September 11th, 1974. Yet, despite being in contention for the majority of the season, the Indians did not offer Ken Aspromonte a contract extension. On September 12th, Seghi agreed to a trade that had been in the rumor mill for some time. The Indians swapped Ken Suarez, a player to be named later (Rusty Torres), and cash, for Frank Robinson. Robinson had been on the Indians' radar for some time - not just as an addition to the offense. The future Hall of Famer had just turned 38 and had been in the league since the age of 20. He could still hit - as his 30 homers and 97 RBI in 1973 - had shown. Robinson had openly discussed his desire to be a manager - and one in the era when players could continue to play and manage (can you imagine a player/manager in 2024?). Robinson had been on good terms with Angels GM Harry Dalton, who had traded for him in 1965 when he was with the Orioles. Robinson had bumped heads with Angels Manager Bobby Winkles, who was fired in June. But the Angels did not promote Robinson, who had managed the Puerto Rican squad and seemed destined to become a major league manager with the Angels. Instead, they traded him to Cleveland who, unlike the Angels, had definite plans to give him a chance.[89]

Robinson debuted as a player for the Indians on Friday, September 13th, going hitless in a loss to Baltimore. A couple of weeks later, Gaylord Perry and Robinson nearly came to blows in the clubhouse. On the afternoon of Friday, September 27th, with the Yankees in town for a three-game series and rain blanketing Cleveland, Perry and Robinson may have had too much time on their hands. As the players waited for Aspromonte to speak to them about what was

---

89 The Indians could have also honored World Series hero and coach Larry Doby as the first black manager, but didn't. In 1978, Veeck gave him the chance, hiring him to manage the White Sox and making him the 2nd black manager in Major League Baseball. Given the job in the middle of the season, it didn't go well. The White Sox were 37-50 under Doby. "I can't truly say what kind of manager I was or could've been because I didn't have enough time," Doby said. "I thought I could have been successful. I thought I had those intangibles." Doby never managed again.

essentially his termination, Perry and Robinson began arguing, motivated by comments that Perry had made publicly about Robinson's salary. The Indians had paid a $20,000 price for Robinson and were paying him $20,000 of the $173,000 Angels salary he came with (for the final three weeks of the season). Moving forward, though, Robinson stated that he wanted $180,000 and a no-cut contract in his contract. The amount of money the Indians were poised to pay Robinson rankled Perry. "I think I should get as much as Robinson, and a dollar more," he told a crowd in Akron. Robinson didn't care for the comments. "I simply told Gaylord," Robinson said, "That I didn't want my name used by anybody in the newspapers about how much money I make, or how much money somebody else makes." Perry reportedly countered that he would "use anybody's name I want in order to get the money I think I'm worth."

Despite the news that he would not manage the Indians again in '75 and the presence of the manager-to-be as a player in his clubhouse, Aspromonte stuck around to finish the season - a classy move that did not go unnoticed by many. When asked about the expected change in leadership, most players expressed regret about Aspromonte's departure, saying that Aspro had gotten a "raw deal". But they also thought that Robinson would be quite capable in leading the team and recognized the milestone.

"It doesn't matter if he's black or white," said pitcher Tom Buskey. "I don't particularly like the idea of him trying to be a designated hitter and manager because I think being a manager requires 100 percent concentration. But maybe he is capable of doing both." Pitcher Bruce Ellingsen said Robinson's biggest challenge would be in handling the team's pitchers, a comment that seemed to be reinforced as he and Perry tried to work out their differences. Maybe one of those pitchers was Hilgendorf, who didn't mince any words: "Robinson has got to be better than that man (gesturing toward Aspromonte's office) and I hope he uses pitchers better." African-American infielder Tommy McCraw focused on the milestone: "I think it's a helluva move for black people. This compares to Jackie Robinson and Larry Doby getting their chances to play in the big leagues. But it's also a good move for the Cleveland club. Nobody around her cares what color he is, and I have no doubt Frank will do a good job." Charlie Spikes postulated that it would be rough for Robinson because he was "breaking the black barrier." Alan Ashby said he had no comment because it wasn't his right to judge someone he didn't know personally. Wilcox added that he was happy but that it didn't matter to him as he didn't expect to be in Cleveland in '75. Peterson said he liked the idea of Robinson taking over. He added that at one point, thinking that Robinson would take over as manager of the Angels, he had even requested a trade to California to play for him. Lowenstein, as only he could, put his usual spin on the matter: "I'm happy they're finally going to name him. As a leader, he's more than qualified. If I think of anything more profound, I'll call you."

In the final home game of the year, the Yankees blasted the Indians by a touchdown and a field goal, 10-0. Former Indian Graig Nettles, who could have just as easily still been in Cleveland, hammered two home runs. Broze played "Auld Lang Syne" for the 8,746 fans, or whoever was left in the stands, and the Indians shut off Municipal's lights for another season. The 1974 Indians, who had been through a lusty brawl in Arlington and one of the most infamous nights in baseball history in Cleveland, finished the season 77-85, 14 games behind the division-winning Orioles. They had lost 10 of their last 14. It was a finish that really didn't do justice to the season, one in which they were "in it" for the majority of the campaign.

A few weeks later, over 100 reporters were present for a monumental official announcement: the Indians had named Robinson as their new manager. It made him the first black skipper in Major League Baseball history. Bonda and the Indians were extremely proud. Bonda's son Tom chuckles a little about his father's assessment of his baseball accomplishments. "He always said that the best four things he was known for in baseball were hiring the first black manager, firing the first black manager, having the ugliest uniforms in baseball, and 10 Cent Beer Night." Of the hiring, Bonda adds, "It was just the right thing to do. My father was very big into the Civil Rights movement. And he felt it was the right time."

When he took over in 1975, Robinson stressed physical fitness, which didn't go over well with Perry. "I'm nobody's slave," Perry said. In his first game at the helm he wrote himself in as designated hitter and hammered a home run off of Doc Medich. The Indians defeated the Yankees 5-3 in the opener in front of over 56,000 fans and many thought a new era in Cleveland had begun. But the Indians finished 79-80 in '75 and 81-70 in '76. They struggled out of the gate in '77 and Bonda and the Indians fired Robinson in the third week of June. Few would realize until later that the Indians actually fired Robinson on Juneteenth, the day that has become a celebration of African-American culture.

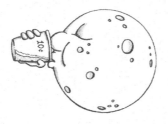

15

THE LEGACY

"Desperation is like stealing from the Mafia: you stand a good chance of attracting the wrong attention."

– Douglas Horton

On Thursday, August 22, 1974, a Lakewood High School social studies teacher named Jerry Rampelt clicked through Municipal Stadium's turnstiles when several men with walkie-talkies suddenly descended upon him. Rampelt's wife freaked out, thinking he was being apprehended by the police or FBI. But, it had only been team employees, stopping the one millionth fan to attend an Indians game in 1974. The Indians honored a relieved Rampelt by giving him a Honda X-100 motorcycle, compliments of Rick Case Honda. To balance things out, they also honored a woman, 16-year-old Patti Allen from Chardon, presenting her with a leather and fur coat from I.J. Fox. Everyone who entered received a "Thanks A Million" leather keychain. Fazio, Bonda, and the rest of the Indians staff had reached their lofty goal. In July, the team blew past the meager 1973 attendance total of just over 605,000 fans. By season's end, over the course of 81 home games, 1,114,262 fans clicked through Municipal Stadium's turnstiles, placing the Indians 7th out of 12 American League teams. It was a whopping improvement from 1973's total of just over 615,000. An exciting season on the field and the new efforts to attract and entertain fans - including four Ten Cent Beer Nights - had paid off. The Rangers also showed enormous improvement at the gate, welcoming 1,193,902 fans, ranking them 4th in the American League and nearly doubling their total from the previous year.

From a record-keeping standpoint the game of June 4, 1974 was recorded as a 9-0 forfeit win in favor of the Texas Rangers. Forfeits in baseball are extremely rare, but the reasons surrounding them certainly enrich the sport's history. In a 1978 article for the Society for American Baseball Research, Paul Doherty noted some of the many causes which contributed to forfeits: anger (at umpires), laziness (by players), absenteeism, boredom, and playfulness (by fans). Whether Ten Cent Beer Night could be categorized as playfulness is certainly debatable, but that's how Doherty defined it.

In 1903, Detroit and Cleveland were locked in an extra inning battle when Detroit put "an old black ball" into play. Umpire Tommy Connolly, a diminutive English immigrant who often umped alone in those days, didn't see anything wrong with the ball and allowed it. Cleveland star Napoleon Lajoie, who was so popular that the team had earlier in the season renamed themselves The Naps, vehemently disagreed with Connolly. Lajoie took the black ball and hurled it over the grandstand - a dramatic gesture that Sam McDowell or Indians pitcher Trevor Bauer[90] surely would have approved of. After that, Connolly promptly declared the game a forfeit in favor of Detroit.

In 1907 famed New York Giants manager John McGraw and the opposing Chicago Cubs manager Frank Chance were both unhappy with the performance of umpire Jimmy Johnstone and sought to ban him from the next day's game. When Johnstone arrived at the Polo Grounds, he was barred from entering the park. As a result, he declared the game a forfeit in favor of the Cubs. McGraw countered by suggesting that both teams appoint a player from each side to act as umpires. The Cubs refused to do this, at which point

---

90 Bauer was in the midst of a rough outing in Kansas City in late July of 2019. When it appeared that Manager Terry Francona was headed to the mound to replace Bauer, he turned toward the outfield and fired the ball over Kauffman Stadium's centerfield wall. The Indians traded Bauer a few days later.

both teams claimed the forfeit. Eventually, though, the game was recorded as a win for the Cubs.

"Rowdyism" is a thread that runs through baseball history and includes aggressive behavior toward umpires. The thump Chylak took on the head is like something that may have happened decades earlier. In 1921 Umpire Billy Evans, who would later serve as the Indians General Manager when they opened Municipal in 1931, got into a fist fight with Ty Cobb. Cobb, angry about being called out after he tried to steal second base, wanted to brawl at home plate but Evans invited him to meet under the stands later. They did and players from both teams formed a circle and the two went at it, reportedly bloodying one another and fighting to a draw.

Fifty years later, elements of Ten Cent Beer Night continue to resonate in the world of sports. On February 10, 2024, overserved fans at the PGA Tour's Waste Management Open careened out-of-control, urinating in public, running onto the course and through bunkers, The Phoenix Police Department arrested 54 fans during the course of the tournament and ejected 211 people. The next day, two streakers interrupted Super Bowl LVIII between the 49ers and Chiefs. And a few weeks later, the Wake Forest men's basketball team upset Duke at home, prompting excited Demon Deacon fans to flood the court, injuring a Duke player and leading to widespread calls for more security and a ban on "court storming."

Looking back, Ten Cent Beer Night was simply part of a continuum of promotions and ball park shenanigans that continues to 2024, a colorful timeline of official and unofficial ways to get fans excited and into the ballpark: from the kerosene-doused flaming brooms of the Portland Mavericks to the chaos of Disco Demolition Night at Comiskey in 1979, and right up to the showmanship of the Savannah Bananas. Today, every professional and not-so-professional sports team fills their home schedule with promotions and entertainment. Just a few years earlier, the Indians and many other teams, hosted Nickel Beer Nights. (Damn you, inflation.)

In *Places I Can't Return To*, comedian Sean Blair-Flannery writes about how he wished he had been at Ten Cent Beer Night. "It was one of those traditions - like smoking on airplanes or the way zoos used to have lions in cages that you could reach into - that no one had questioned yet. And just as we needed Ralph Nader to come along and show us that seatbelts in cars are a good idea, we needed the city of Cleveland to show us, yes, if you sell beer for ten cents, you will get a riot."

Again, there are those quick, dismissive, unfair summaries: "There have been some pretty bad promotions over the years — New Coke, the Kendall Jenner Pepsi ad, and the Hoover free flight promotion just to name a few. But in 1974, the city of Cleveland took it to the next level with Ten Cent Beer Night."

Fazio, who is still a die-hard Cleveland fan, is resolute.

"Our goal was to save baseball in Cleveland and everything has to be viewed through that lens. They were moving to Seattle or New Orleans. It was our last chance to get it right and thankfully all our hard work and planning paid off. Nick Mileti, Ted Bonda, The Blossom Brothers - those are the real heroes. We all should be proud of our role in helping to save baseball in Cleveland."

Horsburgh, Fazio's friend and fellow baseball dreamer, followed the wild events of June 4, 1974 from Texas. "When people criticize Carl and the Indians, they just don't know the facts. The exaggerations and the blanket criticisms are just wrong. The assumption that it was the dumbest promotion in the world is just wrong - it was just another night. Promotions just don't always go well. You could do that promotion ten times - and nine times out of ten it would go well."

And though Ten Cent Beer Night is an easy target for humor, it is also celebrated as a sort of '70s beer and baseball legend. Tell anyone anywhere that you are a Cleveland fan, and there is a decent chance that they may bring up the infamy of Ten Cent Beer Night when a group of drunken fans, akin to the "band of desperados under the hill" who helped settle the city nearly 174 years earlier, stormed the field. Luckily the desperadoes of June 4, 1974 didn't hurt anyone too badly. Fans walking to Progressive Field can stop and buy Ten Cent Beer Night shirts. And perhaps somewhere in a dusty Cleveland attic - or proudly displayed in a man cave? - is one of the three bases stolen that evening.

Daniel Epstein, who celebrates the 1970s in *Big Hair and Plastic Grass*, notes that "a combative energy was in the air. People were just on edge. And that was manifesting itself in a variety of ways." But, Epstein points out, Ten Cent Beer Night felt different than Disco Demolition Night, a failed and chaotic promotion by the White Sox in 1979. "I don't think I could go out and wear a Disco Demolition shirt - there were all kinds of cultural elements involved. I own a Ten Cent Beer Night and I feel completely comfortable wearing it. I can wear the shirt - my tribute to this iconic mess."

Paul Jackson wrote about Ten Cent Beer Night for ESPN in 2008 and likens the allure of it to Kirk Gibson's legendary 1988 World Series home run off of Dennis Eckersley. "It has an incredible cinematic quality to it. What I loved about Ten Cent Beer Night is that it is just as cinematic as something like Gibson's home run, but in the complete opposite direction. There's no glory, no pride, no tradition." Jackson said that the infamous night in Cleveland is also incredibly compelling because of the era and the details that led to the crescendo.

"This was not a particularly innovative promotion - these were happening all over the place. A lot of them didn't go awesome - but *this one* went so remarkably bad and I've been so fascinated by that. I don't necessarily feel like it was just about Cleveland (and its woes). There was so much anger that was coming in sporting events in this era compared to eras prior and since. There were just so many little moments that night - Burroughs falling down and because of the curve of the field the Rangers seeing that and charging out - to me, that's the butterfly's wings where you say, 'Oh, this day is going to go very differently.' The story hinges on some little moments like that."

Perhaps the late famed Indians drummer John Adams - may he rest in peace - summed it up best. Sitting in a Brecksville, Ohio restaurant with a corned beef sandwich in front of him, Adams thought carefully about why Ten Cent Beer Night continues to interest people. He leaned back, shook his head, and laughed, noting that it has achieved legendary status with Cleveland fans - similar to Len Barker's 1981 perfect game: seemingly hundreds of thousands of fans claim that they were there, that they were drinking cheap beer and stormed the field - at the infamous Ten Cent Beer Night.

But John Adams was there. He shakes his head a little.

"Ten Cent Beer Night? Well, it's just a story like any other. I don't even try to tell them the truth anymore."

Adams spreads out the hands that patiently and optimistically drummed for thousands-upon-thousands of Indians games, decade-after-decade.

"The story grows. And who cares? It's just a *great* baseball story."

ON THE HOUSE

(Appendix)

Ten Cent Beer Night Hall of Fame

Indians superfan **John Adams** passed away on January 30, 2023. Adams had started drumming for the Indians in late August of 1973. He was 21 and said he wanted to add to the tradition of seat banging - yet he mostly preferred to sit in the bleachers where there were no seats. Shortly after his debut, Bob Sudyk featured Adams in *The Cleveland Press*, applauding his fresh and much-needed enthusiasm, adding that Adams promised to return to drum, even though Adams had not exactly agreed to do that. But he did and over the next 5 decades became a fixture in the bleachers and a fan legend, nicknamed "Chief Boom Boom" by former Indians' pitcher and radio announcer Herb Score.

Adams did have one interaction with one of baseball's most famous managers.

One night after a game against the Yankees Adams recalled that he was leaving the stadium when he was suddenly stopped by Billy Martin. "I thought, 'Oh shit,' but then he said, 'Hey drummer, I really like what you're doing.' "

In a 2019 interview about Ten Cent Beer Night, Adams joked that "...of the 612,423 people that were at that game, all on the field, but me. I was the only one in the stands." The random number that Adams pulled out was actually very close to the Indians' total attendance in '73. Adams also quipped that, "If they'd ever drill there they'd have struck beer because more beer was spilled than drank."

Adams drummed for thousands of Indians games but never saw his beloved team win a World Series. When they do, he'll be banging his drum from heaven. Adams willed his famous bass drum to the Guardians, who named the bleachers of Progressive Field in his honor.

The Rangers never played a postseason game at **Arlington Stadium,** but beyond the May 29, 1974 Indians/Rangers brawl, it was the site of another significant fracas in its final season. On Wednesday, August 4, 1993, the Chicago White Sox squared off against the Rangers and arguably the most famous player in franchise history, the fireballing 46-year-old righthander, Nolan Ryan. Ryan was in the twilight of his incredible 27-year career when, in the third inning, he plunked 26-year-old Robin Ventura. Ventura considered just making his way to first base. He turned, though, dropped his bat, then ran toward Ryan. The Texan native, who had dealt with a steer or two in his life, immediately navigated the charging Ventura into a headlock and began punching him. Much like the brawl between the Indians and Rangers some 21 years earlier, all hell broke loose. When things finally settled down, the umpires ejected Ventura and allowed Ryan to continue. The career strikeout leader didn't give up another hit in the game and went on to earn the win, his 322nd career victory. He would go on to finish with 324 wins when he finally hung up his cleats.

The Rangers played their final game at Arlington Stadium on October 3, 1993. Hall of Famer George Brett recorded the final hit in the building, a ninth inning single. The stadium was demolished in 1994, although the foul poles, parts of the bleachers, and home plate were moved to the new Globe Life Stadium, built fairly close to Arlington Stadium. Globe Life served as the home of the Rangers from 1994 to 2019. In 2020, the Rangers began the season in the new Globe Life Stadium, a $1.3 billion facility with a retractable roof. Tucked away in the shiny and vast new stadium, amidst a myriad of places to eat, drink, and spend money, is a dark saloon adorned photos celebrating Texas Ranger brawls: from Ryan's taming of Ventura, to Rougned Odor's massive punch of Toronto's Jose Bautista, to images from Ten Cent Beer Night. Stop by and you can buy beers there that cost way more than a dime.

Randy Adamack worked in professional baseball for nearly 50 years. After his early days with the Cleveland Indians as an intern, assistant PR director, and ultimately PR director, Adamack headed west in 1978 to work for Kip Horsburgh and the Seattle Mariners. During the next 44 years he saw Lenny Randle blow a fair ball foul in the Kingdome (1981) and Gaylord Perry win his 300th (1982). Adamack helped the Mariners land the 2023 All Star game. As for Ten Cent Beer Night he says, "I've never seen anything like it before and I've never since." "25,134? (in attendance) That was probably one of our biggest crowds of the season. From that perspective I guess you could say it was a success."

Oddly enough, **Ken Aspromonte's** post-baseball career involved (insert John Adams drum roll)...beer. Aspromonte and brother Bob, who also played in the Major Leagues, were selected among 950 applicants to own and operate a Coors Distributorship in Houston. Aspromonte recognized the irony of him being involved in the beer industry in addition to being in the midst of Ten Cent Beer Night. "Baseball and beer go together - but not like that. Ours was controlled beer. When you give away beer for nothing, that's a problem. I wanted to forget the whole thing." As for retirement, he says, "I golf, I fly a plane. I'll keep at it until the Good Lord says, 'That's enough.' " He also still enjoys watching baseball, marveling at the athleticism of today's players. "This is the best crop of major leaguers ever. Stronger, more agile, more acrobatic. In ten years as a player I never saw an outfielder dive for a ball. Now you see it every night. It's a wonderful thing to watch." Aspromonte always praised the fans of Cleveland, despite their rough treatment of him. "The fans in Cleveland are tremendous. Hard-working...they spend every discretionary dollar to support the Indians or the Browns. Cleveland isn't like New York, Boston, Chicago or L.A. They have fans with plenty of money. As for Ten Cent Beer Night, Aspromonte said that he and Martin had always been good friends, but after that night they were "like brothers." He also remembers the unification of two teams that night: "We had 50 ballplayers fighting about a thousand hooligans and we were knocking them down like bowling pins." Aspromonte added that he and Martin often talked about having a temper, a tag that early in his playing career he was saddled with. "I don't know many Italian Americans who don't have a temper," Aspromonte laughed.

After leaving the world of professional baseball, **Ted Bonda** continued to thrive in business. When he finally retired, he printed up business cards that said "Favors Inc." and passed them out to people. He listed his title as "Chairman of the Bored." After he sold his interest in the Indians, Bonda did not put in the contract rights to any tickets. When he wanted to go to a game, though, he would simply reach out to John Adams and go to the game with him and sit in the bleachers. Bonda died in 2005 after complications from Alzheimer's. He was

88. "He was just the consummate gentleman to the end," a nursing director at his care facility said. John Adams said one of his favorite Ted Bonda moments came when Bonda landed at nearby Burke Lakefront Airport and came right over to Municipal in the midst of a miserably cold and not-so-well attended game. Bonda looked around at the hardy fans in the stands, including Adams, then went to the public address announcer to declare free coffee for everyone. Adams said Bonda got a big kick out of doing that and it was something he always wanted to do - buy drinks for the whole "house." Bonda's son Tom said his father wasn't a drinker and that he never saw him have a drink in his life. Bonda's legacy is reflected in the letters from AL President and former manager Frank Robinson (see Appendix).

Jack Brohamer played nearly 3 ½ seasons for the Indians at the start of his career then spent time with the White Sox and Red Sox, who traded him back to Cleveland in 1980 when he retired. Once, after he helped the Indians beat the hated Yankees with a walk-off walk, Cleveland Press writer Bob Sudyk queried, "What kind of pitch didn't you hit?" Brohamer smiled. "Fastball. Low and away."

Art Broze, was appreciated by the fans for many years, but may have been the only baseball organist fired in the middle of a game. Gabe Paul allegedly fired Broze during a game after Jim Bibby, who was then on the Indians, was pulled from a game and Broze played a song that Paul considered racially insensitive.

Jeff Burroughs struggled in the weeks that followed Ten Cent Beer Night, perhaps because of the jammed thumb sustained in the melee. He had entered that game hitting .332, but in his next 51 at bats he hit just .151. But he recovered and went on to win the American League MVP. He played for the Rangers through 1976 when he was traded to the Atlanta Braves for five players and $250,000. Burroughs played his final season as a member of the Toronto Blue Jays. 1974 was the best overall season in his 16 year career. In 1992 Burroughs coached his sons and a squad from Long Beach to the Little League World Series where they lost 3-2 in the championship to the Philippines, who were ultimately deemed to have violated the age and residency rules, leading to a Long Beach title.

Nestor Chylak received the Purple Heart and Silver Star for his service in World War II. He first umped a collegiate game, for which he was paid $25, then worked his way up from there. Chylak was considered one of the best umpires of his era, drawing praise from players, managers, and fans throughout - and after - his career concluded. Chylak had memorized the rule book and was known to let players and managers express themselves then would somehow get the game to move along. Yogi Berra called Chylak "an umpire's umpire." "He kept the game under control, but would also listen to you when you had a beef." Over a 25-year career Chylak umped 3,857 games, ejecting just 24 players and managers in that span. He also umped in five World Series (1957, 1960, 1967, 1971, and 1977).

He was perhaps the only umpire ever to get a standing ovation from the players (which he got after returning from an illness). Hargrove recalls giving Chylak a hard time about a call at first base. For the next three innings, Chylak stood behind him, chattering and giving Hargrove a hard time about his critique of him. "Finally, I said, 'Nestor, I got it!' "

Chylak retired, at least as an on-field umpire, in July of 1978, but took a position with the American League as an assistant supervisor for umpires. Fittingly, Chylak was present in 1979 when the White Sox's Disco Demolition Night, one of the other infamous promotions-gone-wrong, went awry. Chylak died suddenly of a heart attack just before his 60th birthday in 1982. In 1999, the Veterans Committee elected Chylak to the National Hall of Fame. His plaque there bears this quote: "This must be the only job in America that everybody knows how to do better than the guy who's doing it."

Following the embarrassing 1978 default, the **City of Cleveland** slowly worked its way back in terms of fiscal responsibility. In 1979, Mayor George Voinovich managed to put together a plan to repay the debt and by 1988 the city had reclaimed financial credibility. In 1986, though, the Cleveland United Way chapter organized a fundraising event known as Balloon Fest. The organization accepted donations ($1 for two balloons). Then, with the help of local kids, they inflated over 1.4 million balloons. The organization suspended a massive 250' x 150' woven mesh net about 150 feet up in the air in Public Square to corral the balloons. When they were finally released early in the afternoon of September 27th, some of the balloons caused traffic accidents and many landed in Lake Erie and ultimately floated over to Canada. The Coast Guard had been busy looking for two fishermen but were thwarted by the "asteroid field" of balloons in the lake. Their boat had been found but it wasn't until the next day that their bodies washed ashore. Cleveland was again the subject of ridicule. In the mid-'80s and into the early '90s, though, places like The Flats, Tower City, and ultimately the new home of the Indians, Jacobs Field, brought new life and respectability to downtown Cleveland.

David Clyde, the #1 overall draft pick of the 1973 draft, debuted with the Texas Rangers just a few weeks after graduating from high school. The Rangers selected the 18-year-old from Houston's Westchester High School ahead of future Hall of Famers Robin Yount and Dave Winfield. Clyde's high school numbers were off the charts. Rangers radio broadcast of Clyde's debut conveys the massive expectations and tremendous excitement. Radio announcer Bill Mercer's classic narration introduced the phenom on June 27, 1973 and reflects the whirlwind timeline and massive expectation that been heaped on Clyde (insert AM radio static):

> David Clyde, Westchester High School of Houston. He has not pitched competitively now since June 7. He defeated Galena Park five to nothing on a one-hitter, and pitched Westchester into the state finals, in which he did not appear. That victory - five to nothing over Galena Park - climaxed eighteen wins and no losses this season, his 14th shutout of the year. He was the number one choice of the Rangers and the top selection in the nation. He signed on June the Twelfth. He joined the club last Sunday June the Seventeenth. His scholastic baseball achievements are on the miraculous. As a senior he finished with a zero point one eight Earned Run Average. Three earned runs in one hundred and forty-eight and one third innings. Among his fourteen shutouts he had five no-hitters. In five playoff games Clyde permitted two hits - both singles. He struck out three hundred and twenty eight. An average of 2.2 per inning. High school games are seven innings. Had he been pitching nine inning games he would have averaged 20 strike-outs per game. He finished with fifty-five and a third consec-utive scoreless innings. In Clyde's four year scholastic career he fanned eight hundred and forty three in four hundred and

seventy three and a third innings. He had a zero point six five Earned Run Average. He had nine no-hitters and two perfect games. Clyde won his last twenty nine successive starts, and he had twenty-four shutouts the past two years.

Dick (Risenhoover - Mercer's radio broadcast partner) and I will both attest to the fact that he is a very mature young man at eighteen. I have a boy, twenty one, another nineteen. David certainly has all the presence and all the assurance of a young man who has already spent a deal of a so-called professional life. He has adapted very quickly to the professional ranks. He has a good sense of humor. He goes along with the players who have kidded him quite a bit on occasion quite a bit over some incidents. He has been a very fine gentleman. He is just about as perfect a person to have in this situation as you could have. We are very proud to have met him and to be here on this occasion tonight.

And with that the Rangers rushed Clyde to the mound. His first Major League start - just 20 days after a Texas high school state championship game - brought 35,698 excited fans to Arlington Stadium. It was, *in short*, precisely what the Rangers owner had dreamed of. The Rangers were en route to a 57-105 season that year, but Short saw dollar signs when he signed Clyde. The parking lots and highways were so packed that the Rangers delayed the game by 45 minutes. When Clyde finally took to the rubber against the Minnesota Twins, he walked the first two batters (including Rod Carew) then promptly struck out the side.

The general consensus is that Clyde was rushed to the big leagues too quickly by a cash-strapped franchise. Clyde delivered precisely what the Rangers had hoped for - in his first three Arlington starts for the Rangers he drew over 100,000 fans, going a long way toward paying his $65,000 signing bonus.

But Clyde struggled in ensuing starts and finished the season 4-8 with a 5.01 ERA. Perhaps more importantly he threw 93 ⅓ innings - an awful lot of pitches after also having played throughout the spring in high school.

When the ensuing owner, Brad Corbett, hired Martin to lead the Rangers in '74 and the irascible manager and pitching coach Art Fowler were unimpressed with Clyde. At one point they didn't pitch him for 30 days. "He wanted to send me down," Clyde recalled of Martin. "The front office wouldn't let him. In my opinion Billy wanted to prove I couldn't pitch in the big leagues," Clyde recalled. "I'd get to pitch about once every two weeks." Clyde finished the season 3-9 with a 4.38 ERA and continued to spiral downward, landing in the minors and eventually undergoing surgery for a pinched nerve in 1976.

In late February of 1978 the Rangers traded Clyde and Willie Horton to the Indians for John Lowenstein and pitcher Tom Buskey. The Indians were more interested in Horton but were certainly intrigued and hopeful regarding the once-promising Clyde. Tribe manager Jeff Torborg and pitching coach Harvey Haddix proceeded slowly with him. "If he still has the type of arm he had when he was a kid," said Torborg, who had faced Clyde when he was a player with the Angels, "He could make it back. Lefthanders are a commodity that's very scarce."

Early in the '78 season, Clyde pitched in relief then finally made his Indians debut as a starter on May 16, 1978 against the AL West leading Oakland A's (22-10). Clyde struck out seven over six innings as the Indians won 3-2 and the press went wild. "Comeback Kid Stymies A's," blazed the Plain Dealer headline. Five days later he did it again - another six innings and a 3-2 win over the Orioles. And six days from that, on May 27, Clyde threw a complete game, notching another win against the Orioles. "I ordered a new arm three years ago and it finally arrived," he joked. He had a 1.36 ERA over 33 innings.

But Clyde's strong start to the season evened out as it went on but pitching for the Indians in 1978 was clearly his best year in the big leagues. In late September he pitched another complete game, giving up just one run to the New York Yankees, who, led by Reggie Jackson and former Indian Chris Chambliss would ultimately go on to win the World Series. He finished the season 8-11 with a 4.28 ERA.

"I was just thankful to be in the big leagues again," said Clyde in 2020.

As for Municipal Stadium, Clyde recalls that "it wasn't a bad ballpark to pitch in." Overall, though, he considered the playing field to be awful.

"The playing surface was always soft. When we got back from spring training it had just thawed enough for them to sod. Guys wore plastic baggies inside of their socks to keep their feet dry. Otherwise you might be ankle deep in mud."

Clyde said he rented a house in Rocky River then built a home in suburban Cleveland, but never lived in it. On being rushed to the major leagues, Clyde later said, "It was like taking a kid and throwing him into brain surgery without going to medical school."

Clyde struggled in '79 and in January of 1980 the Indians traded him back to the Texas Rangers who released him later that spring. He signed with the Astros but ultimately walked away, 27 days short of an MLB pension.

1974 Rangers owner **Brad Corbett** sold his majority stake in the Rangers in 1980. His tenure was adventurous, often getting very involved in making trades and player personnel decisions. Corbett famously made a trade with the Indians GM Gabe Paul while standing at a urinal. "We'd been at the Old Swiss House restaurant in Fort Worth," recalled Corbett. "Haggling over the trade for hours. It was after midnight, the place was fixin' to close and we still hadn't finalized anything. Before we left, both of us had to take a leak. While we were in the john, we decided, 'Oh hell, let's make a deal' and we shook on it.'" In 1977, Corbett was so frustrated after a July 4th loss and told the press, "I'm selling this team because it's killing me! They are dogs on the field, and they are dogs off the field."

Dan Coughlin wrote for The Plain Dealer from 1964 to 1982 then switched over to TV sports. "Baseball was really a great beat to cover. You could go for a long time without having to pay for a meal. They'd have a pregame meal, a nice meal. Then they'd have a snack and beer during the game. We called it the Wigwam. Most ballparks after you wrote your stories you could stop and have one more on them." As for Municipal, Coughlin and others miss it. "One of my kids said to me long after the stadium was torn down, 'I really miss the stadium' - because we owned it. And they did. They knew every nook and cranny in it. And a lot of old timers say they miss it. It wasn't perfect for football or baseball but it was our place and we knew it."

The **Cuyahoga River** continues to proudly course through the heart of the Cuyahoga Valley National Park, a 32,000-plus acre creation north of Akron and south of Cleveland. It is the only national park in Ohio. Combined with nearby amazing metroparks, the park forms an "Emerald Necklace" that nestles up to Cleveland.

In early June of 1976, **Carl Fazio** and the Indians celebrated Bill Veeck and the glory days - particularly '48 and '49 when the Indians drew a stunning total of 4,850,000 fans. They honored Veeck on Ten Cent Beer Night. "Nickel beer now costs 20 cents," Fazio told *The Plain Dealer.*

The cherry red uniforms that Fazio and Horsburgh used in Twin Falls and again in Elmira, also appeared in the Major Leagues, in a way. "I showed Ted Bonda the look and he loved it. We started to wear several different combinations. Red and white. Navy blue and white bottom." The red, white, and blue are still part of the Guardians color scheme today.

Fazio left the Indians in 1978 to join the family business. Ten Cent Beer Night and all of the promotional efforts, he said, were all part of an effort to save baseball in Cleveland and he is proud of his role in it. He thinks the Indians made the right move hiring Frank Robinson at the end of the 1974 season. "Frank Robinson made us relevant both locally and nationally and got us back. He understood the gravity of the situation (being hired). He was a fierce competitor who wanted to win."

In a 2024 reflection, Fazio summed up Ten Cent Beer Night:

> Let's be clear, we were on a quest to save baseball in Cleveland, and after the last 14 seasons of mediocrity and mismanagement (1960-1973), we knew deep down that this might be our last chance. New ownership, now headed by Nick Mileti and Ted Bonda, embarked on a comprehensive, focused plan to sell tickets and attract fans back to the ballpark. We scheduled many promotions and special events. Ten Cent Beer Night was one of them. We modeled it after what other teams did, but surely we could have executed ours better. Given the previous week's fight with the Rangers and the ensuing buildup of hostilities in anticipation of their visit to Cleveland, we could have anticipated problems - but it's difficult to anticipate that which you can't imagine happening. This crowd was looking for trouble. Concession stand personnel were

overwhelmed and intimidated by rowdy fans. Security personnel in those days were nothing like we are used to today. By contract, half of the ushers, who were middle aged to older men, and some of the police, would leave after the 5th inning of a game. And communications were a challenge as only one Indians' employee had a walkie talkie. Of course, there were no cell phones. This was normal in those days - 50 years ago. Security, umpires, teams - we were just trying to get through the game, but finally things got out of control in the last two innings, as the Indians came from behind to tie the game in the 9th inning. In the end, it was the players who restored order. Additional police - mounted police - finally arrived. The lights were turned down and exhausted fans finally cleared the field.

After 20 years in Cleveland, **Pete Franklin** left WWWE in 1987 for a $600,000 job at New York's WFAN. He struggled mightily, though, to pull in listeners. There was some speculation that Franklin would return to Cleveland, which he would often say was his home. If he did, Bob Dolgan wrote, he would be a hypocrite. "He bashed Cleveland and its sports teams when he went to New York. When he was here, he said he hated the New York Yankees. In New York, however, he said (sic) rooted for all New York sports teams." Franklin did return to Cleveland, though, for a couple of brief stints. He died in 2004 at the age of 76.

After retiring as a player, **Tom Grieve** served as the General Manager of the Rangers from 1984 to 1994 then as a Rangers TV broadcaster from 1995 to 2022. He is unsurprised that people continue to revisit the Ten Cent Beer Night. He also notes that players today don't have quite as much fun as they did back then. "You look back on wacky things that have happened in baseball and that era has had a bunch of them. There were just more characters back then. Players today are bigger and stronger and can hit it farther but as far as interesting characters that era had it. As for the horror of the night, Grieve says that "I always felt in the middle of that looking around most of the people were just drunk and happy and laughing and looking around," yet acknowledges that things might have been very different if the Indians players hadn't helped. That's right, the Indians saved the Rangers.

In September of 1974, a woman in Baltimore accused **Oscar Gamble** of rape. He denied the charges and called it a "frame up." The charges were later dropped at the request of the accuser. Gamble also reported - also in September of '74 - that his car had been stolen in Cleveland.

While playing later for Martin and the Yankees, Gamble was a bit surprised to walk into the clubhouse and see that his locker was missing a uniform. Martin told him that Owner George Steinbrenner said that when Gamble got a haircut he would then get a uniform. But Gamble had a commercial lined up with Afro Sheen. Gamble cut his hair, adhering to Steinbrenner's hair and facial hair policy, and Steinbrenner gave him $5,000 to compensate for the lost endorsement.

Gamble played for the Yankees, White Sox, Padres, and Rangers. Trying to explain the craziness of the New York clubhouse, Gamble once famously said, "They don't think it be like it is, but it do."

Gamble died in 2018 after a battle with a rare tumor of the jaw.

Laugh In writer and Cleveland native **Jack Hanrahan** also came up with the show's popular "Flying Fickle Finger of Fate" award, presented by hosts Rowan and Martin to, well, "jerks" (or the craziest news item of the week). Winners included the Pentagon, the drug industry, and, of course, The City of Cleveland. He won an Emmy in 1970 for his *Laugh In* efforts. A graduate of Cathedral Latin High School, he got his first writing job with the *Cleveland Shopping News*. He always liked writing about Cleveland. "And it's so much easier writing from the truth. The humor flows. You don't even have to make jokes up. It flows. It flows like water through the sewers of Cleveland." Ironically, Cleveland played a role in a show that Hanrahan contributed to getting yanked off the air. In 1969 Laugh In producer George Schlatter had created an unusual, forward-thinking, and edgy show called *Turn On*.[91] Hanrahan had written for the show. One episode included a sketch where a woman was aggressively and unsuccessfully trying to get "the pill" from a vending machine. A producer at WEWS in Cleveland

---

91 For a wild glimpse of '70s TV, check out an episode of *Turn On* via YouTube: Turn On, Episode #1

saw the first episode and allegedly also did not want the show to replace *Peyton Place*. He stopped the episode midway through and filled the final 15 minutes of airtime with an organ player. He called California and the show was canceled before it even reached the West Coast, certainly putting a damper on the watch party of Hanrahan, Schlatter, Conway, and others.

Needless to say, Hanrahan did not care for Cleveland's "conservatism." " 'Best location in the nation,' " he grumbles sarcastically. "Sometimes I wonder for what?" After *Laugh In* Hanrahan wrote for a variety of TV shows, including cartoon series like Dennis *The Menace*, *The Yogi Bear Show*, and *Dinky Dog*. In 2004 Hanrahan lost his wife and was overwhelmed with grief. Hanrahan spiraled downward. After a garage fire, he was evicted and his landlord seized all of his possessions, including his Emmy. Some friends pooled money together and bought him a bus ticket to Cleveland where he was homeless until his death in April of 2008.

Mike Hargrove played for the Rangers from 1974 through 1978 when, in October, the Rangers traded him to the San Diego Padres. Hargrove opened the 1979 season with San Diego but in June the Padres traded him to the Indians for Paul Dade. He was an enormously popular and sweet swingin' player in Cleveland, holding down the first base position from 1979-1985, when he became known affectionately as "The Human Rain Delay." Players, fans, announcers, and members of the media chuckled as just before at bat or in between pitches Hargrove conducted a symphony of nervous movements with one foot out of the batter's box and time granted by the home plate umpire. A YouTube compilation celebrates it all: "...bangs the barrel of the bat against his left shoe, reaches behind him to the left hip pocket, readjusts the glove, readjusts the donut he wears on his left thumb, flexes the shoulder, touches the helmet, readjusts the glove again, goes to the nose, again a readjustment to the glove, again a readjustment to the glove, a readjustment to the donut, a readjustment of the glove, bangs the barrel of the bat against the shoes...and now Hargrove is ready."

Needless to say, Hargrove's style probably would not have meshed well with new rules, implemented in 2023, which discourage batters and pitchers from slowing down the game. In 1991, just six years after he retired as a player,

Hargrove took over as Indians manager. He said he was always amazed at Billy Martin's managerial skills. "Billy, tactically, was the best manager I ever saw. One time we were in Oakland playing the A's and there was a man on third and we had a hitter at the plate. Twice they thought we were going to squeeze, but we didn't. Then, on the third (opportunity), Billy said, 'OK, now we squeeze.' He squeezed and we won the game. I would just sit there and marvel that he could get ahead of the other manager. He did that real often during the season. I played for 11 managers, but I learned a lot from Billy and talking to Billy. I thought he was so interesting and so intense. He used to say he would give the players the first five innings to play the game. But from the sixth inning on it was his game."

Hargrove navigated the franchise through some very tough years - the end of playing days at Municipal Stadium and a horrific spring training boating accident that killed two Indians pitchers and severely injured a third.

Hargrove led the Indians to a 100-44 season in 1995 and a World Series appearance against the Atlanta Braves (they lost the series 4-2). His 1997 Indians also won the American League pennant, but lost in 11 innings of the 7th game of the World Series to the Florida Marlins.

Hargrove's 721 career wins, notched from 1991 to 1999, placed him just seven games shy of tying Lou Boudreau's mark from 1942 to 1950 as the winningest manager in franchise history. (As of 2024, recently retired manager Terry Francona sits atop the list at 921 wins, placing Hargrove as the 3rd all-time winningest manager in team history).

After Ten Cent Beer Night, Hargrove learned that his wife Sharon and Hargrove's father-in-law listened to the game - and were horrified by what they were hearing - by driving around the countryside near Perryton, Texas. It was the only way they could pick up the radio signal. Hargrove and wife Sharon split time between Arizona and the Cleveland area, where he continues to help the Guardians as a special advisor.

Kip Horsburgh, while with the Rangers, organized an old timer's game that included Mickey Mantle, Stan Musial, Casey Stengel, and Joe DiMaggio (among others). "It was just about perfect. They'd never been treated like this, even at Yankee Stadium. Bobby Brown (Rangers president and former Yankee pitcher) wanted the best for these guys and for a month he didn't care about anything else." The highlight of the affair, Horsburgh recalled, is when DiMaggio called him over in the locker room. "Kid, you have anything to do with this?" DiMaggio asked Horsburgh. "Yes," Horsburgh said. "Best I've ever been to," DiMaggio concluded.

Horsburgh went to Seattle to help start the expansion franchise Seattle Mariners and, after a management shakeup, served as the President of the Seattle Mariners in 1978.

And of his early career baseball days with Fazio?

"Carl and I had lots of great experiences. I don't think I'd trade it for the world." He and Fazio remain great friends.

Indians PA announcer **Bob "Sarge" Keefer** wrote a column called "As Seen and Heard by Bob Keefer" in *The Plain Dealer* in which he let readers in on what he was privy to from his third base field box. In the July 8, 1973 version, "The Lowdown on Visiting Dugouts," Keefer said that "Some of the things you hear, burn your ears, especially when the Detroit Tigers and Baltimore Orioles are in town and things aren't going their way." In particular Keefer was referring to managers Billy Martin, then with the Tigers, and Earl Weaver, the skipper of the Orioles. "Martin, especially, maintains a belligerent attitude. He constantly harasses the umpires, and when a decision goes against his team; goes into a tirade (sic)." Keefer only worked for the Indians on a part-time basis. His day job was "supervisor of employee activities," which he termed "all the fun stuff," at General Electric's Lamp Division in Cleveland's Nela Park ("the first industrial park in the world"). Keefer, like Chylak, served in the Battle of the Bulge. He once tried to class up Municipal by requesting that Indians fans, who were hanging their jackets over the front-row railings, take them down. Keefer announced, "Will the fans in the front row box seats please remove their clothing?"

Keefer announced for the Indians from 1963 to 1965 and again from 1972 to 1975 and said that during one game Martin asked him to stop rooting for the Indians. The Indians had rallied to defeat the Tigers when Martin started swearing at Keefer. "You're supposed to be impartial!" Martin demanded. "I yelled back at him, 'I'm not impartial - I want the Indians to win!' " Martin was ready to throw down with the announcer. Keefer also announced for the Cavs from 1972 to 1978. After he moved to Wilmington, North Carolina in 1991, he became the public address announcer for the University of North Carolina baseball games.

After the Indians released **Mike Kekich** on March 28, 1974, guess who picked Kekich up? Why, the Texas Rangers, of course. He didn't pitch for the Rangers until '75, though.[92] After it appeared he was done in the major leagues, the Mexico City Reds, a franchise which one might think is right out of the opening of the hit film *Major League,* wanted to sign Kekich. But the gritty travel arrangements seemed to discourage him. "I've heard the Mexican League is a bus league," he told Russell Schneider. "The shortest trip is 9 hours, the longest 36. That's not very appealing." But after he labored in the Texas farm system for nearly two years Kekich did pitch in the Mexican League in Nuevo Laredo and Ciudad Juarez. He also pitched in the Dominican Republic and had a couple of stints in the Pacific Coast League (AAA). He also, however, did return to the major leagues and pitched briefly for the Mariners in 1977.

John Lowenstein stole 36 bases for the Indians in 1974. He played 16 seasons for the Indians, Rangers, and Orioles. Lowenstein generally loved to make light of everything, perhaps because he spent a decent portion of his career with the Indians - what else could one do, at times, but flout convention? In 1979, though, Lowenstein experienced a high-level glorious baseball moment while playing for Earl Weaver and Baltimore where he had played five positions during the season. In Game One of the ALCS, the Orioles and Angels were tied at 3 when Weaver pinch hit Lowenstein for Mark Belanger. Steiner fouled off the first two pitches then laced the third offering just over Memorial Stadium's left-field wall for a walk-off three-run homer. Lowenstein, approaching third, raised his arms in triumph, then leapt slightly - as if jumping over a very low hurdle - then briefly embraced Weaver who had run out onto the field. After being mobbed at home, the bespectacled Lowenstein made his way to the dugout then popped back out and raised both arms like a conquering boxer. The crowd of 52,000-plus chanted, "We want John! We want John!" and after a few minutes Lowenstein appeared again, pumping both arms into the air. Later, regarding

---

92 Wouldn't it have been an amazing side story if Kekich and Peterson had met on the field at Ten Cent Beer Night? Damn.

the enthusiastic Weaver on the field, he said, "I never saw such a little man in the baseline."

In early December of 1976, the Indians traded Lowenstein and Rick Cerone for Rico Carty. A few months later, though, the franchise decided they wanted Lowenstein back, so they completed a complicated three-way trade - one of the kinds of trades that might be best explained by someone with a PhD. Fortunately, Lowenstein was willing to explain it all: "A Mexican to a Canadian team for a Jewish Gringo to a Tribe of Indians. Now figure that out. It's a three-nation deal, at least. It involves money as well. Pesos, Canadian, and American money. In fact, I'm the first Jewish Indian traded for a Mexican ever."

After this, Indians organist Art Broze would play "Hava Nagila" as Lowenstein strode toward home plate. Lowenstein, though, quickly reported that he was actually a Roman Catholic. Broze responded by playing the theme to *Jesus Christ Superstar*. Lowenstein batted .242 in 1974. The next season he did it again: .242. He dropped to .205 in 1976. In 1977, Lowenstein stood at the plate in Toronto with a remarkable opportunity to - you guessed it - hit .242 again. He batted four times, striking out three, ensuring a smatch of baseball infamy by finishing the season with another .242 average. His teammates, fully aware of what was on the line, mobbed Lowenstein after he struck out swinging to end the game. Afterwards, of course, Lowenstein delivered a classic: "Naturally, team success always takes priority. However, there is something to be said for personal glory as well."

Some other great Steiner-isms from over the years:

- On baseball: "Baseball is reality at its harshest. You have to introduce a fictional reality to survive."

- On birthplaces: "You never know where you are born. You have to take your parents' word for it."

- On home runs: "I have noticed that there are a lot of outfielders in the American League with great mobility, and the best way to immobilize them is to hit the ball over the fence."

- On statistics: "Nuclear war would render all baseball statistics meaningless."

- On failing to get a bunt down: "Sure, I screwed up that sacrifice bunt, but look at it this way. I'm a better bunter than a billion Chinese. Those suckers can't bunt at all."

- On staying ready on the bench: "I flush the john between innings to keep my wrists strong."

- On discovering whether he was in the lineup: "I glance at the lineup card, I look for length. If I see a very long name, I know I am playing. I also see a misspelled name. Earl (Weaver) always puts the "i" before the "e." Sometimes I'll correct it, but the next day it's still misspelled.

Lowenstein and Altobelli won the American League pennant in 1983. The Orioles lost the first game of the World Series to the Phillies, but in Game 2 Lowenstein went 3-4 with a home run to lead the birds to victory. They then won three more in a row to capture the series. Two years later, on May 21, 1985, the Orioles released Lowenstein, ending a 16-year career. When asked what he planned to do next, he said, "There's part of The Smithsonian that I haven't seen yet." Also, "I'm going to be a player agent, go to Taiwan and sign up with the Little League champions." Over 16 seasons, Lowenstein batted 3,989 times and had 881 hits. He had a .253 average with 116 home runs.

Over his three-season tenure with the Rangers, **Billy Martin** notched a 137-141 record. In 1975, his third and final season with the Rangers, Martin had begun to wear out his welcome. According to Shropshire, "A one-for-all and all-for-one spirit was not manifesting itself on this team. What the Rangers needed was a good Ten Cent Beer Night Riot to unify the troops. Unfortunately happenings like this are somewhat rare in baseball." Throughout his 16 seasons as a manager, Martin finished 1253-1013 and led the Yankees to the World Series title in 1977. Martin was fired numerous times throughout his managerial career - five times by his beloved New York Yankees (or at least pressured to resign). "He just wasn't happy unless he was in pinstripes," Billy Martin Jr. said about his father. Regarding his firings, Martin said that the best way to know that you were fired is to arrive at the ballpark and find your name had been removed from the parking list. On Christmas Day in 1989, in the early evening, Martin and an old Detroit pal named William Reedy, drank in a local bar near Fenton, NY then got into Martin's truck. Reedy drove the icy roads until the truck slid on a turn then plummeted some 300 feet into the woods, flipping then landing on its right side, killing Martin. "It's well documented that he had occasional drinking problems, and I think there were times that got in the way of success," Grieve said. "There were times in '75 where we were taking batting practice not knowing what the lineup was because he wasn't at the ballpark yet." Jim Sundberg also said as much: "Billy began drinking. He lost control of the team. Came to the ballpark under the influence…from my observation it (his firing) was his drinking." There is significant anecdotal evidence that Martin's reign in Texas actually ended when he angrily demanded that John Denver's "Thank God I'm a Country Boy" be played before the bottom of the 7th inning (rather than "Take Me Out to the Ballpark"). According to an autobiography by Bill Pennington, Umpire Ron Luciano heard Martin call upstairs and shout, "I don't care what the owner says, play the Goddamned John Denver song."

On October 27, 1974, **Nick Mileti** wore a brown mohair tuxedo and stood in the middle of a fairly new arena concept - something called a "loge" (in this case a "double-tiered loge") - situated above the floor, but with an excellent view of, the heart of the Midwest Sports Coliseum. It was opening night and the building would eventually be called the Richfield Coliseum, then simply just The Coliseum. Mileti starred that evening, as much as one could, with the headlining performer, Frank Sinatra, who had flown in that afternoon with an entourage of 20, to help open northeast Ohio's newest attraction in style. Mileti sold his own stake in the Indians to Bonda in 1975. He has written three books. In 2019, he was elected to the Cleveland Cavaliers' "Wall of Honor."

Municipal Stadium hosted other notable events, including the World Series of Rock from 1974 to 1980. The Rolling Stones headlined the 1978 affair as 83,000 fans helped Mick Jagger and his crew rock the stadium. In 1981 the Indians hosted the 52nd All Star game at Municipal. Art Broze's friend Rocco Scotti (who wrote to *The Plain Dealer* defending Broze), sang the national anthem. Indians radio announcer **Joe Tait,** with the assistance of Terry Pluto, revisited Ten Cent Beer Night in *It's Been A Real Ball.* Tait didn't care for the Indians saying that the beer was only 3.2 beer - "as if it were unsweetened Kool-Aid." "I was sickened to my stomach. It was the worst thing that I ever saw during a broadcast. Martin wielded a fungo bat. Fans swinging chains."[93] Bonda, because Tait had called it a "riot", wanted Tait fired. Tait blamed the alcohol. "Without fuel, it's hard to have a fire." 65,000 beers (5 per adult). But Mileti, who had been out of town, returned and allegedly spoke to everyone he could (that had been in attendance). He also listened to Score and Tait's broadcast. 'I can't see anything wrong with what Joe said. It obviously was a riot. That was it. I kept my job." According to Tait, he spoke later to Chylak who told him that "as long as they weren't shooting" the game would go off. "Joe, I figured as long as they're not shooting or anything like that, we'll get it done. All of a sudden, I felt some pressure behind the left heel of my shoe. I turned around, looked down and there was a hunting knife sticking in the ground right behind my show. That's when I said, 'Game. Set. Match. We're outta here!' "

The Indians played their final game at Municipal Stadium on October 3, 1993, a 4-0 loss to the Chicago White Sox (this author was there!). They finished the season 76-86. (what was their record at the stadium?) The final game's only highlight (arguably, the *weekend's* only highlight - since the Sox swept the Tribe) came in the form of a walk. Heading into that final game, Indians outfielder Albert Belle led Chicago's Frank Thomas by three RBI in the American League race (129 to 126). Early in the game Thomas notched one RBI in the first and another in the 6th and strode to the plate in the 8th inning with a man on first. Whether Indians pitcher Jerry DiPoto was pitching defensively or actually yielding to the crowd's chants of "Walk him! Walk him!", DiPoto gave Thomas a free pass to 1st base. Thomas threw away his bat in disgust and kicked first base. The crowd, with little else to cheer for, went wild. In the 9th, Mark Lewis struck out to end the game.

Amazingly and fittingly, 83-year-old Mel Harder, who threw the first game pitch when he opposed Lefty Grove in that first game at Municipal in 1931, threw out the final pregame pitch - to Sandy Alomar, Jr. (it bounced about 5 feet short of the plate). A white limo bearing several tuxedoed/sunglassed men wearing red bowties, bearing pickaxes and shovels, got out and dug up home plate. It took a while and considerable effort but it was eventually moved to the new ballpark, Jacobs Field.

---

93 This did not happen, said Fazio.

Then American icon and Cleveland native Bob Hope, 90, came cruising onto the field in a golf cart, his wife Delores by his side. The 90-year-old Hope clambered out and approached the mic, and proceeded to joke about his old football days at Cleveland's East High. "I made one run," Hope reminisced. "One hundred yards. I didn't make a touchdown - but the guy I was chasing did. "I just wanna say this about this beautiful ballpark," Hope added, with Dolores occasionally redirecting him. "I've sang thanks for the memories in a lot of places in this world, but I've never sang it for a ballpark. And I'll tell you, I know this ballpark and I've loved it. And I wanna do this for you. Let me have the music," Accompanied by ballpark organist Jeff Cavallo, Hope began with lyrics written specially for this occasion (feel free to hum along), "Thanks for the memories, it's hard to say goodbye - this you can't deny. Since '31, the job you've done, each man will certify. And we thank you so much. Hey, thanks for the memories - of Bob Feller's fastball, Al Rosen's hits that cleared the wall. It's time to go and this we know: history will make you stand tall and we thank you so much. You can sing along if you wannuuuuu. We won't forget popcorn and peanuts we bought here. And sportsmanship lessons taught here. Well, you've been so swell, and now it's farewell. So thanks for the memories. At this ballpark's final day, how good things pass away, but they'll always be in our memory, any place the Indians play. We'll make a harsh cheer, no matter where they play. And thank you so much."

With the winds whipping up the waves of nearby Lake Erie, the Indians lowered a Chief Wahoo flag down toward an enormous Marlboro man billboard and that was it - at least for baseball. The tenuous relationship between the Art Modell, the city, and Municipal Stadium had already begun to crumble. In 1995, Modell, displeased with the fact that the City of Cleveland seemed to be willing to build a new baseball stadium, but not to help improve Municipal for football (or build a new football stadium), moved the Browns to Baltimore (where they became the Ravens). On December 17, 1995 Browns fans "began the initial demolition" of Municipal Stadium when, after the final home game, rabid members of the renowned Dawg Pound began to dismantle bleacher seats for souvenirs - or out of just plain anger. Fittingly, the city hired Osborn Engineering, which had built Municipal Stadium in 1931, to oversee its official demolition. By early March of 1997, the Stadium was completely razed. The once glorious Donald Gray Gardens, built near the stadium for the 1936

Great Lakes Exhibition, were also wiped out. And despite Bob Hope's hope, the vision of the city leadership in the '20s, one would scarcely be able to tell what had once stood there. Yet, a quarter of the stadium lives on: construction crews pushed about 5,000 cubic yards of concrete into Lake Erie where it now forms two 600-foot fishing reefs - one near Edgewater Park and the other near Euclid General Hospital. (Perhaps that's what inspired the good folks of Pixar in Finding Dory - although those colorful saltwater fish would never make it in Lake Erie.)

Spanning the years that encompassed the end of DiMaggio's famous streak, the glories of '48, the promotional shenanigans of Veeck, the Browns' many victories (and numerous disappointments), the chaos of Ten Cent Beer Night, and the drugged-out World of Rock concerts, Hope's farewell song for Municipal Stadium was appropriate: thanks for the memories..

Gaylord Perry retired in 1983, closing the book on a 22-year career highlighted by 314 wins (including a stunning 303 complete games). Perry had 3,534 strikeouts and was the first pitcher to win the Cy Young in both the American and National leagues. He was not elected to the Hall of Fame immediately - probably because of the sense that he relied so much on the spitball. In 1991, his third year of eligibility, Perry was finally honored, admitted to Cooperstown - fittingly - alongside Fergie Jenkins and Bill Veeck (as well as Tony Lazzeri and Rod Carew). Perry's wife Blanche was tragically killed after a car ran a stop sign and hit her vehicle in Lake Wales, Florida. She was just 46. Perry remarried a few years later and died on December 1, 2022 at the age of 84. Perry had some classic lines about his alleged doctoring of the ball. He once said, "I reckon I tried everything on the old apple, but salt and pepper and chocolate sauce topping." He also said, "I'd always have grease in two places, in case the umpires would ask me to wipe one off. I never wanted to be caught with anything, though. It wouldn't be professional." Also, "There is a difference between jaywalking and grand larceny."

Fritz Peterson went 14-8 for the Indians in 1975, but struggled in 1976. The Indians eventually traded him to - where else? - the Texas Rangers for Stan Perzanowski and cash. Perzanowski never pitched for the Indians. No one knows what happened to the cash. Peterson had a flawless 1-0 record for the Rangers in 1976 before retiring. Peterson's career numbers are certainly above average.

He finished with 133-131 in a major league career that spanned 11 seasons, highlighted by his All Star team selection in 1970. Peterson coached one year of collegiate baseball serving as the head baseball coach for Rock Valley College in 1993. The team finished 3-22. The Peterson/Kekich wife swap story attracted the attention of Hollywood superstars Ben Affleck and Matt Damon as the subject for a potential film. Peterson went 9-14 for the Indians in '74 and 14-8 for them in '75. He won one game for the Rangers, who released him in early February of 1977. The White Sox signed Peterson a couple of weeks later, but he never pitched in the majors again. He was successful, however, in a long marriage to the former Susanne Kekich. They are still married today.

Lenny Randle was the focus of an MLB feature titled, *"Lenny Randle: The Most Interesting Man in Baseball."* Randle famously got down on his hands and knees and blew a dribbler by Amos Otis foul at the Seattle Kingdome in a game between the Mariners and Royals. Randle also stood at home plate as a Met when the lights went out at Shea Stadium in 1977 - the outage was part of a blackout that impacted most of New York City. Randle claimed that right at that moment he hit the ball between third and short and that he should have been credited with a single. He had been traded to New York earlier that year after he punched Rangers manager Frank Lucchesi so hard that he shattered his cheekbone.

Randle gets asked very frequently about Ten Cent Beer Night - and the Shea Stadium blackout. "Some of the guys were too macho to say they were hurt," said Randle, adding that even President Nixon asked him once about Ten Cent Beer Night. "I used to get away with calling him 'Tricky Dick.' He even asked what was going on." Randle has become a baseball legend in Italy. He first played there professionally, winning a batting title with a .477 average. He has continued to promote baseball there, telling *Rolling Stone* in 2015 that he was there trying to find the next Joe Dimaggio, Mike Pizza, or Yogi Berra.

The '74 **Texas Rangers** proved - at least for a season - that they were *not* a Kurt Vonnegut/ Erector Set of a ball club at all. The Rangers surprised everyone, apart from themselves, and nearly won the American League West. Their 84-76-1 record was a far cry from the 100-plus loss seasons of 1972 and 1973. Baseball heaped individual honors all around. Jeff Burroughs won the American League MVP. Fergie Jenkins won 25 games and finished second in the American League

Cy Young race to the Oakland A's Catfish Hunter. Both pitchers were 25-12. Jenkins had struck out 225 to Hunter's 143. Jenkins had 29 complete games to Hunter's 23. But Hunter had a slightly better ERA (2.49 to 2.82). Perryton's paladin, Mike Hargrove, batted .323 and was picked as the American League Rookie of the Year. Catcher Jim Sundberg was honored as an All Star and also strongly considered for the Rookie of the Year.

The '74 Rangers finished just five games behind the cantankerous Oakland A's, who went on to win the World Series for the second straight year. The franchise finished 4th out of 12 in the American League in attendance, drawing 1,193,902 fans. Whatever momentum and promise they had amassed in '74, shriveled up in the hot Texas summer of '75. Tensions between Corbett and Martin had simmered. For his part, Martin resented Corbett's meddling with his managerial decisions. At one point Martin said, "He knows as much about baseball as I do about pipe." After losing the second game of a late July doubleheader, Corbett fired Billy Martin. They were 44-51 at the time. Frank Lucchesi took over and, though he fared better than Martin, the squad finished the season 79-83 in 1975. The franchise mostly struggled for several decades, although they did go 94-68 in 1977, finishing second in the AL West (but Corbett also employed four managers during that season). The Rangers made the World Series in 2010 and 2011, losing in 2010 to the San Francisco Giants. In 2011, they were one strike away from a title but ultimately lost to the St. Louis Cardinals in 7 games. In the fall of 2023 the Rangers slipped into the playoffs as a Wild Card team then proceeded to win every one of their eleven road games en route to winning the first World Series title in franchise history.

Journalist **Tim Russert** was in law school at Cleveland State in 1974 and attended Ten Cent Beer Night. Asked how much beer he drank, Russert is famous for saying, "I had $2 in my pocket. You do the math."

Phil Seghi served as the Indians General Manager for 13 seasons, during which the team finished above .500 just three times (1976, 1979, and 1981). Early in his career, Seghi signed a young Pete Rose. Unfortunately Seghi's great trade of '74, as so often seemed to be the case for the Indians, turned out to be a bust (unless you were a New Yankee fan). **Chris Chambliss** had begun the 1974 season with a .329 average for the Indians. He would go on to play an integral role for the Yankees, who played in three straight World Series (1976-1978) with Chambliss at first base (losing to the Reds in '76 but defeating the Dodgers in '77 and '78). Chambliss, who came up through the organization, knew most of the guys, and was attached to Aspromonte, was stunned and saddened by the trade. His wife, Audrey, contributed regularly to the *Plain Dealer* in a "Baseball Wife" feature. In fact, on the day he was traded, Audrey Chambliss wrote a gentle description of how she and Chris spent the winter in Puerto Rico where he and George Hendrick, Tom Hilgendorf, and Charlie Spikes played baseball and hung out by the pool. She closed the column with, "It was a pleasure being around people who cared about baseball and their team. I'm not saying they didn't have harsh words on the bad plays, but they always seemed to be there to cheer on their team when needed. We could use some of that feeling in Cleveland (this weekend for starters)." Later that day, Chambliss suited up for the New York Yankees against Martin and the Texas Rangers. Another player in the trade, Dick Tidrow, also contributed nicely to the Yankees. In Cleveland, Peterson was 9-14 in '74 and 14-8 in '75. It was downhill from there; he picked up just two wins in '76. Kline struggled with the Indians. Former Indians GM Gabe Paul was now the GM with the Yankees and seemed to know the exact value and potential of Chambliss, commenting that in his mind he was already an All Star. The general manager was incompetent," Aspromonte said about Seghi in 2018, adding that he "resented" his decisions. "We had a good young ball club and we could have given the top clubs a run for their money, but we had impatient people that don't know baseball very well. He gave himself a new two-year contract. I asked him, 'How do you justify that and you don't give me one?' and he said, 'Well, Ken, it looks like we have to make a change' (Frank Robinson). It hurt the ballclub completely and they all recognized it. That was the end of it."

Mike Shropshire covered The Rangers from 1973-1975. In 2013 Dan Epstein and *Esquire* named *Seasons In Hell,* about the early days of the Rangers, as one of the 20 best baseball books ever.

In December of 1974, the Rangers traded **Don Stanhouse** to Montreal, where he pitched for the Expos from 1975 through 1977. Stanhouse was 10-10 in '77 - his best season as a starter - then traded to the Baltimore Orioles in December of that year. In 1978 Earl Weaver used Stanhouse as a very effective closer - he finished third in the American League in saves in both '78 and '79. In 1979 Stanhouse was an American League All Star and helped the O's capture the AL pennant. Stanhouse got the win in relief in Game 1 of the ALCS, but lost Game 3. The Orioles beat the Angels 3-1 in the series, though, to advance to the World Series against the "We Are Family" Pirates, who were led by Willie Stargell, Dave Parker, and side-arming closer Kent Tekulve. In one of the more dramatic series of the era, the Orioles fell just short, losing in Game 7 at home. Stanhouse pitched in three of the '79 World Series games.

In Baltimore, Stanhouse would frequently greet folks who came early to the ballpark with a primal scream, a habit which contributed to his being dubbed "Stan the Man Unusual." On the mound he also tended to walk batters whom he didn't like to face, prompting Weaver to pace nervously back and forth in the dugout - a habit that ultimately earned Stanhouse another nickname, given to him by Weaver - "Full Pack" - a reference to the number of cigarettes Weaver would apparently smoke while Stanhouse pitched. Weaver is also on record as calling Stanhouse "an asshole" who ruined his health.

Stanhouse loves to talk about his baseball career and laughs. "I played for Ted Williams, Whitey Herzog, Billy Martin, Gene Mauch, Dick Williams, Earl Weaver, and Tommy Lasorda - some of the greatest managers in the history of baseball could not do anything with my amazing talent. But I had great hair. Oscar (Gamble) had great hair, but I was right there with him."

Like old teammate Grieve, Stanhouse revels in the glory and uniqueness of 70s baseball. "Brooks Robinson started the MLB baseball alumni association (in 1982) and he said 'We played baseball when baseball was baseball.' I never heard it said any better than that."

After 60 years, **The Wahoo Club**, the Indians fan club, changed its name to the 455 Club in 2023. The number 455 represents the number of consecutive sellouts the Indians notched in the glorious mid to late '90s.

After the rainy night in Cleveland, **The Great Wallenda** continued to ply his unique trade. In 1970, Wallenda tossed back his requisite two martinis then tightroped his way 821 feet along and some 750 above the Tallulah Gorge in northern Georgia. Guinness declared it a world record.

Before his walk above Municipal Stadium, *Plain Dealer* reporter Dan Coughlin spent time with him. "I've been 54 years on the wire and people ask me why I do it. It's my job. I can't walk away from it," Wallenda reflected. "It gives me a chance to make money and care for my children. But if someone gave me more money to do something else, I wouldn't take it. I will do this kind of work as long as the Good Lord gives me strength. Is it not a nice feeling to know you are respected by the American public so much. You cannot buy this."

Previewing his walk in Cleveland, *Press* writer Bob August wrote a column titled, "Finally Found - Error Free Athlete." August noted, "He will walk carefully because he does not permit, as the rest of us do, the luxury of carelessness or bad days." Sadly, Wallenda did have a bad day. In 1978, Wallenda attempted to walk the wire between two towers of the Condado Plaza Hotel on a very windy day in San Juan, Puerto Rico. Inching along, ten stories up as the nearby Atlantic Ocean pushed strongly in his direction, The Great Wallenda lost his balance and tragically fell to his death. A video of the attempted walk and the ensuing fall is on YouTube, but this author has never been able to bear to watch it.

Milt Wilcox pitched for 16 years in the Major Leagues, throwing strikes for the Reds, Indians, Cubs, Tigers, and Mariners. At one point, fairly early in his career, Wilcox concluded that he had lost it. He was with the Cubs in '75 and appeared headed for the minors when a coach named Freddie Martin took him and Bruce Sutter aside, ready to impart upon them something special. "Boys," Wilcox recalled Martin telling him and Sutter, "I'm going to teach you a pitch that will get you back to the big leagues." Wilcox said he had never heard of what Martin wanted to show them but Sutter picked it up right away. It was a split-fingered fastball. "It tumbles and you push up with your thumb. It has topspin on it. So when the topspin hits the wind, it's kind of like a knuckleball. When you throw it like a fastball they think in their brain it's a fastball and it breaks six inches to a foot." Wilcox said he didn't start throwing the pitch until 1981. He added that he taught it to Tigers teammate Jack Morris. In 1984, Wilcox was 17-8 for the Tigers, who beat the San Diego Padres in the World Series. Wilcox won Game 3 of the 1984 World Series and the Tigers won the series, defeating the Padres in five games. In 2005 Wilcox started a company called Ultimate Air Dogs, featuring dogs jumping off of docks and into water.

In the post-game chaos, **Terry Yerkic** took the Rapid Transit Authority back home and didn't see his friends until he got back to his neighborhood. The day after, his former high school principal called Jim Bede, one of Yerkic's friends, who was still in high school, into the dreaded principal's office. Yerkic laughs, "We were legal. We had just a wonderful principal. First thing in the morning Jim gets called up to the office and Jim says, 'Oh no, what did I do?' Our principal asks, 'What did you do last night? You go to the game? No? I'm gonna give you one last shot at this. Next time,' he says, 'Don't wear your letter jacket on the field, you idiot.' " Yerkic said he never intended to be disrespectful or to ignite the powder keg that led to the forfeit. "I can't say I'm ashamed because we've had such a laugh. There's been a lot of publicity about it. I didn't do anything malicious. I wish I hadn't done it when I did it. It was - and is - a black eye to the city and I'm sorry for that. It wasn't premeditated. And we never thought about the consequences. But we do laugh about it." Yerkic managed to hide his involvement in Ten Cent Beer Night from his parents for quite some time. When they did find out about his role, it wasn't a big deal. Yerkic was a machinist who made medical devices and continued to live in the Cleveland area. He has been very involved in Richmond Heights youth sports, so much so that he was formally honored by the city.

Jackie York remembers exactly what outfit she wore on the day and evening of June 4, 1974. "Isn't that funny? It was a sleeveless dress with apples on it. Red apples against a sort of beige." York worked a few more years for the Indians then eventually took a job at Cleveland's famed Playhouse Square. "It's an amazing success story," she says. "They've restored the theaters to their original beauty. They were popular in the '40s and '50s and now people are coming back downtown." York is very proud of Cleveland and its resilience. "That's the one thing about Cleveland: you can't beat the guts and the enthusiasm and you can't beat us down. You can try but you ain't gonna win."

Hugo Zacchini died on his birthday, October 20, 1975, just a year and a half after opening the 1974 season in Cleveland by blasting through the bitter April air and across Municipal Stadium on Opening Day. Although Zacchini was probably best-known as "The Human Cannonball," he was also a respected artist who taught art at Chaffey College in Rancho Cucamonga, California.

Letters of Protest, Letters of Praise

June 11, 1974

Mr. Leland S. MacPhail, Jr.
President
American League
280 Park Avenue
New York, New York 10017

Dear Lee:

There is no question that all of us connected with the
Cleveland Ball Club, and all thinking citizens of this area,
deplore the conduct of the very small group of exhibitionists
who disrupted the June 4th game at Municipal Stadium. It was
a most embarrassing situation for our city and a step backwards
in our efforts to reestablish baseball as the major summer sport
in Ohio.

That we deeply regret the conduct of some over-enthusiastic
fans is obvious, and we certainly hope baseball fans here and
across the nation will not harbor any lingering bad feelings
against the game because of this foolish episode.

Our organization has been striving to restore interest and
enthusiasm in baseball in Cleveland, and we will not let June 4th
dampen our efforts. You have our pledge on this.

Cleveland Indians Co. - The Stadium — Boudreau Boulevard, Cleveland, Ohio 44114 - 216/861-1200
Member: The American League of Baseball

The purpose of this letter is to urge you to reconsider the forfeiture of the game between the Texas Rangers and the Cleveland Indians on June 4th. To blame and therefore penalize the Indians for spontaneous combustion caused by a number of factors beyond our control is, in our opinion, a most unfair action.

Permit me to present our case:

(1) It always has been and always will be our intention to realize the responsibilities that are ours in guarding the safety and welfare of our fans and the ballplayers who participate in games at the Stadium. On the afternoon of the June 4th game, we doubled our security and sincerely felt that measures had been taken to keep everything in control for the ballgame. There was some concern about the intensity of the game because of the episode between the two ball clubs in the game played in Texas. Of the 25,000 fans in attendance we had a game sale of 19,000. Realizing this, we took immediate action to reinforce our security measures.

(2) The punishment dealt to the Cleveland Club was too severe when you stop to consider that the opposing team had much to do with inciting the fans behavior. It should be kept in mind that the on-rush of the Texas Rangers, lead by Manager Billy Martin, with bats onto the field is what really triggered

the on-rush of the fans from the stands. It also should be
noted that Manager Martin threw gravel into the stands behind
the Rangers' dugout, as well as thumbing his nose at them. In
addition, he swung his bat over the top of the dugout attempting
to strike some fans, breaking his bat with the force of his blow--
we have this documented. At the time of the outbreak, two of
our staff were on the field; namely, Dan Zerbey, our Stadium
Supervisor, and Carl Fazio, our Director of Sales and Marketing.
After hearing their stories of the incident, I still believe
that a more concerted effort should have been made to clear the
field; that is, that both clubs should have been sent to the
clubhouses until the field had been cleared and order had been
restored. In view of these circumstances, I strongly feel that
the umpires should have called it a suspended game rather than
a forfeited game.

(3) I feel that these experienced umpires should have handled
this matter in a more efficient manner long before the 9th inning.
At those time, when there were minor interruptions beginning with
solo runs across the outfield which increased from the 3rd inning
on to the 7th inning, there were no warnings given by the umpires.
I am sure that in the history of baseball there has never been a
forfeited game without prior warning to the crowd by the umpires.

It is our contention that had there been warnings of suspension of play when a few people were running over the outfield, it would have been possible to ward off the incident which occurred in the 9th inning.

I regret very deeply not taking it upon myself to call down sometime between the 3rd and 7th innings and inform the umpires to take the action necessary to have avoided the deplorable incident that developed. Yet I felt all along that they would take the game in hand as had been done so many times in other incidents on other fields by the umpiring crews.

(4) There is precedent for reversing the forfeiture ruling, which I am sure you are aware of. I sincerely hope that you will study this matter most conscientiously and thoroughly, and realize that we have a most valid protest of the forfeiture of the June 4th game.

Cordially,

Phillip D. Seghi
Vice President-General Manager

PDS:tjh

"It really is a whole new ball game."

June 18, 1974

Mr. Leland S. MacPhail, Jr.
President
The American League of Baseball
280 Park Avenue
New York, New York 10017

Dear Lee:

Thank you for taking the time to meet with Phil Seghi and myself last
week in your office.

Though you had predetermined your decision and we should abide by it,
I came away from the meeting feeling stronger than ever that you are
backing a very bad decision by the umpires. Since returning, I have
gone over all the facts we have, all the evidence we have, I have talked
to additional people, I've looked at TV tapes secured from Channel 7 in
Detroit and they make the umpires reports look a good bit off base.
Just sighting two obvious statements; (1) the exemplary conduct of the
Texas Rangers, and (2) more than a thousand fans on the field in the
9th inning. The evidence shows the conduct of the Rangers "anything"
but exemplary and no one claims nor do pictures show that more than
two or three hundred fans were ever on the field at one time.

I also feel that your personal investigation was rather shallow, and
no attempt was made to find in many cases, what the true facts were.
As an example, your statement that Jeff Burroughs missed a number of
games after the June 4th incident. Just a cursory look at the subsequent
box scores would show that he played in every game thereafter. Additionally, your statement that announcements warning against spectators going
on the field were not made in Cleveland - was erroneous. Did you make
any attempt to check Nestor Chylak's stories and observations? The head
of our police and security forces claims Chylak was not hurt on the field.
You have done Cleveland a great disservice by your seeming dependence on
hearsay and newspapers for your determination.

-- continued

Cleveland Indians, Inc. • The Stadium — Boudreau Boulevard, Cleveland, Ohio 44114 • 216/861-1200
Member: The American League of Baseball

I promise that I won't belabor this issue any longer and we in Cleveland have learned some good and valuable lessons and have since implemented old procedures and started new ones. However, all of this will be of no avail unless the League also learns from the incident and will also institute crowd control instructions and procedures to umpires who in certain situations must be in stronger control of the players. I don't want you to think that we in Cleveland condone what happened. In fact, we deplore it and apologize for our apparent negligence and lack of foresight, but we were treated very harshly for conditions that were not entirely under our control and in fact, were in many ways inspired by others.

Sincerely yours,

Ted Bonda
Executive Vice President

ATB:sh

P.S. *Incidentally, your observation that our incident would hurt Cleveland and the rest of the leagues attendence is certainly off base. Ours is higher than before and apparently, so are the others.*

baseball

Office of the Commissioner
Bowie K. Kuhn
Commissioner

August 1, 1974

Dear Ted:

Several weeks ago, your club staged a fan scramble for money scattered about the field. I have intentionally let some time slide while I thought about whether I should write you on this subject. While I am quite reluctant to get involved in club promotions and while I believe that imaginative marketing is a critical need of our game, I have a real question about the desirability of this particular event. Even though it has been used in the minors, I think it reflects badly upon the image of Major League Baseball and that is something about which I have to be concerned as all of us have a common stake in that image. I would appreciate your giving serious thought to the views I have expressed in this letter.

Sincerely yours,

Mr. Alva T. Bonda
Executive Vice President
Cleveland Indians
The Stadium
Cleveland, Ohio 44114

BKK/ms

15 West 51st Street, In Rockefeller Center
New York, N.Y. 10019
(212) 586-7400

```
                    FRANK ROBINSON

                 15557 Aqua Verdes Drive
                Los Angeles, California  90024


        June 20, 1977


             Mr. Alva T. Bonda
             Investment Plaza
             Suite 1700
             Cleveland, OH  44114

             Dear Ted:

             I know that others have taken full credit for my
             hiring as the Indians manager; however, I know
             that you personally were responsible for my
             hiring.  Although I am still somewhat stunned by
             the events of this past weekend, I suppose I am
             slowly beginning to realize that my termination
             as manager of the Indians was simply one of the
             hazards of the job.  As I think about it, I should
             not be too disappointed since this is my first
             firing after more than two decades in the game of
             baseball.

             I do want to express my thanks to you for your
             support as I know that many people were anxious
             to see me fired.  I can tell you in all honesty
             that I gave my very best and did everything I
             could to make the Indians a winner.  I am sorry
             I was not able to achieve greater success; but
             you may be assured that I will continue to try to
             lead another team in baseball to the ultimate goal
             ...the World Series Championship.

             I would like to wish you and the Indians success
             throughout the remainder of the 1977 season and,
             of course, in the years ahead.  I am confident
             Jeff will do a good job at the helm provided he
             is given the support that is needed from the front
             office.

             Sincerely,


             Frank Robinson
```

A kind letter from Frank Robinson, the first black manager in the American League, to Ted Bonda, who hired him and fired him.

THE AMERICAN LEAGUE OF PROFESSIONAL BASEBALL CLUBS

280 PARK AVENUE   NEW YORK, N.Y. 10017

February 23, 1978

MAR 1 1978

Mr. Ted Bonda
c/o Cleveland Indians
The Stadium
Boudreau Boulevard
Cleveland, Ohio   44114

Dear Ted:

I would like to congratulate you on the extremely difficult job
you did in keeping the Indians afloat and arranging new financing
for the club. Further, you are to be congratulated on the caliber
of the people you brought into your ownership. You piloted the team
through a real crisis period and have succeeded in establishing
the club on its best footing in modern baseball history.

I believe your years of struggle in baseball have made a real
"baseball person" out of you and it is my fond hope that
we will continue to see you at meetings and at the Stadium.
Please call me if I can ever be of any personal assistance to you.
I am counting on our meeting occasionally for lunch at the
Gloucester House or for dinner in Florida.

Sincerely,

L. S. MacPhail, Jr.
President

LSM/pkm

P.S. - I do not feel it would be fair to ask you to continue on
       The Player Relations Committee. We are just about to go
       into a new round of bargaining for a new Basic Agreement and it
       is going to be very, very hectic and very time consuming. With
       a new man on board to be indoctrinated, it is going to be even
       more difficult. Thank you for your past service on the most
       thankless assignment in baseball and I will proceed to try to
       find someone else to do their bit for the cause.

**AL President Lee MacPhail recognizes Bonda's contributions towards saving
baseball in Cleveland.**

ALVA T. BONDA

1700 INVESTMENT PLAZA · CLEVELAND, OHIO 44114 · (216) 696-6346

March 14, 1978

Mr. L. S. MacPhail, Jr.
President
The American League of
    Professional Baseball Clubs
280 Park Avenue
New York, N.Y. 10017

Dear Lee:

Thank you very much for your nice letter of
February 23. For some reason it didn't come to my
attention until now.

I always was a baseball fan and since I am still
somewhat involved with the Indians, I will still be a
real "baseball person" as you pointed out. I very much
enjoyed my association with many baseball people that I
came in contact with, especially the President of the
American League.

I do hope we can have lunch or dinner in New YORK,
Cleveland or Florida.

Kindest Regards.

Bonda's response to MacPhail.

From A Crown to A Frown: Performance, Attendance & Notes on 1947-1975

Year	Record		Attendance	Notes
1947	80-74-3	1st	1,521,978	First full season of Veeck ownership - buys team for $1.1 million; Larry Doby is the first African-American player in the American League; Veeck installs outfield fence, shrinking the spacious dimensions of Municipal; Feller throws two one-hitters, 9th & 10th of his career
1948	97-58	1st	2,620,627	World Series Champs, defeating Boston Braves in 6 games; Player/Manager Boudreau is AL MVP. Veeck: Executive of Yr.; Indians sign Satchel Paige in July; Bob Lemon emerges as another ace; Indians are the talk of baseball
1949	89-65	3rd	2,233,771	Indians get off to slow start and can't quite recover; Veeck sells team at the end of season for $2.2 million to Ellis Ryan; from '49-53 Indians average over 90 wins per season
1950	92-62	4th	1,727,464	Hank Greenberg named GM; Manager/Hero Boudreau's last season as manager; succeeded by Al Lopez. Al Rosen (37 HRs) and Luke Easter (28 HRs) burst onto the scene, joining Doby (25 HRs).
1951	93-61	2nd	1,704,984	Finish 5 games behind Yankees, who win World Series
1952	93-61	2nd	1,444,607	Finish 2 games behind Yankees, who win World Series
1953	92-62	2nd	1,069,138	Finish 8 ½ games behind Yankees, who win World Series
1954	111-43	1st	1,335,472	Incredible 111 win season, Lopez declares the pitching staff of Feller, Early Wynn, Lemon, Mike Garcia, Art Houtteman, Hal Newhouser & rookie relievers Ray Narleski & Don Mossi as "the greatest ever assembled." Exhausted by their run to a record-setting season, the team falls flat in the World Series, losing to the Giants in 4 straight.
1955	93-61	2nd	1,221,780	Herb Score has a superb rookie season (16-10) with an incredible 2.85 ERA. Team finishes 2nd to the Yankees for the fourth time in five years.
1956	88-66	2nd	865,467	Feller retires, Colavito hits 21 home runs in rookie season; despite 2nd place finish behind Yankees (yawn…again); franchise sees big drop in attendance

1957	76-77	6th	722,256	Score hit with line drive in eye in May, ending his season; Roger Maris, who will go on to break Babe Ruth's single season HR record in 1961, is a rookie; GM Greenberg fired after the season; Indians rumored to move to Minneapolis; Frank "Trader" Lane named GM
1958	77-76	4th	663,805	Lane executes 19 player transactions, including trade of Maris to Kansas City A's; attendance continues to drop; Houston group makes bid for Indians but Indians chairman William Daley & Board of Directors reject it
1959	89-65	2nd	1,497,976	Lane trades amazing 33 players; team and attendance bounce back; Colavito thrives with 42 HRs & 111 RBIs; Tribe acquires promising 1B Norm Cash after the season
1960	76-78	4th	950,985	Year from Hell: Lane blows up the team; trades fan favorite & AL HR leader Colavito as well as Cash; attendance down again; Lane, after a total of 51 transactions involving 118 players in 3 seasons - and a rare swap of Manager Joe Gordon for Tigers Manager Jimmy Dykes - does not have his contract renewed. The seeds of destruction are planted.
1961	78-83	5th	725,547	The Gabe Paul era begins; Paul fires Manager Dykes on the morning of the final game of the season & hires 1B coach Mel McGaha. The Indians trade fiery outfielder Jimmy Piersall, who hit .322, to Washington. Attendance drops precipitously.
1962	80-82	6th	716,076	Paul fires McGaha with with two games left in the season, names Birdie Tebbetts manager. Ownership, including former owner William Daley & Paul and others, reorganizes.
1963	79-83	5th	562,507	Sam McDowell's first full season; Fleet-footed Vic Davalillo's rookie season; Max Alvis hits 22 HRs; all-time attendance low
1964	79-83	6th	653,293	Greater Cleveland Growth Association heads up major preseason ticket drive but team still loses over $1 million, attendance languishes; team rumored to move to Seattle, Oakland, or Dallas
1965	87-75	5th	934,786	Rocky Colavito returns but at the price of losing top prospects Tommy Agee & Tommy John; McDowell is 17-11 with 2.18 ERA and leads league in strikeouts (325)
1966	81-81	5th	903,359	Cleveland businessman Vernon Stouffer buys team and promises to keep it in Cleveland; pitching strong with McDowell, Luis Tiant, and Sonny Siebert leading the way, Colavito hits 30 HRs

1967	75-87	8th	662,980	Paul hires Joe Adcock as manager, but is fired at the end of season and replaced by Alvin Dark; Indians finish last in league in attendance
1968	86-75	3rd	857,994	Attendance up & pitching strong again - led by Tiant (1.60 ERA) and McDowell (1.81 ERA)
1969	62-99	6th	619,970	Dark and Paul engage in a power struggle resulting in Dark's new responsibility over player personnel. Attendance plummets again; new OF/1B Ken "Hawk" Harrelson acquired to provide offensive clout (has 27 HRs) but hits for low average (.222); Pitching struggles but McDowell is still 18-14 (2.94 ERA).
1970	76-86	5th	729,752	Hawk breaks ankle early & misses most of season; Catcher Fosse demolished at plate by Pete Rose in All Star Game; McDowell still has another 20 win season.
1971	60-102	6th	591,361	Manager Al Dark fired after poor start, Ken Aspromonte named new manager; Paul regains full GM responsibility; Chris Chambliss is AL Rookie of the Year; Graig Nettles emerges (28 HRs); attendance plummets.
1972	72-84	5th	626,354	Paul negotiates to play 30 games in New Orleans. McDowell swapped to Giants for Gaylord Perry, Graig Nettles traded to Yankees for Charlie Spikes & three others. More turmoil. Attendance untenable; at season's end, the Mileti Group purchases the team from Stouffer for $10 million. Mileti cancels New Orleans move. Paul leaves to join Steinbrenner Group in purchase of Yanks.
1973	71-91	6th	615,107	Youngsters Chambliss, Gamble, Hendrick, & Bell show promise; Perry goes 19-19 (3.38 ERA); attendance poor. Mileti spread too thin, so, at season's end, Ted Bonda, one of the Indians' partners, named executive vice president; Carl Fazio hired as sales & marketing director
1974	77-85	4th	1,114,262	Indians owners/partners vow to do whatever is necessary to get franchise back on track & keep team in Cleveland; Massive promotional efforts & a strong first-half performance on field (40-24 start) lead to first season over 1 million fans since 1959
1975	79-80	4th	977,039	Frank Robinson takes over as player/manager; first African-American manager in baseball

Excerpt From Indians Radio Broadcast Transcript

June 4, 1974

Tait: Tom Hilgendorf has been hit on the head. Hilgy is in definite pain. He's bent over, holding his head. Somebody hit Hilgendorf on the head, and he is going to be assisted back into the dugout. Aw, this is absolute tragedy. Absolute tragedy...I've been in this business for over 20 years and I have never seen anything as disgusting as this.

Score: I haven't either.

Tait: And I'll be perfectly honest with you: I just don't know what to say.

Score: I don't think this game will continue, Joe....The unbelievable thing is people keep jumping out of the stands after they see what's going on!

Tait: Well, that shows you the complete lack of brainpower on the parts of some people. There's no way I'm going to run out onto the field if I see some baseball player waving a bat out there looking for somebody. This is tragic...The whole thing has degenerated now into just - now we've got another fight going with fans and ballplayers. Hargrove has got some kid on the ground and he is really administering a beating.

Score: Well, that fellow really wants a piece of him - and I don't blame him.

Tait: Boy, Hargrove really wants a piece of him - and I don't blame him.

Score: Look at Duke Sims down there going at it.

Tait: Yeah, Duke is in on it. Here we go again.

Score: I'm surprised that the police from the city of Cleveland haven't been called here, because we have the makings of a pretty good riot. We *have* a pretty good riot.

Tait: Well, the game, I really believe, Herb, now will be called. Slowly but surely the teams are getting back to their dugouts. The field, though, is just mobbed with people. And mob rule has taken over.

Score: They've stolen the bases.

Tait: The security people they have here are just totally incapable of handling this crowd. They just, well- short of the National Guard, I'm not sure what would handle this crowd right now. It's just unbelievable. Unbelievable...

Score: [As soon as] people go back in the seats, others jump down and take their place.

Tait: The bases are gone. Both teams are back in the respective dugouts...

[Keefer announces that the game has been declared a forfeit. The crowd boos.]

Tait: It will go into the books as a 9-0 forfeit to the Texas Rangers. So the Indians battle back, tie the game in the ninth [explosion rings out], and then the game is ruled a forfeit. That's it. It's all over. Well, there's no sense wrapping it up because it goes into the book as a 9-0 forfeit. Now, what about records in a game like this? I'm not up on this because I've not been in one before.

Score: I have never seen this before. I suppose we will just have to await a ruling from the American League office...

Tait: Well, that's it...[another cherry bomb goes off]. The final score, in a forfeit, ruled by the umpires after a riot broke out here in the ninth inning after the Indians had tied the game 5-5, final score in the books then will be Texas 9, Cleveland nothing.

(from The Top 20 Moments in Cleveland Sports by Bob Dyer)

Double Duty: Rangers Who Played for the Indians & Indians Who Played for the Rangers

Both franchises, perhaps because they were fairly mediocre, shared a remarkable number of players during the 1970s. Many Ten Cent Beer Night participants (or witnesses from the bullpens or dugouts) had played for both teams already - or were playing for the one side and would eventually play for the other.

Mike Kekich
Indians, '73
Rangers, '75

David Clyde
Rangers '73-74
Indians '78-79

Jim Bibby (traded for Gaylord Perry)
Rangers '73-775
Indians '75-77

Jackie Brown
Rangers '73-75
Indians '75-76

Larry Brown
Indians '63-71
Rangers '74

Leo Cardenas
Indians '73
Rangers '74

Steve Dunning
Indians '70-73
Rangers '73-74

Steve Hargan
Indians '65-72
Rangers '74-77

Mike Hargrove
Rangers '74-78
Indians '79-85

Toby Harrah
Rangers '72-78
Indians '79-83
Rangers '85-86

Alex Johnson
Indians '72
Rangers 73-74

Dave Nelson
Indians '68-69
Rangers '72-75

Duke Sims
Indians '64-70
Rangers '74

Stan Thomas
Rangers '74-75
Indians '76

Merl Combs (Coach)
Rangers Coach '74
Indians '51-52

Buddy Bell
Indians '72-78
Rangers '79-85, '89

Dick Bosman
Rangers '72-73
Indians '73-75

Rico Carty
Rangers '73
Indians '74-77

John Ellis
Indians '73-75
Rangers '76-81

Oscar Gamble
Indians '73-75
Rangers '79

Bill Gogolewski
Rangers '72-73
Indians '74

Jim Kern
Indians '74-78
Rangers '79-81
Indians '86

John Lowenstein
Indians '70-77
Rangers '78

Gaylord Perry
Indians '72-75
Rangers '75-77, '80

Fritz Peterson
Indians '74-75
Rangers '76

Willie Horton
Rangers '77
Indians '78

THE AFTER PARTY

Celebrate the 50th anniversary of Ten Cent Beer Night
with this limited edition run of bobbleheads!

Ten 10¢ Beer Night Bobbleheads

Bobblehead #1: Billy Martin blows kisses to the Municipal Stadium crowd!

Yes, the legendary manager who was twice thrown out of games before the contests even
began, shows why he was one of the best - and the worst.

Bobblehead #2: Poor ol' Nestor Chylak!

Yes, here he is - the extremely well-respected Hall of Fame umpire and Ten Cent Beer
Night crew chief. Temporarily blinded in the Battle of the Bulge, this WW II veteran
thought he had seen it all (after his vision came back to him, that is) - *until* he visited the
normally placid shores of Lake Erie. Press the bloodstain on his head and hear Chylak's
famous TCBN line: "They were (bleepin') uncontrollable beasts!"

Bobblehead #3: The Texas Cavalry charges!

Here they come! A rare multi-headed, uh, bobblehead bunch? The bat-wielding Texas
Rangers charge into battle to rescue right fielder Jeff Burroughs! Or was the ol' mastermind Martin simply trying to win the ball game via forfeit?

Bobblehead #4 The ol' greaser, Gaylord Perry!

Be careful! Squeeze this bobblehead in the right spot and a little vaseline shoots out! (But
you have to guess where that spot is.)

Bobblehead #5: Roll The Dice!

The Greatest Afro to ever grace the field. Oscar Gamble. Come on! Look at it! Try to
top it! Forget about it! (Note: This bobblehead will not contain styrofoam packaging...
it has its own padding!).

Bobblehead #6: Two Moons Over The Cuyahoga!

The father/son mooning duo. On a full-mooned, legendary night, why not add a 2nd
and 3rd moon?

Bobblehead #7: My Broz-eph!

Municipal Stadium organist Art Broze poised over his powerful instrument. Naturally, this bobblehead plays some of your ballpark favs.

Bobblehead #8: State Champ!

Wrestler Terry Yerkic in his Richmond Heights singlet.

Bobblehead #9: Abandon Ship!

The beer truck girls fleeing their posts!

Bobblehead #10: The Well-Hung Harrier!

The one-socked naked bandit in full stride. That's right, we've saved what is likely to be the most coveted bobblehead of them all for last. He stripped, he streaked, he wore a single black - or was it blue? - sock. It's hard to tell when a photo is black and white! He looked like one of Ohio's best cross country runners in form (Ohio has fantastic cross country, by the way).

Beer Night Recipe

Ingredients

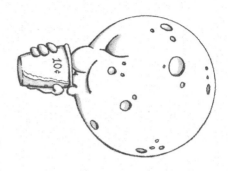

1 Full Moon, slightly yellow

2 Middling professional ball clubs

1 Stick-It-Their-Ear Manager

1 Rabble-rousin' Sports DJ

1 Experienced ballpark organist

1 Umpire crew, led by World War II veteran

Assorted firecrackers/M-80s/Smoke bombs

Tennis balls

1 Drummer (must be named John Adams)

1 big breasted woman

25,134 "Uncontrollable Beasts" (including dozens of streakers)

A handful of security guards and Cleveland Police

Unlimited 3.2 beer (BYOC!)

Directions:

1. One week or so ahead of beer night, mix together both teams violently, then set aside to fester.
2. Marinate fans, preferably on AM radio - newspaper and word-of-mouth also OK. Brine fans slightly in opposing manager's salty comments. Remind fans of Cleveland sports history. Sprinkle with "burning river" jokes.
3. On beer night, admit fans early, preferably two hours ahead of the first pitch.
4. Open up beer taps.
5. Send streakers across field.
6. Play a little baseball, allow the visiting team to get a lead.
7. Throw tennis balls, firecrackers, etc., at the visiting manager.
8. Beat drum.
9. Send buxom woman out to kiss home plate umpire.
10. Send more streakers but have them slide into bases (ouch).
11. Abandon visiting bullpen.
12. Fire up the home team (fans take position on top of visitor's dugout); tie game.
13. Steal the visiting rightfielder's hat.
14. Visiting squad, grab bats. Charge into right field!
15. Pour fans out of stands.
16. Strain with Rangers and Indians players.
17. Send in mounted police.
18. Turn off stadium lights.

Ten Cent Beer Night: A Tragi-Comedy in Five Acts

<u>Cast of Characters</u>

Bello Martino, a Ranger

Aspromonte, an Indian

Chylak, an adjudicator

Gaylord, an Indian

Lowenstein, a jester

Wilcox, an Indian

Randle, a Ranger

Fazio, Manager of Mirth

York, Lady of Promotions

Lord Bonda, a lord

Broze, a musician

Shopshire, a scribe

Prince MacPhail, a prince

The Prologue

Two fam'lies, both alike in dignity,
On the shores of Erie, where we lay our scene.
Mix in a slight, prompting malignity -
Throw in beer that could be drunk by a teen.

From forth the fatal dugouts of these foes,
A pair of star cross'd players took offense.
Randle dug in and dodged Wilcox's throws -
Both families charged and sought recompense.

Fearful promotion of suds: just a dime!
A field built long ago, 'neath a full moon.
Patrons could even bring their own beer stein!
The organist played fun, happy tunes.

What ensued was to some a laugh riot -
If you've never streaked, you oughta try it!

Act I
Arlington Stadium

Two families, one from Cleveland, another from Arlington, meet.

Bello Martino: Thy ol' greaseballer, I spit upon thy spit! I hate thy spit, as I hate all marshmallow salesmen - and thee! (Unless, of course, thou wanteth to spit on balls for us. Then I approve of thy spit - if you give us, say, 20 wins a season.)

Gaylord: Shutteth up, thou wretched little man! Wilcox, silence their tongues!

Wilcox: I will, my lord, I mean, Gaylord.

Wilcox throws behind Randle. Randle bunts then tackles Wilcox. Brawl ensues. Both families ultimately separate.

Bello Martino: Thy family is weak and we shall continue this in a week.

Gaylord: I shall withdraw, but this willful choler will not be forgotten.

Lowenstein: Yeah, we'll get y'all on the shores of Lake Erie.

Act II
Cleveland's Municipal Stadium

Fazio: Hark, the moon is full! Come, crush a cup of suds with us.

Bonda: Behold, this night, lusty men and women do imbibe, while cheering heartily for the Tribe!

Act III
Cleveland's Municipal Stadium (on the shores of Lake Erie)

Bello Martino (to the crowd): I bite my thumb and thumb my nose at ye!

Aspromonte: Thou should not hath done that. Hark! The crowd! Yerkic, no!

Chylak: The battlements forthwith are akin to me the he Battle of the Bulge.

Bello Martino: Get out thy bats and charge!

Broze: Peace! Turn thy ears to my merry tune!

Cleveland Po-Po: Ride! Ride! Ride! Subdue and quell their pernicious rage!

Act IV
Cleveland and New York

Prince MacPhail: Rebellious subjects, enemies to peace!

Thy fountains of yellow hath besmirched our reputation.

Thou shalt not have any other beer nights. Plus, you lost that game.

Bonda: We protest! Victory wouldst hath been ourn!

Act V
New York & Cleveland

Prince MacPhail: I deny thy protest.

Bonda: We protest your denial of our protest!

Prince MacPhail: Nope. Sorry. You lost.

Shropshire: A glooming peace doth the new day's sun bring.

One things's for sure: these two teams are a long way from a ring!

Well, never was there a story of more woe

Than Ten Cent Beer Night & Bello Martino.

Bonus: To streak or not to streak? That is the question!

Questions for Reading Groups & Roadtrips!

1. Why is beer so delicious?
2. In the midst of the riot, should the father have put his four-year-Old on the field to run the bases? Why or why the hell not?
3. Take the letters in STROHS then rearrange them to sort of create the last name of someone in this book. (Hint: he owned the Texas Rangers.)
4. What color was the one-sock streaker's sock?
5. Take two other early '70s promotions then combine them with Ten Cent Beer Night to make the best/worst imaginary promotion ever. For example:

    > TEN CENT BEER NIGHT + THE GREAT WALLENDA + HOT PANTS NIGHT

6. Is it a coincidence that one of the game's most annoying managers played for one of the game's most annoying franchises? Could you take him in a fight?
7. What songs did organist Art Broze play while the riot ensued?
8. Which streaker captivated the crowd the most?
9. What song did Bonita Gamble sing at the night club shortly after the riot and what were the players drinking as they unwound?
10. Will the Cleveland Guard-Indians ever win the World Series?

Also in 1974

Nixon created a national speed limit of 55 (a response to the oil embargo).

On March 6, 1974, 1,543 streakers ran naked at the University of Georgia, setting a record.

Hank Aaron broke Babe Ruth's long-standing career home run record, hitting his 715th homer on April 8th in Atlanta. "What a marvelous moment for the country and the world," said Hall of Fame announcer Vin Scully. "A black man is getting a standing ovation in the Deep South."

On April 14th, Tiger outfielder Willie Horton killed a pigeon via a foul ball at Fenway Park.

Carl Douglas hit it big with the release of "Kung Fu Fighting" - a song that could easily have applied to Ten Cent Beer Night.

Peter Benchley published *Jaws* and Stephen King published his debut novel, *Carrie*.

The first UPC was scanned to buy a pack of chewing gum in Troy, Ohio.

A few weeks before Ten Cent Beer Night, David Bowie released *Diamond Dogs*. Featuring songs like "Rebel, Rebel" and lyrics describing urban chaos and urban wastelands - of course Bowie scholars might view it otherwise - but it seems a slightly appropriate soundtrack for TCBN.

On June 20, 1974 a total solar eclipse passed over the Indian Ocean and Western Australia.

Erno Rubik, a Hungarian inventor, created the Rubik's Cube.

A group of farmers discover the "Terracota Army" in Xi'an China.

West Germany defeated The Netherlands, 2-1, to win The World Cup & Ali defeated George Foreman in the "Rumble in the Jungle."

Jack Nicklaus won the first-ever Players Championship, then known as "Tournament Players Championship." Charlie Sifford, who joined Ted Bonda in trying to hit a five-iron over Municipal's scoreboard, finished tied for 58th. Sifford served as the head pro of Sleepy Hollow Golf Course in Brecksville for many years.

The Symbionese Liberation Army abducted Patty Hearst, who ultimately said she had joined the terrorist group.

An American jeweler hatched an idea for a type of ring which would change colors depending on a person's mood.

Tactical Studies Rules, Inc. published a game known as "Dungeons and Dragons."

Movies that made their mark included *Blazing Saddles, Godzilla vs. Mechagodzilla, The Texas Chainsaw Massacre,* and *The Godfather Part II.*

A nod to Why Is Daddy So Sad on Sunday?
(a few coloring book pages)

BIBLIOGRAPHY

Seeking footage of Ten Cent Beer Night is like trying to find a Honus Wagner card in some rural American attic. Some great clips of it might be out there, but good luck finding it. In 2024, we are used to every sporting event from pickleball to frisbee golf being broadcast and recorded. In 1974, though, mid-week baseball games in early June were just not on TV very often. The Indians televised 40 of the 162 games in '74, including 25 home games - all on WJW (Channel 8). Most of these were weekend games and Ten Cent Beer Night was not one of the non-weekend games shown. Bummer. A short commentary by Harry Reasoner on the ABC Evening News does feature a little bit of the beer night riot and some beer night scholars (who, like streaking scholars, are a sordid lot that you would be best to avoid!) have located some footage at a Detroit TV station. For the most part, though, TCBNS (Ten Cent Beer Night Scholars) are limited to photographs. Photos by Paul Tepley are from the Cleveland Press Collections, courtesy of the Michael Schwartz Library Special Collections, Cleveland State University.

I *loved* interviewing folks - primarily players, fans, journalists, former front office personnel. Piecing together what happened during the infamous game was a little bit like trying to triangulate various accounts after a raucous college party. Did the well-endowed woman flash the crowd in the second inning or the fourth? Did the father and son team moon the crowd in the 3rd inning, or was it the 4th? The details were sometimes a little murky the day after and maybe even murkier after 50 years. Then again, I spoke to many people who would say stuff like, "I remember it like it was yesterday."

Please see my Ten Cent Beer Night Book website for a list of chapter notes/citations.

It was enormously fun combing through various databases, newspapers, records, scrapbooks, and documents from various sources. The primary ones included:

Baseball-Reference.com

The Cleveland Press (via The Michael Schwartz Library @ Cleveland State University)

Cleveland Magazine (via The Michael Schwartz Library @ Cleveland State University)

CPL.org (The *Plain Dealer* Historical Archive via Newsbank & The Cleveland Public Library)

The Encyclopedia of Cleveland History (case.edu/ech)

Kip Horsburgh Scrapbook

Paperofrecord.com (*The Sporting News*)

Sabr.org (The Society for American Baseball Research)

Sports Illustrated Vault (vault.si.com)

Ted and Tom Bonda Scrapbook

Wikipedia.com

YouTube.com

Radio, Social Media, Television & Film

"ABC Evening News." Commentary by Harry Reasoner. *"ABC Evening News."* ABC, June 6, 1974. Vanderbilt Television News Archive.

CBS News. 2014. "Richard Nixon's Resignation Speech." YouTube.

Corning, NY, PBS. 2024. "Upstate History Documentaries | Agnes: The Flood of '72 | WSKG." Video.wskg.org.

Fox 10 Phoenix. n.d. "More Arrests at the WM Phoenix Open than Last 2 Years, PD Says." Accessed February 25, 2024.

"Jean Shepherd's America - Chicago (White Sox)." n.d. Www. youtube.com. Accessed April 5, 2024. https://www.youtube.com/watch?v=O2e3Ov1lFyg.

"1979 ALCS Game 1 (EDITED)." n.d. YouTube. Accessed February 26, 2024.

Porter, Ben. 2021. "Ten Cent Beer Night Footage." https://twitter.com/Ben13Porter/status/1347939067456073733?s=20&t=1VQd2KgOf1g737asAmxZ8Q.'

"Ray Stevens - the Streak (Live)." n.d. Www.youtube.com. Accessed April 3, 2024. https://www.youtube.com/watch?v=RwZFKY0qhvU.

Rhetty for History. 2023. "1970s Fashion Fads!" *YouTube*. https://www.youtube.com/watch?v=ZNgR9WIIJxY.

Shropshire, Mike. 2005. *Seasons in Hell : With Billy Martin, Whitey Herzog and "the Worst Baseball Team in History"- the 1973-1975 Texas Rangers*. Lincoln: University Of Nebraska Press.

Sundberg, Jim. 2023. Jim Sundberg (2023) Interview by John McMurray. *Society of American Baseball Research*. https://sabr.org/interview/jim-sundberg-2023/.

"Ten Cent Beer Night Post Game Interviews." Cleveland, OH, June 4, 1974. John Carroll University Northeast Ohio Broadcast Archives.

Tepley, Paul. Various photographs. Cleveland Press Collections, courtesy of the Michael

Schwartz Library Special Collections, Cleveland State University. http://ClevelandMemory.org.

"Ten Cent Beer Night: An Oral History." 2021. OHIO v. The WORLD. Evergreen Podcasts. October 12, 2021.

"The 'Ten Cent Beer Night' Riot." n.d. YouTube. Accessed February 27, 2024. https://www.youtube.com/watch?v=nx_zzHjqFRk.

Newspaper, Database, Magazine Articles & Recordings

Admin. n.d. "April 9, 1974: Padres Owner Ray Kroc Throws a Tirade – Society for American Baseball Research." Society for American Baseball Research. Accessed January 31,2024.

Armour, Mark. n.d. "Gaylord Perry – Society for American Baseball Research." SABR.org. Accessed February 27, 2024. https://sabr.org/bioproj/person/gaylord-perry/.

Baldassaro, Lawrence. n.d. "Ken Aspromonte (2016) – Society for American Baseball Research." Accessed February 6, 2024. https://sabr.org/interview/ken-aspromonte-2016/.

Blumenau, Kurt. n.d. "July 18, 1972: Home Sweet Home: Elmira Ends 28-Day Flood Displacement with Win – Society for American Baseball Research." SABR.org. Accessed February 27, 2024.

Boissoneault, Lorraine. "The Cuyahoga River Caught Fire at Least a Dozen Times, but No One Cared Until 1969." *Smithsonian*, June 19, 2019.

Cappadona, Bryanna. 2015. "Matt Damon, Ben Affleck to Make Yankees Wife-Swap Movie." Boston Magazine. April 9, 2015.

Clinic, Cleveland . 2022. "Does the Moon Affect Humans?" Cleveland Clinic. October 24, 2022. https://health.clevelandclinic.org/moon-effects-on-humans.

Coughlin, Dan. "Wind, Not Height, Worries Wallenda." *The Plain Dealer*, May 30, 1974.

Deford, Frank. 1975. "Love, Hate and Billy Martin." *Sports Illustrated*, June 2, 1975. https://vault.si.com. "Did a John Denver Song Get Billy Martin Fired?" n.d. MLB.com. Accessed February 6, 2024. https://www.mlb.com/news/billy-martin-rangers-firing#:~:text=And%20yet%2C%20the%20strangest%20of.

"Evolution of the NFL Rules | NFL Football Operations." n.d. Operations.nfl.com. Accessed February 1, 2024. https://operations.nfl. com/the-rules/evolution-of-the-nfl-rules/#:~:text=In%201974%2C%20 the%20NFL%20implemented.

Fimrite, Ron. 1972. "Circle the Wagons! Indian Uprising: A Long Dormant Lake Erie Tribe Is on the Move." *Sports Illustrated*, May 29, 1972. https:// vault.si.com.

Gallo, Bill. 1974. "'Owners Can Blame Themselves' & 'Cleveland Hangs Big Head in Shame.'" *New York Daily News*, June 6, 1974.

Gerlach, Larry. n.d. "'Batter Ump': Basebrawls Involving Umpires – Society for American Baseball Research." SABR. Accessed February 9, 2024.

Guerrieri, Vince. n.d. "March 29, 1973: MLB Experiments with Charlie Finley's Orange Baseballs – Society for American Baseball Research." SABR.org. Accessed February 4, 2024. https://sabr.org/gamesproj/ game/march-29-1973-mlb-experiments-with-charlie-finleys-orange-baseballs/#_edn9.

Heiling, Joe. "Lee May Homers - Drinks on House," *Sporting News*, June 22, 1974; p. 18.

Hersh, Gene, "Indianettes aid Stadium beautification program," The Plain Dealer, June 30, 1974. (page?)

Jackson, Paul. n.d. "Page 2: Remembering 10-Cent Beer Night - ESPN Page 2." https://www.espn.com/espn/page2/story?page=beernight/080604. "June 04, 1974, Tuesday: Do You Remember That Day? | TakeMeBack. to." n.d. Takemeback.to. Accessed February 27, 2024. https:// takemeback.to/04-June-1974.

Keefer, Bob . 1973. "The Lowdown on Visiting Dugouts." *Plain Dealer*, July 8, 1973.

Lubinger, Bill. "The Strange Tale of Ten Cent Beer Night." Www. ohiomagazine.com. June 2014. https://www.ohiomagazine.com/ohio-life/article/brawl-game.

Nasaw, Daniel. 2012. "How Offensive Is the Word 'Lunatic'?" *BBC News*, May 8, 2012, sec. Magazine. https://www.bbc.com/news/magazine-17997413.

The New York Times. n.d. "10 Years Later, Cleveland Is in Financial Health." Accessed March 14, 2024. https://timesmachine.nytimes.com/timesmachine/1988/12/15/778988.html?pageNumber=20.

McPherson, Myra , and Tom Huth. 1971. "WashingtonPost.com: Rowdy Fans Hand Senators Final Loss." Www.washingtonpost.com. October 1, 1971. https://www.washingtonpost.com/wp-srv/sports/redskins/history/rfk/articles/baseball.htm.

O'Day, Joe. n.d. "'Now They're All Crying in Their Beer' ." *New York Daily News*. "Raw Hide." 2009. The Sydney Morning Herald. January 2, 2009.

Reichard, Kevin. 2017. "The Glory Days of Baseball and Beer Marketing." *Ballpark Digest*. February 2, 2017.

Sporting News, p. 22, June 22, 1974, AL Flashes.

Sporting News, "Beer Bust or Ball Game?", *Sporting News*, June 22, 1974; p. 14.

Sporting News, "Caps and Diablos Hold 'Golden Gloves' Night; p. 40.

Schneider, Russell. "'Aspromonte New Tribe Manager: 'I Have a Phobia About Losing' "." *The Plain Dealer*. November 10, 1971.

Staff, S. I. n.d. "The Mouth That Always Roars." Sports Illustrated Vault | SI.com. Accessed April 10, 2023. https://vault.si.com/vault/1982/11/22/the-mouth-that-always-roars

Sudyk, Bob. "'The Bad Boys of Summer Back Then, the Indians Were out of the Pennant

Race by June, but They Had a Lot of Fun Losing.'" *Plain Dealer*, September 22, 1996.

Vickrey, Eric.. n.d. "Oscar Gamble – Society for American Baseball Research." SABR. Accessed February 7, 2024.

Walders, Joe. "The Man Who Made Cleveland a National Joke." *Cleveland Magazine*, January 1,1976.

Wancho, Joseph. n.d. "John Lowenstein – Society for American Baseball Research." SABR.org. Accessed February 27, 2024.

Weird History. 2022. "TIMELINE 1974 - Nixon's Resignation, 10 Cent Beer Night & Blazing Saddles." https://www.youtube.com/watch?v=yp8diPBgQUA

Weller, Steve. 1974. "'Mental Giants: Frown, Frown.'" *The Buffalo News*, June 14, 1974.

Western, Case . 2020. "HOLLENDEN HOTEL | Encyclopedia of Cleveland History | Case Western Reserve University." Case.edu. February 10, 2020.

Whelan, Bob, and Steve West. "Bob Short." Society for American Baseball Research. Accessed April 10, 2020.

Whisnant, Scott. 1993. "Former Sports Announcer Did More Than Talk." Greensboro News and Record. May 29, 1993.

Wilson, Herb. n.d. "Nestor Chylak – Society for American Baseball Research." SABR.org. Accessed February 27, 2024.

Wikipedia Contributors. 2019. "Tommy Hilfiger." Wikipedia. Wikimedia Foundation. December 23, 2019. "Why the Word 'Lunacy' Comes from the Moon." n.d. Science Friday. Accessed February 18, 2024.

Wild, Matt. 2017. "Remembering the Milwaukee Brewers Ill-Fated 'Ten Cent Beer Night.'" *Milwaukee Record*, June 21, 2017.

Wilson, Herb. n.d. "Nestor Chylak – Society for American Baseball Research." SABR.org. Accessed February 27, 2024.

Wild, Matt. 2017. "Remembering the Milwaukee Brewers Ill-Fated 'Ten Cent Beer Night.'" *Milwaukee Record*, June 21, 2017.

"1973 Oil Crisis." 2024. Wikipedia. February 13, 2024.

Zitrin, Richard . 1974. "'Fan: Frustrating, but It Was Fun' ." *Akron Beacon Journal*, June 6, 1974.

Books

Ballparks Yesterday and Today. Edison, NJ: Chartwell Books,, 2007.

Clark, Jim. *Rally 'Round Cleveland*. Cleveland: Great-R Good Publishing Inc., 2018.

Dyer, Bob. *The Top 20 Moments in Cleveland Sports: Tremendous Tales of Heroes and Heartbreaks*. Cleveland: Gray & Company, 2007.

Epplin, Luke. *Our Team*. New York: Flatiron Books, 2021.

Epstein, Dan. *Big Hair and Plastic Grass*. New York: Thomas Dunne Books, 2010.

Franklin, Pete (with Terry Pluto). *You Could Argue But You'd Be Wrong*. Cleveland: Gray & Company, 1988.

Ingraham, Jim. 2019. *Mike Hargrove and the Cleveland Indians*. Gray Publishers.

Pennington, Bill. Billy Martin: *Baseball's Flawed Genius*. Boston: Houghton Mifflin Harcourt, 2015.

Schneider, Russell. *The Cleveland Indians Encyclopedia* (Collector's Edition). Norwalk, CT: The Easton Press, 2002.

Shropshire, Mike. *Seasons In Hell*. Lincoln, NJ: University of Nebraska Press, 1996.

Pluto, Terry and Joe Tait. *It's Been A Real Ball.* Cleveland: Gray and Company Publishers, 2011.

West, Steve (& several others). *The Team that Couldn't Hit: The 1972 Texas Rangers*

Edited by Steve West and Bill Nowlin

Torry, Jack. 1996. *Endless Summers : The Fall and Rise of the Cleveland Indians.* South Bend, Ind.: Diamond Communications.

Interviews

Adamack, Randy. Interview by Scott Jarrett. Phone. Seattle, WA, September 20, 2018.

Aspromonte, Ken. Interview by Scott Jarrett. Phone. Houston, TX, July 30, 2018.

Blossom, Bun. Interview by Scott Jarrett. Phone. Cleveland, OH, August 29, 2020.

Bonda, Tom. Interview by Scott Jarrett. Phone. Cleveland, OH, April 13, 2020.

Brohamer, Jack. Interview by Scott Jarett. Palm Desert, CA, August 13, 2020.

Coughlin, Dan. Interview by Scott Jarrett. Phone. Rocky River, OH, August 22, 2018.

Epstein, Dan. Interview by Scott Jarrett. Phone. Chicago, IL, October 5, 2018.

Fazio, Carl. Interview by Scott Jarrett. Phone. Florida, August 28, 2018.

Fazio, Carl. Interview by Scott Jarrett. Phone. Cleveland, July 26, 2020.

Fazio, Carl. Interview by Scott Jarrett. Phone. March, 2024.

Foulk, Rich. Interview by Scott Jarrett. Phone. Lorain, OH, October 22, 2018.

Grieve, Tom. Interview by Scott Jarrett. Phone. Arlington, TX, February 17, 2020.

Hargrove, Mike. Interview by Scott Jarrett. Phone. Tucson, AZ, December 5, 2023.

Horsburgh, Kip. Interview by Scott Jarrett. Phone. September 27, 2020.

Horsburgh, Kip. Interview by Scott Jarrett. Phone. December 31, 2020.

Jackson, Paul. Interview by Scott Jarrett. Phone. Chicago, IL, February 27, 2024.

Knuff, Jim. Interview by Scott Jarrett. Phone. Cleveland, January 31, 2021.

Konyha, Bill. Interview by Scott Jarrett. Phone. January 9, 2020.

Krslovic, Ken. Interview by Scott Jarrett. Phone. Cleveland, n.d.

Nagy, Greg. Interview by Scott Jarrett. Phone. Elyria, OH, October 23, 2018.

Powers, Gary. Interview by Scott Jarrett. Phone.

Powers, Greg. Interview by Scott Jarrett. Phone.

Randle, Lenny. Interview by Scott Jarrett. Phone. Rome, Italy, September 13, 2019.

Robinson, Paul. Interview by Scott Jarrett. Phone. Chicago, Illinois, February 27, 2024.

Stanhouse, Don. Interview by Scott Jarrett. Phone. Trophy Club, TX, May 2, 2023.

Sundberg, Jim. 2023. Jim Sundberg (2023) Interview by John McMurray. *Society of American Baseball Research*. https://sabr.org/interview/jim-sundberg-2023/.

Wilcox, Milt. Interview by Scott Jarrett. Phone. Jacksonville, FL. July 31, 2020.

Williams, David. Interview by Scott Jarrett. In person. Austin, TX. March 17, 2024.

Yerkic, Terry. Interview by Scott Jarrett. Phone. Cleveland, OH, August 7, 2018.

York, Jackie. Interview by Scott Jarrett. Phone. Rocky River, OH. September 25, 2019.

RAISE YOUR STEIN!
(ACKNOWLEDGEMENTS)

I owe a bunch of 10¢ beers - and many of the more expensive kinds - to many people. Thank you to everyone - players, fans, former employees, journalists and others - who took the time to speak with me. Please see the Bibliography for the list of interviews. This book would not have been possible without Carl Fazio and Kip Horsburgh, who were both incredibly patient, encouraging, and just overall awesome - not to mention very appreciative of Tiffin's finest export: Ballreich's potato chips. Thank you to Tom Bonda for a great interview and the amazing stuff from his father's time with the Indians.

Several librarians were extremely helpful. They include William Barrow and Beth Piwkowski at Cleveland State University, various librarians at Cleveland Public Library, as well as folks at the UT's Dolph Briscoe Center For American History. When I descended into various rabbit holes (which was part of the fun of this project), the folks at the Baseball Hall of Fame were always willing to scan and send me anything they could find.

Although I sensed that the current Cleveland's current MLB team did not exactly want to embrace the 50th anniversary of Ten Cent Beer Night, I really appreciate the help of Bob DiBiasio, Nate Jonoso, and Jeremy Feador of the Cleveland Guard-Indians. The Cleveland chapter of the Society For American Baseball Research was also fantastic. Thank you to Cleveland SABR's Joe Shaw for helping me contact and meet John Adams before he left us for the great ballpark in the sky. Having lunch with him in Brecksville in late December of 2019 was a real treat. It got even better when we were about to say goodbye and I asked about his famous drum. "It's in my trunk!" he said. "Want to bang on it?" What Cleveland baseball fan wouldn't be over the (full) moon at such an invitation?

Filmmakers and fellow TCBN devotees John Dauphin and Seth Moherman were terrifically enthusiastic and supportive with incredible documents. I sure hope you make your film someday. Thank you to Alex Hastie, host of the Ohio v. The

World podcast. Paul Jackson and Dan Epstein, fellow "70s baseball enthusiasts, were both very inspiring.

Thank you to several proofreaders, editors, and advisors, including Lance Brown, Don Dingee, Chuck Eddy, Aaron Gardner, Darrel Mayers, Greg Melville, Paul Worland (who, I think, gave me my first beer) and, on the shores of Lake Erie, Dan Morrison. Muchas gracias to advisor and proofreader Marshall Harrell, whose enthusiasm for baseball and life is infectious. How about a new duty? Are you up for selling books at the corner of Carnegie and Ontario?

Thank you to my family, including the LOCH, for putting up with and encouraging me in this scavenger hunt. The Guardians will win it someday, Jeff Dawson, and you and I will be there and celebrate it with a cold beer. College pal Andy Cope created incredible drawings that I am honored and thrilled to include. Throughout the process, Cope (!) put up with a line of questions that he is accustomed to from our Gambier days: What about this? What about that? Could you draw this? I started this project in 2018 and it was an extremely welcome diversion during the pandemic. It seems that there are still many rabbit holes I would like to explore, but the 50th is coming up, so I am shutting down the beer truck. My apologies if I have left anyone out.

ABOUT THE AUTHOR

Scott Jarrett began studying baseball at the age of one and is still slightly upset that his parents didn't take him to Ten Cent Beer Night when he was three. He began studying beer at the age of 17 at Kenyon College. He is the author of the hit 2017 Austin traffic poetry collection, *Traffickwocky*, and believes that he is one of Austin's Top 10 traffic poets. Others disagree with this ranking. He is also the author of *Asking For Bread and Getting Beaten*, a lighthearted travel guide to Bulgaria that met with mixed reviews from his Bulgarian bride. He may or may not be allowed to return to Bulgaria. He has lots of great memories of Cleveland's Municipal Stadium, including attending the 1981 All Star Game with his Dad. And then there was that typically frigid April day when he and some Kenyon pals jammed a leftover senior party keg in their car trunk and dragged it from Gambier to Cleveland for a doubleheader against the Red Sox. Boston's Matt Young no-hit Cleveland, but somehow the Indians won 2-1, a classic Municipal moment. He also has lots of great baseball memories, including the summer when he was 12, his brother Jim mowed base paths in the lawn (much to their Dad's dismay), and he and the Kookamongas played nearly every day, until the sun went down - and even after.

He and his family of ballplayers live in Austin, Texas.

Hark! Mounted police, approacheth!
Municipal Stadium lights…OUT!

(The End)